Advance Praise for

Talmud, Curriculum, and The Practical

"This lovely book is a great relief. Alan A. Block's words re-affirm for me a terrible amnesia in education. We have forgotten how deeply formed we are by our spiritual ancestries and bloodlines, with all the ghosts and hopes and dreams that haunt such formation. This is a book of deep, sometimes troubled, sometimes troubling remembering, rooting the work of Joseph Schwab back into the ages of Judaism. *Talmud, Curriculum, and the Practical: Joseph Schwab and the Rabbis* is not only itself an act of great rabbinic scholarship—it is an act of great courage to say out loud and in such loving detail what we already know: that our images and understanding of language, our love of the word, and our energetic concerns over the shape and nature of interpretation, our sometimes near-panic over the fragile and blossoming lives of our children (their "course," their "curriculum") comes from somewhere that is richer, more complex, more difficult, more interesting and more ancient than the bare bones of what often counts as educational theory. Read this. It is a beautiful work."

—David Jardine, Professor of Education, University of Calgary, Canada

"On the surface, the concept of a curriculum is rather simple. But, thanks largely to Joseph Schwab, the question of curriculum grew from simply 'what do students learn' to 'how do students learn the skills of learning?' In this book, Alan A. Block demonstrates the important place of Jewish roots in Schwab's theory of curriculum. Citing examples from the Talmud and Jewish classical literature, Dr. Block clearly ties the classic method of Jewish dyadic learning to the methodology which Schwab championed."

—Rabbi Paul Drazen, Executive Director, Mid-Continent Region, United Synagogue of Conservative Judaism

Talmud, Curriculum, and The Practical

Complicated Conversation

A Book Series of Curriculum Studies

William F. Pinar
General Editor

Vol. 2

PETER LANG
New York • Washington, D.C./Baltimore • Bern
Frankfurt am Main • Berlin • Brussels • Vienna • Oxford

Alan A. Block

Talmud, Curriculum, and The Practical

Joseph Schwab and the Rabbis

PETER LANG
New York • Washington, D.C./Baltimore • Bern
Frankfurt am Main • Berlin • Brussels • Vienna • Oxford

Library of Congress Cataloging-in-Publication Data

Block, Alan A.
Talmud, curriculum, and the practical: Joseph Schwab and the rabbis /
Alan A. Block.
p. cm. — (Complicated conversation; v. 2)
Includes bibliographical references.
1. Schwab, Joseph Jackson, 1909– 2. Education—Philosophy.
3. Education—Curricula—United States. 4. Talmud. I. Title. II. Series.
LB885.S382B56 370'.1—dc22 2003022439
ISBN 978-0-8204-6181-6
ISSN 1534-2816

Bibliographic information published by **Die Deutsche Bibliothek.**
Die Deutsche Bibliothek lists this publication in the "Deutsche Nationalbibliografie"; detailed bibliographic data is available on the Internet at http://dnb.ddb.de/.

Cover photos: "Rabbis Learning" reprinted courtesy of Steve Karro/ Karro International Fine Art;
Portrait of Joseph Schwab reprinted courtesy of the Special Collections Research Center, University of Chicago Library/ Stephen Lewellyn, photographer
Cover design by Lisa Barfield

The paper in this book meets the guidelines for permanence and durability of the Committee on Production Guidelines for Book Longevity of the Council of Library Resources.

29 Broadway, 18th floor, New York, NY 10006
www.peterlang.com

Printed in the United States of America

To the memory of my father,

Sidney David Block

זכרונו לבררכ

May his memory be for a blessing

TABLE OF CONTENTS

	ix	ACKNOWLEDGEMENTS
	1	HAKDAMAH
CHAPTER ONE	5	BY WAY OF AN INTRODUCTION
CHAPTER TWO	31	THE VALUE OF SCHOOLING
CHAPTER THREE	47	WHAT IS JEWISH ABOUT JOSEPH SCHWAB
CHAPTER FOUR	67	GOLD ACQUIRES SILVER
CHAPTER FIVE	95	"THEY PELT HIM WITH STONES": STANDARDS, HIGH-STAKES TESTING, AND CULPABILITY
CHAPTER SIX	125	"WHO HOLDS THIS BOOK": ETHICS, READING AND RESPONSIBILITY
CHAPTER SEVEN	159	"THEY SOUND THE ALARM IMMEDIATELY": ANTI-INTELLECTUALISM IN TEACHER EDUCATION
CHAPTER EIGHT	175	OBLIGATION'S TIME
AFTERWORD	209	*by Peter Appelbaum*
HOSAFAH	221	BY WAY OF AN INTRODUCTION
	223	REFERENCES

ACKNOWLEDGEMENTS

Hebrew is a consonantal language. That is, in Hebrew, all of the letters are consonants and its vowels are all signs placed above and below and about the consonants. The Rabbi of Rizhyn said: "Just as the holy letters of the alphabet are voiceless without the vowel signs, and the vowel signs cannot stand without the letters, so zaddikim and hasidim are bound up with one another. The zaddikim are the letters and the hasidim who journey to them are the vowel signs. The hasidim need the zaddik, but he has just as much need of them. Through them he can be uplifted…"

I do not know if I am anything at all like a zaddik, but whatever wisdom I possess, of whatever consonants I am composed, I am always in need of vowel signs to breathe life into them. I have been blessed to have been given voice by dear, dear vowel sounds. Bill Pinar remains a constant stimulus to my thought and work, and his support of this manuscript gave it the breath to become a viable text. I cannot express my gratitude to him; it would forever lack sufficient voice.

I tricked Sali Mounce into formatting this text, and though she might never forgive me for that skullduggery, I am forever indebted to her. She has been kind, and patient, and cheering, even when the headers became footers, and the justified margins didn't warrant justification, and even when we both ran out of breath. She has worked innumerable hours on this manuscript for raspberry muffins and pumpernickel breads.

I thank Marty Springer and Bill Wikrent who cheerfully changed my jpegs to tiffs and my tiffs to jpegs. It was Marty who had me stand knee deep in newly-fallen snow for the portrait which graces the back of this text. He made me look better than I deserve.

I am grateful to Rabbi Steven Karro and Karro International Fine Art for the use of the painting, *Rabbis Learning*, and to the University of Chicago archives for the photo of Joseph Schwab. The photographer was Stephen Llewellyn.

Gary Welch has heard this book told over the many miles we ran together at absurd hours of the day and in unspeakable temperatures. He has been a remarkable friend.

Finally, I thank my family, Beth, and Emma and Anna-Rose, who have given me the time and space and care to consider, to compose and to complete this book. I am forever grateful…

HAKDAMAH[1]

In Tractate *Berakhot* (3A) of the Babylonian Talmud there appears this story. Rabbi Jose recounts that once he was traveling along a road when it came time to pray. In order to prevent being interrupted in his daily prayer, he stopped in an abandoned ruin. While he was thus praying, the prophet Elijah appeared, and stood in the crumbling doorway of the ruin and awaited the completion of Rabbi Jose's prayer. When he had concluded, Elijah cautioned Jose that he ought not to pray in dangerous and suspicious ruins but rather, when traveling, should stop and pray by the side of the road. And furthermore, Elijah said, when praying by the side of the road, so as to avoid being beset upon by bystanders or highwaymen, Jose must say a shortened prayer. R. Jose concludes:

> I then learned from [Elijah] three things: One must not go into a ruin; one may say the prayer on the road; and if one does say his prayer on the road, he recites an abbreviated prayer.

I have spent my entire life in school as student and as teacher. It is not difficult to take note of the ruinous state of many of our educational establishments. It has been estimated that 75% of our school buildings are in need of some structural repair. And if there were no clear evidence of physical decay, certainly we might discover there some educational break down. Celebrants of both the political left and right decry the state of the schools in the United States. The national "No Child Left Behind" law, and the Wisconsin "Every Child Deserves a Great School" propaganda are both premised on the reputed inadequacies of the present state of education. There is no lack of alarm sounded concerning the present structures and states of education in the nation.

Of course, the state of our schools and our educational system has been a perennial topic for jeremiads. From the published letters of James

---

[1] A Hebrew word which means 'forepiece,' as in a moving forward.

Carter in the early years of nineteenth century, to the plaints of Horace Mann through the mid-years of that same century, to the moanings of Arthur Bestor and Robert Hutchins and William Bennett, Diane Ravitch, Allen Bloom, and Rod Paige, in the century recently passed, the ineffectiveness and insufficiencies of the public schools have been a common subject in the world of politics and social critique. Joseph Schwab's book, *College Curriculum and Student Protest* (1969b), soberly castigated the state and practice of education in the United States. This book, he writes, is "an examination of the style, the expression, and some of the content of student protest as presenting symptoms of evils of their education; student ineptitudes and ignorances indicating neglects by the curriculum; perversities indicating distortions and mistreatments"(1969b, 3). Indeed, it was in that same year that Schwab would declare the curriculum field itself moribund. Given the desperate descriptions of the education system in the United States, one might expect that Elijah would have cautioned that it was not safe to pray in there. And yet Schwab spent his entire professional life within the walls of academia; I think he often said his prayers there. I do not think Schwab ever retreated to the sides of the road.

I, too, have spent my entire professional life in schools. I have never thought that I stood amidst ruins; the rhetoric notwithstanding, I do not now believe that our schools are in a state of ruin and decay; I have over the years prayed often there. I continue yet to do so. In the schools, engagement in study is engagement in prayer. I have written lately (see Block, 2001) on the relationship of prayer and study. Study, I aver, is a prayerful act. Study, like prayer, is a stance we assume in the world. Study, like prayer, is a way of being—it is an ethics. When we learn, as when we pray, we acknowledge in public our sense of wonder and awe. Wonder, as Abraham Joshua Heschel teaches me, is a radical amazement; wonder is a state of maladjustment to words and notions, the recognition of their fluidity. Wonder arises in the awareness of the world's glory, which always exceeds our comprehension and our grasp. To our sense of wonder we respond with awe, and when we stand in awe, we acknowledge that even in the smallest particle there is meaning that we can never fully understand. In prayer and in study, we acknowledge how little we know, and we then stand in awe at the complexities of our lives that we only, in part, can realize.

A blessing, as is study, is a moment of insight and an opportunity for direction. Study, as is prayer, is the awareness that we live amidst daily miracles, and that there is more to the world than we will ever know. Abraham Joshua Heschel (1959, 52) writes that "*The beginning of awe is wonder, and the beginning of wisdom is awe.*" Prayer is an expression of awe; prayer sacralizes the mundane. So, too, does study. When we pray and when we study, we take a stance in awe and humility, and we actively acknowledge that "our lives take place under horizons that range beyond the span of an individual life, or even the life of a generation, a nation, or an era" (Heschel, 1959, 52). Prayer and study emanate from the silence of awe and wonder. If contemporary chaos theory argues that there is order in the universe, and that that order is only recognizable in time, then engagement in prayer and study acknowledges our patience and our hope.

Prayer and study set standards to which we might aspire but never reach.

I think it is not for lack of trying that the standards cannot be achieved; it is that the standards must always elude us. They are a consummation devoutly to be sought for, but never to be achieved. Both engagement in study and prayer acknowledge that there is far more in the world than we will ever know. In prayer and in study, we acknowledge that our knowledge will never suffice and that what we undertake in the classroom is merely a hint of all that exists outside it. We ought to stand in our classrooms in awe and wonder. I like to think that Joseph Schwab would have appreciated this thinking.

I go regularly into public school buildings, and I study regularly there. I do not think these buildings will soon crumble, though perhaps they could do with some repair. Schwab devoted his life to the repair of education in the public and private schools of the United States. He has had remarkably little influence. Perhaps, it would be argued, this failure is due to the paucity of his ideas, though I do not hold to this position. I will have a great deal more to say about this later. Ian Westbury and Neil Wilkof state (1978, 2) that for some, "the character of [Schwab's] thought seemed unusual and puzzling." I do not think either adjective represents a fair measure of Schwab's thought. I will argue that Schwab's ideas were mistranslated, appeared in a tongue foreign to their fecund sources, and were, as a result, misinterpreted, dismissed or, for lack of better understanding, dismissed as commonplaces in educational circles. Wilkof and Westbury state that to fully appreciate the cogency and breadth of Schwab's ideas demands an understanding not of any on particular essay, but the intertextual character of all of Schwab's essays, the "complex back-and-forth between the particular and the more general." I will speak to the power of Schwab's ideas, and I will attempt to situate these ideas in the grounds from which they took root and from which they flourished. That soil is generally Jewish and specifically Talmudic, and I think Schwab's ideas are best appreciated when they are viewed in this specific context. I think Schwab's educational prescriptions have greatest potency when these sources and roots are revealed. And further, because I am concerned with the progress of education in the United States, I want to employ these same Talmudic methods to study issues currently troubling education: issues of curriculum, issues of standards and high-stakes testing, issues of reading and scholarship, and issues of ethics. I think these methods are implicit in Schwab's thinking, but they are also methods to which for various reasons upon which I will later speculate, Schwab could not give authentic voice.

The schools are not in ruins, as I have said, but they are in need of some repair. It is to that repair that this book speaks. I like to think Joseph Schwab would have supported this effort.

A story is told of the Maggid of Zlotchov:

> One of his disciples asked: "In the book of Elijah it is said that 'Everyone in Israel is in duty bound to say: 'When will my work approach the works of my fathers and mothers, Abraham and Sarah, Isaac and Rebecca, and Jacob and Leah and Rachel?' How is it possible," the disciple asked, "to ever imagine that we could achieve what our ancestors achieved?" And the Maggid responded: "Just as our fathers and mothers invented new ways of serving, each a new service according to his or her own character: one the service of love, the other that of stern justice, the third that of beauty, so each one of us in our own way shall devise something new in the light of the teachings and of service, and do what has not yet been done" (Buber, 1991, 147).

It is my hope that in this book something new will be offered and something new will be seen. Perhaps this abbreviated prayer may satisfy that service.

Chapter One

By Way of an Introduction

One of Joseph Schwab's more illustrious students, Eliot Eisner (1984, 203) attributes the origin of Schwab's ideas to the influences of Aristotle and John Dewey. He is not incorrect; Schwab earned his baccalaureate and graduate degrees at the University of Chicago. There, he was immersed first in the reformed undergraduate humanities curriculum and then in the great books seminars advocated, developed, and offered by Robert Hutchins and Mortimer Adler for the newly formed undergraduate programs in general education at the University of Chicago. The University of Chicago was also where Joseph Schwab taught until 1974, and where he served as the first chair of the Great Books extension program. This program, proposed and implemented by Robert Hutchins, the influential president of the University of Chicago, was inspired by the belief that "only philosophical and metaphysical arguments offered the prospect of escape into a realm of permanence, justice and truth" (McNeill, 1991, 151). This curriculum, dominated by the works of classical Western philosophers and writers, was designed to "impose a rational order on the world" and to seek that intellectual certainty and moral guidance that would, it was hoped, sustain civilization. Schwab participated energetically and centrally in the development of the University's general education program based upon these held beliefs. Schwab believed strongly in the liberal arts curriculum. I am certain that Schwab's curricular prescriptions are founded heavily on the *works* of Western civilization, of which that of Aristotle is foundational. It is no accident, I think, that Schwab's exemplar in his essay "Enquiry and the Reading Process" comes from Aristotle's *Physics,* a volume translated by the University of Chicago's own Robert McKeon, one of Schwab's mentors and colleagues. The *Physics* is a work of obvious stature in the Western canon. Ian Westbury and Neil Wilkof (1978) note that Schwab read assiduously the works of the philosophers who were influential in and on the Chicago milieu. At the University of Chicago, the curriculum was dominated almost exclusively by the thought of Western civilization and by the liberal education programs which sought, realistically, to offer not merely the artifacts of the traditional culture, but the interrogation of that culture and the development through discussion of resolutions to the problems that culture faced. It was a curriculum based, it was held, on "*culture*, the *person* and the *community*," and its method was to synthesize these elements in the concept of *experience*. The works to be studied were to be interrogated for the problems they presented; students would experience the work, experience the culture out of which that work arose, and experience their thought processes resolving problems presented in the text. This was an idealist curriculum: from theoretical perspectives it would address practical, cultural issues with the intent of resolving the culture's problems. Schwab argued from early on for the efficacy of a liberal education. "Schwab, more than anyone," Westbury and Wilkof write, "was to articulate all of the elements of the rationale" (1978, 12) for a liberal education. What Schwab deplored, however, was the practice of the liberal educator who offered 'discussion' as merely a condiment to the transmission of requisite knowledge, but did not engage in discussion as an essential element in education itself. Schwab argued strongly for the institution of discussion *as* curriculum, "an engagement in and a practice of the activities of thought and communication" (1978, 106). This was the form of liberal education Schwab would advocate throughout his career.

Eliot Eisner says also that Schwab was strongly influenced by John Dewey. Westbury and Wilkof concur, acknowledging that "John Dewey, more than any other thinker, determined the character of the conception of liberal education that Schwab was to develop" (1978, 13). I will have a great deal to say about Schwab's prescription for curriculum reform and curriculum development in American schools, and there is little doubt that Dewey's work had influence on Schwab's thinking. Indeed, Schwab's essay "The Teacher in Progressive Education" seems to me to be, in no small part, homage to the thought of John Dewey. In that essay, Schwab offers a succinct statement of Dewey's educational philosophy, declaring that "the problem of the pragmatic rhetoric is to move men to an informed and reflective practice" (1978, 170). This formulation could also describe Schwab's advocacy for a curriculum reform he referred to as "the practical." It would seem, therefore, that Dewey's influence is direct. And though there is much of John Dewey to be discovered in Schwab's thinking, I also think that this characterization is an educational commonplace from which little might be learned. On the one hand, we would be hard pressed to discover a contemporary liberal educator who does not show influences of Dewey. On the one hand, we would be hard pressed to discover a contemporary liberal educator who does not show influences of Dewey. On the other hand, I will suggest that Schwab's sympathy for Dewey's work might find its original source in an unacknowledged Jewish pragmatics. I will argue that the contemporary portrait of Schwab exemplified by Westbury, Wilkof, Eisner, and others is seriously incomplete because Joseph Schwab spoke, too, from a silenced and invisible Jewish tradition. And it may be true that as a result of the traditionally anti-Semitic culture of American academia, Schwab was constrained to hide his roots.[1] As a result, Schwab's writing was then, and may still be today, misunderstood.

Of course, this experience of the Jew suffering misapprehension, and/or of being denied a space to speak authentically, is particular neither to education nor to Joseph Schwab. We live in a culture organized through the eyes of Greco-Roman and Christian culture. Leslie Fiedler (1991, 70), speaking of another but not unrelated discipline, complains that "not only do the Jewish American writers . . . tend to read Jewish Scripture through Christian eyes, but their perception of their own Jewishness is similarly secondhand." Indeed, original Jewish texts are known only through their Christian translation—the King James Bible the quintessential example. In his meditation on the Book of Job, Fiedler notes that though the King James translation inaccurately represents the text, it has, nevertheless, become the canonical version of that text. Thus, Fiedler points out, the line "Man is born to trouble, as the sparks fly upwards" is a mistranslation of the original, which has been offered in Jewish translations variously as "For man is born to weariness, while spiritual beings soar in flight," or "Man is born for trouble/As the sons of Reshef fly upward." Our cultural knowledge of Job, however, stems from the mistranslation rather than from the original, and the work done with the book is based on that distortion.

---

[1]As I will show below, Jewish texts and wisdom have had no place or influence in Western education theory or practice. Rather, Jewish educational practice has attempted to assimilate into American culture. Emily Bingham's study of the Mordecai family (2003) gives evidence of the struggles of American Jews in American Christian society. Mordecai Kaplan (1994/1934), a professor at the Jewish Theological Seminary in New York City, quotes John Dewey, a professor working down the street as a professor at Teachers' College, but I have not seen a reference to Kaplan in Dewey's work. Perhaps Dewey's pragmatism might be studied in light of Kaplan's reconstructionism. And besides, they must have passed each other as colleagues on the streets on the way to and from lunch.

Other Jews in academe have complained of a similar difficulty. David Bleich writes that "Having internalized a well-documented history of hostility from host societies, the oppositional aspect of being a Jew is familiar to me" (1999, 111). Bleich recounts the difficulty, for example, experienced by Lionel Trilling when he tried to write as a Jew in the decidedly anti-Semitic environment of Columbia University and the New Critics, the latter advocates for the existence of a Platonic ideal of truth and beauty. As Trilling discovered, a Jew in academia is a stranger in an inhospitable land; often, the desire for acceptance threatens to compromise an individual's integrity. At other times, as Bleich suggests, the position of stranger might be used to, albeit, lonely advantage. Maxine Greene (1973) has written on the necessity of the teacher assuming the role of stranger in the classroom, and I have suggested (Block, 1998) that the Jew as the quintessential stranger is, therefore, naturally suited to the educator's role. Furthermore, Roger Simon (1999, 320) warns that "a pedagogy of Jewish particularity must attempt to avoid being rendered a form of academic *shtick*." That is, Simon cautions, what is particularly Jewish about curriculum and method must not be consumed and appropriated by the language and structures of mainstream, Christian academe. Perhaps in attempting to speak to the mainstream, Joseph Schwab may have lost the power that might have derived from a more forthright expression of the origin and originality of his ideas.

Translating Jewish wisdom into the language of the Greco-Christian may have resulted in the turn in Schwab's writing to what has been termed a certain opacity, and might have led to the misunderstanding, or even, summary dismissal of his work. Eisner complains that "Schwab's writing, like his speaking, is exasperating. It is at once a model of erudition and eloquence, and, at the same time, it is pedantic and convoluted. His vocabulary is ineluctably . . . grand, and his syntax is as elliptical and cryptic as one is likely to find in the literature" (1984, 203). This description is from one of Schwab's admirers! Seymour Fox (1985, 63) states that "most of the essays seem to have been overlooked by his critics in recent years. . . We are concerned that some of Schwab's most basic ideas are liable to be distorted if his works are not read in their broader context." And Janek Wankowski and William Reid, in a conversation published in The *Journal of Curriculum Theorizing* (1982, 129), say that "Schwab is too reasonable altogether to have an influence at all. People wouldn't take much notice of his reasonableness." Ian Westbury and Neil Wilkof (1978, 2) claim that Schwab's writings have had "uncertain impact" on the field of education and that "much of what he said often appeared puzzling even to those who half-remembered the idea of general education, and it was opaque to those who did not have any context in which to place Schwab's work." As I will suggest throughout this book, these "puzzlements" are endemic to the methods of Rabbinic scholars. Though it is now, perhaps, impossible to ascribe to Schwab's writings a conscious attempt to practice the Rabbis' methods and to attribute his lack of influence now to his failure to translate that practice into the Greco-Christian vocabulary demanded by the Academy, I will suggest that it is the Rabbis' methods that serves as a context for Schwab's prescriptions and that it is the Rabbis' methods that Schwab urges as the basis and methods of curriculum. The source of Schwab's ideas, however, is never identified as other than Western. The critique of him derives, I argue, from Greco-Christian models of educational practice and decorum.

It is my contention that the radical work of Joseph Schwab finds its foundation not in Greek and Christian thought, but in Jewish practice, specifically in the work of the Rabbis from the early part of the past millennium, whose work resulted in the Talmud. However, as William McNeill writes, at the University of Chicago, where Schwab worked for almost his entire career, "almost no attention was paid to the non-Western world, or to the ancient Orient, or to Judaism. Inattention to Judaism and to the role of Jews in European society may seem odd in retrospect" (1991, 149). It was in just such a hostile environment that Schwab worked and wrote. I am suggesting that to be heard at all Schwab had to employ a language that inevitably would have misstated his ideas. And because Joseph Schwab's work was steeped in Jewish practice and method, and because he could not—or did not—speak openly as a Jew, his work was inevitably made obscure in the translation. In her book, *Leviticus as Literature* (1999), Mary Douglas distinguishes between two types of thought—mytho-poetic reasoning and discursive logical reasoning. Arguing that the two systems of thought serve different purposes, a work that reasons one way (in this case, *Leviticus*), can not be read as if it had been written in the other way (in this case, *Deuteronomy*) (1999, 20). But, should it happen, however, that a work is so read, "it will certainly be misread." Such, perhaps was the fate of Schwab's work in education in general and curriculum in particular. Simply put, as Jew he was misread and misunderstood when interpreted through a Greco-Christian lens.

I SHALL HAVE THREE POINTS

I shall have three points. The first is this: that the field of curriculum has been forever dominated by the discourses derived from Greek, Roman, and Christian principles and by practices and methods that derive from those principles. These are the principles found in the works of Socrates, Plato, Aristotle, Augustine, Aquinas, and Descartes. Much contemporary educational discourses are based in the ideas of these writers. Joseph Schwab worked in the very Greco-Christian environment of the University of Chicago for almost his entire educational career, and though he was a strong advocate of a liberal education, he was constrained to employ the discourses of the culture and traditions of Greco-Christian educational ideology and method if he desired to be heard at all. Schwab was, from early on in his career, a vocal critic of the aim and manner of contemporary education. Speaking for his own discipline—science—he held that the traditional educational program of stuffing students' minds with knowledge disguised "the reality of science as open-ended enquiry into the enormous complexity of living and inanimate nature" (McNeill, 1991, 145). As early as 1943, "Joseph Schwab had the effrontery to challenge 'truths of modern science' that many professors in the graduate departments still deemed to be true forever, needing only to be memorized by undergraduates in their final, perfected form" (McNeil, 152). Schwab advocated that "liberal programs in science consist of (or contain) original records of scientific research, series of papers containing the knowledge of whatever subject matters seem appropriate and treated analytically and critically," for the purpose of learning not subject matter, but the origins of that subject matter in particular ways of thought. In offering process as opposed to product, Schwab argued, "one gains . . . minds aware of what a problem is and what a solution is; men and women committed and habituated to thoughtfulness and flexibility of mind within the limits of their powers" (1978, 102-3). Schwab demanded that schools develop intelligence, a quality that he understood as the ability to ask questions and to seek answers to those questions. The student engaged in such a program "will be teaching himself to read and understand. He will be liberating himself to some extent from the need for a living teacher. And this last is the sign and sense of a liberal education" (1978, 102). Education, to be liberal, must be liberatory; it must open thought with the question.

Schwab's revolt may seem merely academic, but, I will suggest, it was actually cultural at its base. Schwab's notion of "deliberation" may be best appreciated when recognized as based in the traditional Jewish pedagogical methods of the Yeshiva, itself, perhaps, based in ancient Jewish exegetical traditions.[2] In the Yeshivah, "study [is] institutionalized . . . as a performative act carried out by the students' participation, [and] the learning space is shaped by the intensity and quality of the ongoing exchange of its students" (Halbertal & Halbertal, 1998, 459). In the Yeshiva, learning occurs from the activity and commitment of the students to deliberation. Schwab averred that "discussion, in one form or another—with others or with one's self—is indispensable to a good liberal education. For in the last analysis it is not merely a device . . . . It is also the *experience* of moving toward and possessing understanding, and a liberal education is concerned with the arts and skills of understanding" (1978, 105), Indeed, McNeill's (perhaps, idealistic) depiction of a transformed University of Chicago (1942-46) sounds remarkably similar to the Halbertals' description of an actual Yeshiva. McNeill writes, "Lecturing has been almost banished. Instead, discussion—endless discussion, in and out of class—was the preferred vehicle for active learning. Everyone—students and teachers alike—took part" (1991, 141). The Halbertals write that "The discursive mode of study is not restricted to the individual [study] partners; questions and answers circulate across the Beit Midrash . . .Young and old discuss the same problem, which circulates around the hall as the issue of the day" (1998, 458). The Yeshivah, the Halbertals note, "is a fascinating institution because in it a deep link can be seen between the text at its center, the particular discursive form of its creative re-enactment and the mode of reasoning which fits both the text and its re-enactment" (1998, 468). Schwab's practical seems to me very much rooted in the practices of the Yeshivah and varieties of textual practices. But if Schwab spoke from this Jewish perspective, indeed, even if Schwab was not fully aware of the embeddedness of this pedagogy in Jewish culture, he was constrained by the language and culture of the University of Chicago not to discover this connection and was constrained to express himself in a manner that could not fully contain his thought.

[2]See, Michael Fishbane, 1998; David Weiss Halivni, 1997, Susan Handelman, 1982.

If Schwab had that language available, he was not willing or able to use it. And because he spoke a strange tongue, Schwab's work in curriculum could not be adequately expressed in the traditional Greco-Christian language of the academy, and the truly radical character of Schwab's work could not be recognized or appreciated. To most, his work lacked coherence and audience. As Seymour Fox complained, "Most of the (early) essays have been overlooked by his critics in recent years, and thus they have missed a most important source for gaining a comprehensive understanding of [Schwab's] theory of curriculum development. We are concerned that some of Schwab's most basic ideas are liable to be distorted if his words are not read in their broader context" (1985, 63). I believe that context is a decidedly Jewish one. When Joseph Schwab argued for discursive enquiry and discussion as educational practice, he argued, I assert, from a Jewish perspective. When Joseph Schwab urged that enquiry sit at the center of curriculum, he spoke from a completely different tradition than that practiced by an American education that traced its routes from Plato and Aristotle, through Augustine and Aquinas, through the works of Horace Mann and William Torrey Harris and John Dewey and Robert Hutchins, and the multitude of educators espousing advocacy of a liberal arts and/or practical curriculum. Schwab's work in curriculum, I think, derives from a different system of thought than traditional Greco-Christian thought, and his educational program can not be appreciated by viewing it through Greco-Christian eyes. I am myself concerned with the situation and reception of Schwab's work. I am myself concerned with this issue. I am comforted to find a colleague in Joseph Schwab.

Schwab argued vigorously against the traditional curricular focus on the reception of meaning. Examining the student protest movements of the late 1960s as his content, Schwab (1969b, 3) charged that the content of student protest revealed "the evils of their education," that student ineptitudes and ignorances evident in their protests resulted from the "neglects by the curriculum," and that behavioral, intellectual and imaginative perversities manifested in student protest were evidence of distortions and mistreatments by curriculum. Schwab complained that "The practical competences of deliberation are not, of course, traditional obligations of the academic curriculum. I have tried to indicate, however, that there is every reason why they should become so." Schwab devoted his energies to an attempt to reconceptualize curriculum. His prescriptions, I believe, are the methods of the Yeshiva, and they are substantively Jewish. "The first thing the reader of the Talmud notices is the importance of dialogue in the working through of thought. Talmudic thought is the thinking of the questions" (Ouaknin, 1995, 84, 87). Not *the* answer but *another* answer is the goal of study exemplified in Talmud.

What is Greek and what is Rabbinic in language and textual practice are not synonymous. Susan Handelman (1982, 27) writes, "With the deceptively simple words 'In the beginning God created the heavens and the earth,' the Hebrew Bible begins. In fact, however, the statement was *long before Derrida,* (emphasis added) a supreme challenge to the entire classical tradition of Western metaphysics . . . to assert that matter was not eternal, that the world had a temporal origin, that substance came into being through divine fiat, indeed through divine *speech* . . . threatened the foundations of Greek ontology (emphasis in original)." Rabbinic thought, unlike that of Plato in which Western academia has been forever immersed, held that the world could not be perceived through Reason because there were no natural laws that could be rationally explicated or logically deduced: the universe was not naturally formed; rather, the world was created. What the world is, is not as important as what we are to do in it. Learning is the process of seeking answers and not the answer itself: discussion "stirs up the tranquility of a truth that is one, a truth that goes off to sleep and forgets for want of being thought out" (Ouaknin, 1995, 84). The Rabbis taught that everything could have been otherwise and that thought would discover the alternatives and the possibilities. Whatever is ordered, is not naturally so. According to the Rabbis, reason itself might be a human construct and not the manifestation of natural order. There is no answer and therefore, no way to the answer. "The answer suppresses the 'opening,' the richness of possibility; whereas the role of the question is to open up" (Ouaknin, 1995, 87). Rather, there are a variety of interpretations, not all equally valid but all readily acknowledged. Schwab sought to provide a curriculum in which students and teachers would be led to questions through answers. "To the question how big a context constitutes the proper context for a reported inquiry, there is no answer," Schwab stated (1978, 153). The only stipulation that he required was that any answer should acknowledge that there was more that might be known and known about.

Whereas Rabbinic thought saw the world having been created out of nothing, Greek thought, in which I have been immersed throughout my education—indeed, which has defined itself as education—posited a *logos* that preceded the word.[3] There is meaning, Plato suggested, and it must be found. From this Greek foundation derives the Western pedagogy against which Schwab fought. Schwab argued not that answers be discovered but that discovered answers be interrogated. It was always the question and not the answer for which Schwab clamored. David Purpel (1999) quotes a joke familiar in the Jewish community: Two people, one a Jew, the other not, are having a long and heated conversation. In a moment of frustration, the non-Jew asks, "Why is it that every time I ask a Jew a question, they always answer with another question?" The Jew replies, "So, what's wrong with asking questions?" Schwab adored the question.

The search for meaning for the Jew and for the Greek—the project of textual interpretation—are, therefore, two very different processes. However, Western education has traditionally been founded on the Platonic (Greek) belief in meaning and the possibility of the proper search for it. For the Greeks, *logos* is that which we can articulate in words; *logos* is behind the words and inevitably may only be incompletely expressed by them. Meaning is singular, though words are plentiful. For the Greeks, words could represent things, though not be those things; there would always exist things outside of the words. Rabbinic thought, however, teaches that words can never be exhausted by things and that there are always words that exist outside of things; indeed, there even exists words outside other words themselves. Max Kadushin writes that the basis of Rabbinic thought, "the value-concept,"[4] "takes on meaning as it interweaves with the other value-concepts, grows in meaning, expands its idea-content in accordance with its use in combination with other concepts" (1952, 46). For the Rabbis, there is always another use and another interpretation of text because what is at stake is not final knowledge but daily practice. A teacher at a Yeshivah whose opinions of text remain constant would soon have no students.

However, Schwab complained, in the common practice of traditional education, "surveys of knowledge, instillation of 'principles' abstracted from their meaning-conferring structure, or intensive drills in

[3]Emmanuel Levinas (1990b, 144) argues that "This marvelous coincidence of obedience and commandment, subjection and sovereignty [which the Jew feels in faith] bears a well-worn but handsome name: reason…Rationalism does not menace the Jewish faith."

[4]This is, I think, equivalent to the concept "signifier" in structuralist and post-structuralist theory.

'fundamental' facts without the framework which confers significance on them" (1969b, 201), are a sterile experience. Jewish wisdoms were clearly not part of American education practice. Indeed, argue Moshe and Tova Halbertal (1998, 468), the organization of the [Jewish] Yeshiva challenges theories of education in general. "What would other fields of knowledge look like if they were investigated in such a context? How would modes of reasoning, experiences of learning be affected if higher institutions of learning were established in a Yeshiva-like form? How would channels of intellectual exchange and forms of teacher-student relationships be shaped, if our universities had a Beit Midrash at their center." We have only to imagine the arrays of students sitting at their desks in forced silent attentiveness to the pronouncements of their teachers to see how far American educational practice is from that of the Yeshivah. It is my contention that Schwab's work argued for such an unnamed model and that his work was at its core remarkable because of its sources in Jewish practice and wisdoms.

THE SECOND POINT

My second point is that Joseph Schwab's work *in* curriculum, and particularly his exploration *of* curriculum in the four seminal essays that appeared between 1969 and 1984, have been interpreted within the framework of these Greek, Roman, and Christian discourse systems and have been, therefore, either misinterpreted or misunderstood—perhaps even as a result of Schwab's own reticence to name the "J" word in his published work. Westbury and Wilkof acknowledge something of this problem when they admit that "Part of the problem that Schwab faced was, of course, the assimilation of his novel views of the structure of the disciplines into more conventional schemes" (1978, 25). And what was true for this aspect of Schwab's thinking might be generalized to much of his work in curriculum. Though he worked at the Melton Center, the educational arm of the Jewish Theological Seminary, he "was not able to find a way of bringing this work into the clear focus that he needed to write effectively within the somewhat foreign context of confessional education" (1978, 30). I suggest that this inability stemmed from the inability of translating Jewish wisdom—which was not confessional in subject or tone—into the discourses of American education. The Jewish roots implicit in Schwab's essays, essays that have become essential to curriculum history (though *not* to its practice in the United States) have not been revealed, nor is Schwab's practical ever situated in a Jewish culture and practice. Much advantage, however, would be gained by recognizing these roots and developing fruit from them.

In 1973, Joseph Schwab was invited as someone who "has made a major contribution to the scholar-curriculum problem in general education" to a conference entitled "From the Scholar to the Classroom: Translating Jewish Tradition into Curriculum," sponsored by the Melton Research Center for Jewish Education. Seymour Fox (1977, xvii), a conference organizer, said "We asked [Schwab] to open the conference with a discussion of the many problems related to the application of the fruits of scholarship and research to elementary and secondary curricula..." Interestingly, Professor Joseph Schwab, who was Jewish, does not attribute any of those curricular problems to the Christian Western tradition of philosophy or educational ideologies. Nor does Schwab address the particularly Jewish setting or themes of that particular conference. Joseph Schwab (1977, 1) does say, however, that:

> The means by which scholarly materials are adapted to the purposes of education are quickly told but only slowly mastered. The means are easily understood but difficult to use. They are difficult because they require collaboration by men of five different bodies of experience, each such body of experience being alien to the possessors of the others bodies of experience. The collaborators, then, must first learn something of the concerns, values, and operations which arise from each other's experience. They must then, and this is harder, learn slowly to honor these various groupings of concerns, values, operations, and adapt and diminish each his own values to make room in this thinking for the others. Finally, they must bring these partially coalesced bodies of judgmental factors to bear on the body of scholarly materials.

What Schwab argues for in curriculum work is the necessity of deliberation amongst various constituencies and the translation of that discourse into practice. It is, in sum, the practice of Talmud. "Edited as intergenerational arguments, layer upon layer, most Talmudic discussions do not reach a definite legal opinion about the previous controversies. Rather, they preserve and clarify the wealth and multiplicity of approaches to the problem at hand. In many Talmudic discussions, the *sugiya*[5] does not proceed by way of selection aimed at approaching or

[5]"The *sugiya,* or *sugya,* is a self-contained, sustained deliberation in the Talmud" (Kraemer, 1990, xiii).

approximating the right answer . . . they attempt to maintain the validity of opposing interpretations against potential challenges, challenges which are raised and refuted in turn" (Halbertal & Halbertal, 1998, 460). Education in the Yeshivah is a re-enactment of this Talmudic discussion. Schwab's deliberation seems to me to mirror Talmudic practice.

It is helpful, then, to understand Schwab's deliberative method as situated in Rabbinic scholarly tradition. Thus, Schwab cautioned that the meanings of curriculum purposes and reasonings "which matter are those which determined whether a given text, a given pattern of teaching, a given treatment of a topic, when examined and momentarily submitted to, is both felt and seen to be appropriate to the curriculum which has been envisaged. These meanings lie in the whole course of the deliberations which created them. The meanings lie as much in what was decided against, for example, as in what was decided for. They lie in the reasons for rejection of alternatives as much as in the reasons for preferring those which are preferred. They lie in nuances of expression in the course of the deliberation" (1973, 506). David Kraemer, in, *The Mind of the Talmud*, writes (1990, 79), "The Bavli[6] occasionally records brief interpretations of an antecedent Mishnaic text, but such brief interpretations are rare. In the vast majority of cases, brief comments are followed by questions and responses, and then new questions, and then new responses, and so on. It is not only deliberation but the extent of deliberation that so characterizes the Bavli. At every step of the way, the urgent necessity to advance that process makes itself more and more felt." *Deliberation* is the very word Schwab employed to characterize both the curriculum and the means of its creation. He said that "it is unrealistic, in an highly charged and special meaning of 'unrealistic,' to expect that others, not privy to the deliberation, can, like bronze molders, take a terminal statement of purposes as a pattern and from it, realize a curriculum, i.e., construct materials for students, guides for teachers, patterns of teaching and learning which are the appropriate materials guides, and patterns" (1973, 506). Deliberation is the very center of Talmudic discourse, but nowhere in Schwab's talk—nor in the other seminal work that Schwab wrote concerning curriculum—is this tradition noted. Rather, always Schwab appears situated in the Christian

---

[6]The Babylonian Talmud. This edition is distinguished from the related but often divergent text, the Jerusalem Talmud.

Western discursive tradition. The Jewish voice has been effectively suppressed and/or denied in discourses of education. It might, of course, be true that trained as Schwab was in that very Greco-Roman and Christian tradition and trained as he was in the language of American curricular work, and functioning as he was constrained to do within the conventional academic milieu of the University of Chicago, that Joseph Schwab himself may have lacked the vocabulary and/or the opportunity to articulate the radical character of his work in anything but the traditionally accepted discourses of curriculum and education. In *Hutchins' University,* William H. McNeill's memoir of the University of Chicago, McNeill remarks that in the 1940s, when Schwab began his long career at the University of Chicago, "when the Hutchins college was in full flower, the assimilationist ideal that had prevailed in the 1930's still pervaded the consciousness of students and faculty alike. In practice this principle meant enthusiastic exploration of the riches of a rational, liberal version of the Western heritage, starting with the ancient Greeks" (1991, 149). But despite this ideal, McNeill notes, "Almost no attention was paid to the non-Western world, or to the ancient Orient or to Judaism" (1991, 149). But in denying that voice, I believe that Schwab, and we who follow in his paths, deny access to a culture and wisdom that might effectively change the nature of curriculum and help us restructure schools.

As it has been traditionally the case in education, the attempt to speak as a Jew must appear, as it were, as jokes and parapraxes. Freud tells the story of the man whose desire to join proper society led to his public renunciation of Judaism by conversion. Freud's is a story of the failure to suppress the Jewish voice. Despite his conversion, the man felt an emotional tie to Judaism and, at an appropriate time, told his baptized sons about their Jewish heritage.

> One day while we were sitting at tea with our otherwise friendly hosts, the lady of the house, who had no inkling of her summer guests' Jewish ancestry, launched some very sharp attacks on the Jews. I ought to have made a bold declaration of the facts in order to set my sons the example of "having the courage of one's convictions," but I was afraid of the unpleasant exchanges that usually follow an avowal of this sort. Besides I was alarmed at the possibility of having to leave the good lodgings we had found and of thus spoiling my own and my children's . . . limited holiday period, should our hosts' behaviour towards us take an unfriendly turn because of the fact that we were Jews. As however I had reason to expect that my sons, in their candid and ingenuous way, would betray the momentous truth if they heard any more

of the conversation, I tried to get them to leave the garden "*Juden* [Jews]," quickly correcting it to "*Jungen* [youngsters]." In this way I enabled the 'courage of my convictions' to be expressed in a parapraxis (1960, 92-3).

That is, to speak as a Jew requires subterfuge, in which case we are always apt to be misunderstood: if we want to engage in the conversation we must soon correct our discourse; or, conversely, we must speak as a Jew and risk our securities. "The process of cultural assimilation began for us [Jews] long before we reached the university—as early indeed, as the compulsory first twelve years of our education, which typically our classrooms were presided over by gentiles . . . . Even as they taught me to pass by learning to speak the brand of standard English spoken in the gentile suburbs, they sought to impose on me a life-style utterly alien to that of my ancestors," writes Leslie Fiedler (1991, 69). So, perhaps too, for Schwab. And in that passing, Schwab spoke a language that could not communicate the originality of his thought. Perhaps a better understanding of Schwab's work may be had if he can be placed within the Jewish Rabbinic tradition as it is clearly evidenced in the Talmud. Schwab's prescriptions derive, it seems to me, from Talmudic practice; Schwab's educational programs seems to me steeped in Jewish practice.

What Schwab argues as true for curriculum development is true as well for curriculum enactment.

HISTORIES OF THE WESTERN EDUCATIONAL EXPERIENCE

Histories of education almost always begin with the Greeks. Philosophies of education are almost wholly founded on the influence of Greek thinkers. With extremely rare exception, authors and texts begin their philosophical exploration of education with the Greek experience, and trace educational practice from these origins. In my studying, I have learned and learn again that American education has been centrally founded upon Greek metaphysics; indeed, it would seem that a great part of American education does not know philosophers before Plato. "The first proponents of intellectual education were the Greek philosophers Socrates, Plato, and Aristotle," writes John L. Elias (1995, 5) in his text, *Philosophy of Education: Classical and Contemporary*. There are in his text no references to Jewish thought or educational practices, though there is clear evidence that the Greeks encountered the Jews, who had themselves a literary and scholarly tradition. To Elias, however, it is as if the Greeks invented the tradition of an educational experience. Well, indeed, they have, insofar as Western education is concerned. But, as Walter Benjamin (who was Jewish) has said, "There is no document of civilization which is not at the same time a document of barbarism. And just as a document is not free of barbarism, barbarism taints also the manner in which it was transmitted from one owner to another" (1969, 256). Curriculum discourse is not free from that taint. Perhaps I may attribute the dissatisfaction perennially expressed about education to its foundation in Greek ontology and epistemology; our continual sense of educational failure stems from a stubborn adherence to logos, to meaning. Richard Rorty describes the angst experienced by contemporary humans ontologically challenged:

> . . . our Glassy Essence [intellectual soul] remains with us . . . [A] sense of moral failure mixes with a sense of grievance that philosophy—the discipline supremely concerned with "the higher"—has not made us more aware of our own nature. That nature, it is still felt, makes its distinctive character most clearly felt in a certain sort of knowledge—knowledge of the highest and purest things: mathematics, philosophy itself, theoretical physics, anything which contemplates universals. To suggest that there are no universals—is to endanger our uniqueness (1979, 43).

I recognize in Rorty's listings the standard curriculum of the public schools—at least that of the privileged—but that is another story. For here it is significant to recognize that the Greek model upon which much of American education was founded denied the very foundation of Jewish teaching that might have offered an alternative perspective and educational practice. David Weiss Halivni (1997, 83), for example, says that once the Israelite nation had embraced the book, "interpretation took the place of revelation." This event took place with Ezra in the sixth century B.C.E. Henceforth, wisdom for the Jew was a process and not a destination. The Platonic concept of the Real—real concepts and real ideas—a belief in mind that could grasp these concepts and ideas through reason, is opposed by Jewish practice, which seeks not for the truth but a life that is true. The Platonic thrust in curriculum persists, I might suggest, in an effort to deny not only the Jewish voice itself, but to deny even the suppression and silencing of the Jewish voice in the discourses of education.

Socratic teaching/learning is at the heart of most progressive, and even some less progressive prescriptions for schools, but is not central to the Rabbinic method wonderfully displayed in the Talmud, a document redacted between 200-600 C.E. There, conversation may be defined as readaptation and reinterpretation of the Book to meet the kaleidoscopic changes in the Jews' situation. Meaning for the Talmudic scholars is not in the text, but may be made with the text. The Talmud is the written story of that interpretation, of the making of bylaws, of participation in the process that adds forever to the great store of Jewish legislation and legend. Talmud is a way of thinking about how to live in the world based upon an ethical ontology. The question in Talmud is always how might the ethical word be obeyed. God's Levitical directive is a command to be holy because God is holy, but the Rabbis recognized that there were no singular solutions. The Rabbis debate, but they do not resolve. A joke—for in suppression, we speak, as Freud suggests, in parapraxes and jokes—epitomizes Jewish belief and practice:

> The master sits in front of his class of young students. He begins his lesson: "Class, can any one tell me why the first book of the Bible, ***Bereshit***, begins with the letter **gimel**?" The class is silent. From the back of the room a timid hand goes up. "Yes?" asks the teacher sternly. "Can you tell why the first book of the Bible begins with the letter **gimel**?" And in a hushed and tentative voice the child responds, "But, teacher, the first book of the Bible doesn't begin with the letter **gimel**, it begins with the letter **bet**." "Well," says the teacher looking sternly at the student, "that's one answer!"

The Greek logos on which Western education is based premises a right and wrong, a correct and an incorrect knowledge. Allan Bloom, who, like Schwab, was Jewish and worked at the University of Chicago says, "A life based on the Book is closer to the truth, in that it provides the material for deeper research in and access to the real nature of things" (1987, 60). But it is not the Torah to which Bloom refers when he speaks of the book; rather, he speaks of the books that make up the Western canon. His search for the real nature of things—the belief that these books contain a single, discoverable truth—belies Rabbinic thought, which prioritizes a multiplicity of meaning and offers not knowledge but ways to create knowledge. Rabbinic thought, I believe, is the foundation of Schwab's radical alternative: polyfocal conspectus.

But the Greco-Christian language of the schools excludes Rabbinic thought; Schwab spent his life at the University of Chicago: What language did he speak? Schwab sought to reform curriculum, but I think the ceaseless, inexhaustible and fruitless search for new and effective methods and principles is fatally constrained by the hegemony of these philosophical systems that silence the Jewish voice exemplified in Schwab's work. "Our search for ways of implementing philosophical axioms in our classrooms begins with Socrates, Plato, and Aristotle, though philosophy, or the love of wisdom, existed long before their time," states David Jacobsen (1999, 55) in his recent book on the philosophy of education. Acknowledging the existence of other philosophical systems, the author nevertheless ignores their substance and wholly dismisses their influence on education and curriculum. With the exception of Karl Marx, whose relationship to Judaism is at least problematic, Jacobsen's text includes only Western white, male, Greek and Christian philosophers. Similarly, though the authors Ozmon and Carver (1999) acknowledge the influence of Eastern philosophy on Western thought, they minimize its significance by stating that in Eastern philosophy, "If any one idea is paramount, it is a concentration on the inner rather than the outer life. Eastern philosophy, unlike Western, more empirical philosophy, stresses intuition, inner peace, tranquility attitudinal development, and mysticism" (93). Ozmon and Carver argue that though Eastern philosophy has influenced Western education, it has done so mainly as "an antidote to the strong empirical and rational tradition of Western philosophical traditions." Ozmon and Carver describe the dualism that persists between the intellectual and spiritual, and that was established at the outset of the educational philosophical tradition employing the rational tradition of the Greeks as the dominant paradigm. In American educational practice, this dualism is easily traced to the Puritans and the Aristotelianism central to their philosophical position. Our Puritan forebears argued that only right reason could control the will and passions and lead to grace.

Of course, I find the distinction between intellectual and spiritual education interesting and flawed. I certainly see no evidence that Messieurs Ozmon and Carver have explored the intricacies of Talmud in which the intellectual and the spiritual are intimately connected. Rather, in their text, Judaism is named merely as an example of the Eastern philosophy identified not so much with philosophy as with religion—which the authors distinguish as separate disciplines. "The separation (between philosophy and religion) is difficult particularly when we look so far back. One can hardly expect early civilizations to have a very sophisticated or scientific idea about the nature of the universe and humanity's place in it" (1999, 94). There is not a small amount of ethnocentrism here and certainly a large measure of intellectual imperialism. The authors do not show any familiarity with the complex intellectual thought patterns that permeate Talmud. Talmud is not at all concerned with the abstract and merely theoretical; rather, Talmud insists on the particular and on the intimacy of thought and action. Judaism, as Abraham Joshua Heschel reminds us, is not only a way of being; it is simultaneously a way of thinking and of acting, combining the abstract with the practical and the philosophical with the physical. For Ozmon and Carver, however, the Eastern philosophical tradition, in which they include Judaism, is a part of a system in which the rational is opposed to the irrational, the intellectual is opposed to the mystical, and the empirical is opposed to the spiritual.

This dualism has suffused Western educational tradition as a result of the heavy influence of the Greeks and Christians on educational thought and practice, and it is this dualism that pragmatists and post-modernists have been earnestly attempting to dissolve. For example, William Doll (1993, 3), in his widely popular *A Postmodern Perspective on Curriculum*, acknowledges that postmodernism, which calls into question "the sweeping changes affecting art, literature, mathematics, philosophy, political theory, science, and theology—changes questioning the basic epistemological and metaphysical assumptions in those fields—will play themselves out in education and curriculum . . . ." Never does Doll doubt that the changes will be great, but neither does Doll give voice to the idea that postmodernism might itself derive from the thought of Rabbinic Judaism, which developed and was codified from at least the years 200-600 C.E. when the Talmud was being written and compiled. These are, not coincidentally, the years referred to as the Dark Ages in Western Europe. Doll does not give voice to the belief that postmodernism might be couched in Jewish thought and language; that the entire cultural tradition that is called into question by postmodernism is the Christian voice that has usurped and suppressed the Jewish voice. Doll situates the postmodern curriculum perspective in the advances of science and especially the development of chaos theory, but this post modern curriculum may actually be first heard in that silenced Jewish voice. Susan Handelman (1982, 173), drawing relationships between Rabbinic thought and Derrididean textuality, says that "if Judaism is the experience of the infinitely other, it is precisely this irruption of the totally other that threatens the Greek logos, and the Christian holy family as well. Like writing, the Jew is historically the castigated other, intruder, threat, scapegoat, exile, idolater, and it is surely no accident that those who take up arms against the paternal logocentrism of western thought would be Jews." Jewish philosophy has always provided an alternative to the Greco-Christian, but it has historically been rendered silent. The Greeks considered the Bible obscene; the early Christian Church transformed it into a preface. On order of the sitting Pope, the Talmud was publicly burned on 6 June 1242 and again on 9 September 1553. Pope Pius IV permitted the publication of the Talmud on the condition that all sections that affronted Christianity were erased, and in 1592, unsatisfied with the continued existence of the Talmud, Pope Clement II prohibited the study of Talmud in any version or edition.

Nevertheless, it is to the Greeks and Christian theologians that educational philosophers and historians look when they search for origins and influences. If "the first proponents of intellectual education were the Greek philosophers, Socrates, Plato, and Aristotle," as John Elias (1995, 5) writes in his recently published *Philosophy of Education: Classical and Contemporary,* then Elias defines intellectual education from within the discourses of these Greek philosophers. Jacobsen (1999, 59) states that this avowedly Greek discourse holds "that the acquisition of knowledge through intelligent inquiry not only brings us closer to universal knowledge but also improves the human condition by bringing us closer to universal moral behavior." This statement epitomizes the ubiquitous discourse that Kliebard refers to as that of the mental disciplinarians or humanists; this language is what we today know as arguments from advocates for a more rigorous classical education, its contemporary proponents ranging from Allan Bloom, to E. D. Hirsch, to William Bennett, to Diane Ravitch, to Roger Kimball, to George Bush, the latter who acquired only marginal benefit in and from this curriculum. Here, education is understood as the training of correct thinking—the way to Truth. The intellectual midwife in American modern education for this belief was William Torrey Harris. The second point made by his Committee of Fifteen demands that curriculum be constructed so that "the adjustment of the branches of study [occur] in such a manner that the whole course at any given time represents all the great divisions of human learning . . ." (in Willis et al., 1994, 3) Knowledge is complete and requires only transference to the youth.

For Socrates, too, knowledge was to be uncovered not produced. This must be so because truth is not subject to the physical world; rather, it is eternal and constant. Thus, Socrates may absolve himself of all responsibility for teaching anybody anything: "If anyone of these people becomes a good citizen or a bad one, I cannot fairly be held responsible, since I have never imparted any teaching to anybody, and if anyone asserts that he has ever learned or heard from me privately anything which was not open to everyone else, you may be quite sure that he is not telling the truth." The basis of the traditional Western view of education as the appropriate training of intellect resides in this Socratic position and rests on the assumption that knowledge is timeless and universal. The critique made of the sophists by Socrates and Plato inheres in the emphasis of the latter on the relativist nature of knowledge. But the opening words of Genesis suggest that only God—not truth—is eternal and omniscient. And the thrust of Torah suggests that God exists beyond human knowledge; human reason could never comprehend or encompass God. Hence derives a Jewish focus on the practical, on the Deed: How might God's word be best obeyed! From this emphasis derives the Jewish focus on textual interpretation.

Gerald Gutek acknowledges that an alternative to the Platonic philosophy existed in the philosophies of the sophists. Since truth was relative, they held that the main aim of education was to teach the art of practical politics. Education was intended, therefore, to enable participation in the (limited) political arena in which decisions about daily life were to be made. Thus, the ability to develop and to express arguments was the focus of educational theory and practice. Recognizing the personal element in all thought and knowledge, "[Sophists] tended to deny universal and objective standards of morality and behavior, and grounded their educational goals in social utility" (Gutek, 1972/1987, 33). These sophists were concerned with teaching the rhetorical arts—the art of argument. The Sophists held that education ought to enhance political power and was, therefore, intimately tied to the art of persuasion. Gutek argues that "the education espoused by the sophists, with its concentration on language, grammar, rhetoric, and logic, exercised a continued influence on Western educational development. It contributed to the formulation of the liberal arts and the oratorical education that dominated the Roman education of Cicero and Quintilian." (1972/1987, 34) Clearly curriculum energies for much of the first millennium can be traced to the famed trivium-quadrivium focus derived from this concentration.

However, the decline in the reputation of the sophists owes much to the ascendance of idealist education of Plato and Socrates. The antagonism between these two philosophical perspectives on education remains a primary point of contention yet today. American educational practice is based solidly in Greek experience. In the sixth edition of their book, *Philosophical Foundations of Education*, Ozmon and Carver (1999, 93) state that "Most studies of Western philosophy begin with the Greeks." Certainly the influence of Socrates and Plato and Aristotle are incontrovertible in Western educational histories and philosophies. The Socratic method—an inquiry approach to truth—may be summarized as a) focus upon an ill-considered statement; b) questions that point out inconsistency in answers which produces an awareness of inadequacies; c) a redefinition of the original statement, concept, generalization, etc. and d) the new definition of conceptualization that becomes subject to the same critical examination (in Jacobson, 1999, 59). According to Socrates there are principles of thought and action that are true for all men and women, and that the potential for right thinking is within all of us. It is the Socratic teacher who can ask the right questions that prods the task of self-examination. "Well, that's one answer."

As Socrates had said, he must not to be accused of teaching anyone anything: he imparts knowledge to no one, but merely guides each back to what he/she already knew. Platonic idealism suggests to us that there are universal forms and that right reason may lead us to them. For Platonists and neo-Platonists—the ideal world is far more real than the material world. Plato argued for a distinction between the ideal and unchanging world and the world of human action. The former consisted of perfect forms such as truth, goodness, justice and beauty. The latter were conceived to be imperfect approximations or representations of these universal and eternal ideas. Knowledge comes to human beings not through the senses, but by exercise of intellect (reason) which must penetrate beyond the confusing shadows of sense perceptions, experience and opinion. True knowledge is always changeless and eternal. On the other hand, Aristotle held that the "material and spiritual world were inevitably connected, and that from the study of physical material, abstractions might be achieved. Man arrives at concepts by abstracting the form of these objects from the material content that conveys them to the senses" (Gutek, 1972/87, 42). Aristotelian idealism remains yet (in say, the work of Mortimer Adler, another assimilated Jew at the University of Chicago) an important influence on curriculum. We may find a religious version of this Aristotelianism in Puritan ideology in 17th century colonial America (see Perry Miller, 1955). But Maimonides, a 12th century philosopher trying to accomodate Aristotelian concepts to

Jewish philosophy, does not appear in the traditional educational philosophy texts.

In his synoptic text on curriculum, William Schubert, too, traces the history of curriculum back to the Greeks. He writes that "The primary origins of curriculum today can be traced to ancient Greece" (1986, 56). But Schubert makes no mention of the influences of the Hebrew on the Greek. Nor does Schubert make mention of the contempt with which the Greeks held Jewish thought and textual practice, and how Greek thought developed often in opposition to Jewish praxis. That is, the structures of American education might sit atop a silenced, unacknowledged, Jewish foundation. The exclusion of Jewish thought was necessary to re-inscribe the world by the Greeks and early Christians to justify their world view; the Jewish voice threatened the unity to which the Greek aspired and that the Christian sought. Emmanuel Levinas suggests that the process of translating the Talmud into the idiom of today is a process of translating the Hebrew into Greek and the Greek into Hebrew.

Schubert (1986, 59) proceeds: "The educational curriculum of the Middle Ages was indisputably Christianity . . . . To gain perspective on curriculum thought and practice in the Middle Ages, one must begin with the origins of Christianity." Though not exhaustive, Schubert does present the development of Christianity and its developing relation to the Western world. Yet what is not part of Schubert's discourse is how Christianity delegitimized, usurped, and reinscribed the Jewish voice and therefore, altered forever pedagogical purpose and practice. The origins of Christianity in Schubert's account do not note, for example, how Paul's insistence on personal mediation (with Jesus as mediator) replaced the textual mediation of Jewish practice. For Christianity, faith in Jesus substituted for the immediacy of textual authority and the primacy of interpretation, both central principles developing in Judaism especially with the destruction of the Second Temple in 70 C.E. With the rise of Christianity, Susan Handelman (1982, 84) writes, "In place now of textual mediation is personal mediation through the figure of the new redeemer, whose presence has ended the long metonymy of Jewish history . . . ." Interpretation is ended with Jesus' word; the text is made flesh, and meaning is based in acceptance of Jesus' meaning. The whole pedagogical process that will become the Talmud and its methodology is denied. Schubert gives no expression to the early delegitimization of the Jewish voice by Christian belief; he effects and enforces the silences of that voice. He acknowledges (1986, 12) that Jesus "took away the ritual of Hebrew church law and dogma" as well as the Greek and Roman deification of reason and worldly knowledge and granted each person the right to a life sustained by personal communication with God," but nowhere does Schubert discuss what that Jewish law and dogma might be. Nor does Schubert address the pedagogical implication of this linguistic and legalistic shift.

Schubert states (1986, 60) that Augustine "moved in a more reconciliatory direction by attempting to join the teachings of Plato with those of the Church," but Schubert never acknowledges a) how Plato's own philosophy can be distinguished from Jewish philosophy or b) how Augustine interpreted Jewish practice as idolatry. Nor does Schubert note the clearly anti-Semitic bias of Augustine's teachings. According to Augustine, the Jews wrongfully took signs for literal things and, therefore, did not look beyond those signs; they could not, thus, believe in Jesus. Christian practice, following Augustine, interpreted the sign and elevated those signs to actually be the things they represent. Entire curricula, especially in reading, were constructed based in this position; the alternative Jewish tradition that Augustine branded heretical is never given voice and remains yet absent from curricular history and discursive practices. Its postmodern disguise continues the silencing of Jewish wisdom in curriculum discourses and continues the expropriation of and delegitimization of the Jewish voice. Yet, in his text, Schubert writes (1986, 3) that "My primary purpose is to convey the character of curriculum knowledge to those who will need to use it. Clearly it is addressed to those who plan to be curriculum leaders in schools as well as to scholars." It is a knowledge of dubious character talking clearly out of only one side of its mouth.

I do not mean to address the historical motives for the exclusion of Jewish philosophical thought in educational discourses. It is enough here to acknowledge the silences. Schwab worked amidst the silences. For Judaism, no less than for Platonism, the idea that thought is a philosophy is incontrovertible. Heschel (1955, 14) says

> The major premises of Western philosophy are derived from the Greek way of thinking. There is more than one way of thinking. Israel and Greece not only developed divergent doctrines; they operated within different categories. The Bible, like the philosophy of Aristotle, for example, contains more than a sum of doctrines; it represents *a way of thinking*, a specific context in which general

concepts possess a particular significance, a standard of evaluation, a form of orientation; not only a mental fabric but also a certain disposition or manner of interweaving and interrelating intuitions and perceptions, a unique loom of thought.)

In his text, *Ancient Jewish Philosophy*, Israel Efros (1964, 1), situates the origins of Jewish philosophical thought in the Bible. "Jewish philosophy, as a statement of a unified world view, starts not with Rab Saadia Gaon, but with the Bible." But, perhaps, because it starts with a unified world view that is not idealist, it asks a different set of questions to which it might seek answers. Abraham Joshua Heschel (1955, 24) states boldly:

> In reading the works of Western philosophy it is Plato or Aristotle, the Stoics or the Neoplatonists, whom we meet again and again. The spirit of their thinking hovers over every page of philosophical writing. However, we would look in vain for the Bible in the recesses of Western metaphysics . . . . What we mean by the absence of the Bible . . . is the spirit, the way of thinking, the mode of looking at the world, at life; the basic speculations about being, about values, about meaning. Open any history of philosophy. Thales or Parmendes is there; but is Isaiah or Elijah, Job or Ecclesiastes ever represented? The result of such omission is that the basic premises of Western philosophy are derived from the Greek rather than the Hebraic thinking.

From a somewhat different perspective, Steven Katz (1975, 10) argues that Jewish philosophy "arose out of the confrontation between Jewish religion and Greek philosophy (particularly the Stoic-Platonic tradition) and had as its aim the philosophic interpretation of Judaism. It also had an apologetic purpose: to show that Judaism is a kind of philosophy, whose conception of God is spiritual and whose ethics is rational." Nevertheless, Katz acknowledges that Jewish philosophy is authentically Jewish; that it remains unvoiced in Western discourses renders it silent and invisible.

If our educationally defining moment is the Greeks, then all subsequent history is a movement from that beginning, and, indeed, that appears to be how educational philosophical histories are written. Gerald Gutek (1972/1987) does not have the word *Jewish* or *Hebrew* in his entire index, though in the text there are chapters covering educational history from its beginnings (the Greeks) to Twentieth Century Educational Trends. Aquinas and the Venerable Bead and Augustine are, as you might expect, heavily featured. In his more recent book, *Philosophical Foundations: A Biographical Introduction* (1999), Gutek again begins with Plato and ends with Mao Zedong. In between there is not one representative of Jewish philosophy nor Jewish influence on education. Similarly, in Jacobsen's *Philosophy in Classroom Teaching* (1999), the author's time line of philosophers conspicuously divides philosophical time into the traditional Christian demarcation of The Ancients (those who came before Christ), the Moderns, and the Postmoderns. Interestingly enough, there is no philosopher listed from Aristotle to Francis Bacon. That marks a span of almost 1,800 years. It is at least during those years that the entire Talmud was composed, when Philo Judaes, Moses Maimonides, Abraham ben Izra, Saadia Gaon, and Joseph Albo, among many, many others, continued to write. Baruch Spinoza is not mentioned. Martin Buber, Moses Mendelssohn, Abraham Joshua Heschel, Mordechai Kaplan, and an entire host of Jewish writers are rendered voiceless.

THE THIRD POINT

The third point, which constitutes my thesis is that there might be a renascence of the field of curriculum, a renewed capacity to contribute to the quality of American education when curriculum energies are infused with the discourses of Talmudic study. Joseph Schwab argued strongly for this renascence. By the practical, Schwab referred "to a complex discipline, relatively unfamiliar to the academic and differing radically from the disciplines of the theoretic. It is the discipline concerned with choice and action . . . . Its methods lead to defensible decisions where the methods of the theoretic lead to warranted conclusion . . . ." (1969a, 2). If curriculum development and practice were to based in the practical, then "there will be renaissance of the field of curriculum, a renewed capacity to contribute to the quality of American education" (1969a, 1). For Schwab, education had failed American youth and American society. Most of the competence deficiencies and satisfaction deficiencies evident in students, Schwab argues, "point unmistakably to deficiencies of curriculum" (1969b, 29). It is not of these deficiencies I would speak; rather, I would enter into the conversation the methods and discourses of Talmudic study that I believe Joseph Schwab advocated and employed and that might offer to the curriculum field the opportunity for its renascence.

Chapter Two

THE VALUE OF SCHOOLING

Joseph Schwab was concerned with the value of schooling, which to his mind, had lost its significance. Of what worth, he wondered, is curriculum? What purposes ought the school to serve? Of course, Schwab's concern was not original to him. At the veritable beginning of the twentieth century, John Dewey had written (1916/1966) what must have been considered even at that time an historical cliché: education was a necessity of life. Education, Dewey asserted, made possible the constant renewal of social life. All social groups maintained their integrity and vitality by passing on to their young the values and skills which that society esteems. In exchange for the costs of education—these will be financial and social—society receives stability, and even continuity. Education as a social process is, thus, embedded in social vision. As I often recount to undergraduates, education is absolutely unnecessary *unless* there previously exists a vision of a social order that ought to arise as a result of that education.

I have, I suppose, stated yet another cliché. Education must have function, but first it must have purpose. If one is to truly learn, then that learning must somehow be understood as an enhancement to existence. We learn because *what* is learned is immediately important *to our lives.* That is, it is not the material alone but the context in which that material is encountered that defines the engagement with learning. And that context—that relevance—cannot be imposed upon a life; rather, that relevance must be derived from it. "The aim of education," Dewey argued, "is to enable individuals to continue their education—or that the object and reward of learning is continued capacity for growth" (1916/1966, 100). The aim of learning is to learn. The aim of learning is to enhance our capacities to live our lives with greater levels of satisfaction and reward.

Steeped in relevant content—and context—education occurs quite naturally in the act of living a life; education happens because of a human desire to ensure the continuation of life and growth. "Life grows," Dewey avers, "when a temporary falling out is a transition to a more extensive balance of the energies of the organism with those of the conditions under which it lives" (1934/1980, 14). That is, unless we err, we do not learn. Erring creates imbalance, and learning becomes the attempt to restore that balance. Once that balance is restored, the one who has become educated possesses another strategy in approaching the ambiguous, though not wholly strange, future. In America's rural economies, learning had been, for the most part, informal: If we wanted eggs for breakfast, we went out to the barn to gather them. We learned from where eggs derived; we did the work ourselves. We counted the requisite number of eggs necessary hopefully to satisfy the family's hunger. We prepared and breakfasted on the eggs with the adults who had first sent us out to the barn. At that meal, we may have discussed the day and its obligations. We engaged in life and learned from our efforts, which were most likely not always at first fully successful. Many eggs were probably and regrettably broken. But education—learning—occurred in the acts of living. In that context and time, such activities probably did not require the label of education: What happened was life. One participated—retrieved the eggs—one learned a great deal about eggs, and one was satisfied.

I do not mean to oversimplify or romanticize these earlier times. I do not mean to call up breakfast at the Cleaver's as the quintessential American family educational experience. Farms disappeared and cities grew; diminishing chicken coops were seen by fewer and fewer children. And the various histories of the egg were obscured. Formal and intentional organizations known as schools—these are John Dewey's terms—arose, in part, because the complexities of democratic society required knowledges that would be learned only there. The question of what knowledge was of most worth became central. On the farm what had to be learned was obvious and practical, but in the absence of daily practicality the question of what ought to be learned moved to prominence. Curriculum struggles in the twentieth century have arisen over this issue (see Kliebard, 1987, Cracco et al., 1999). Not all requisite knowledge might be eventually learned—nor must all programmed knowledge need be learned.

As society grew in complexity, much of what was necessary to learn required formal instruction. For example, in the burgeoning cities chicken coops were not easily kept, and eggs were acquired not from under chickens but from behind store counters. Outside of rural economies, a different way of thinking about numbers was necessary and must necessarily be taught. The economic and social exigencies of life supplanted the social center of the family farm, and what life required could no longer be acquired so informally in the very natural act of maintaining a life. Dewey (1916/1966, 8) wrote: "Much of what adults do is so remote in space and in meaning, that playful imitation is less and less adequate to reproduce its spirit. Ability to share effectively in adult activities thus depends upon a prior training given with this end in view. Intentional agencies—schools—and explicit materials—are devised." Though in play we often see the mirroring (or mimicking) of adults by our children, too much of the world's necessities are beyond the immediate view and ken of those children. Schooling became a social necessity. Schooling became a preparation, but became also a substitute for living; in schools, students were sequestered away, as it were, in preparation for their life as adults. Adults struggled over the substance and method of that preparation. Curriculum became a central concern of society and the school.

"What knowledge is of most worth?" Herbert Spencer asked in 1860, and we have not ceased debating that issue since. Clearly, however, the answer to that question depends on the nature of the society that that education seeks to produce, and there is no dearth of ideas regarding these educational ends. "[T]he search for a sound general education is as various and unending as the search for the good society itself and there are many roads to Rome," wrote the post-World War II Committee on General Education in a Free Society (Harvard University, 1946, 80). The identity of that particular knowledge to be communicated—and learned—depends on the social vision that should result from that education. A society of workers demands vocational education in skills and values; a society of intellectuals requires a different educational program. Such varied education produces varied societies—of Morlocks and Elois. The dangers intrinsic to the conflicting knowledges and ignorances is aptly portrayed in H. G. Wells's horrifying novel, *The Time Machine*.

It is not my intent to write here a history of curriculum. But it is integral to my purpose to acknowledge that issues of *what knowledge is of most worth* have sat at the center of curriculum controversy since education's inception and are very much tied to the nature of the social ends envisioned for each student. Certainly, curriculum—what knowledge was of most worth—was the concern of Joseph Schwab. He argued against the exclusion of "the practical competences of deliberation" from curricular content. The exclusion of such practical competences left the curriculum effete: "Our systems of lectures, lecture notes, prescribed readings, and examinations must make room for some experience of deliberation and reasonable choice, of mutual criticism, of a pooling of diversities of experience and insights—and do so frequently enough and effectively enough to constitute them as sources of durable satisfaction" (1969b, 30). As they were constituted, however, schools offered nothing that would provide such satisfaction.

I want to posit here that education in the United States has been apparently constructed as a system of trade. For the education each student acquired, she/he is expected to offer something in exchange: time, effort, and/or money. In return for the education it funds, society expects some valued social return. In these terms, education might be considered a commodity with value. Karl Marx (1967, 48) had written, "In order to produce [commodities] . . . he (i.e., the capitalist) must not only produce use-values, but use-values for others, social use-values . . . . To become a commodity, a product must be transferred to another, whom it will serve as a use-value, a means of an exchange." Commodities may be exchanged for other commodities with significant use-values. Education understood as a commodity must have use-value, and that value must be understood by those who make exchange for it. One issue that swirls about in education today concerns the discrepancy between the expected exchange undertaken by those directly engaged within the classroom—students—and the exchange expected from those outside it—society in general. Issues of accountability insist that lists of standards and objectives be constructed and strictly adhered to so as to maintain a specific social vision; education has become a sorting tool.

Joseph Schwab (1969b) decried this form of standardized education as antithetical not only to education, but to democracy as well. For Schwab, the exchange was characterized by inequalities. He complained that in such educational environments, students are infantalized and made incompetent. The function of the school ought to be "the discovery of intellectual competences, discloser of principles and methods, mastery of arts, and the use of these disciplines in the recovery and extension of knowledge," and, Schwab pleaded, curriculum must foster these aims for the sake of the individual and society. At present, however, the curriculum as theorized and practiced was ineffective. Worse, "the field of curriculum is moribund, unable by its present methods and principles to continue its work and desperately in search of new and more effective principles and methods" (1969a, 1). The results of these failures are enormous: Schools have failed in their primary function—to enable competences of "listening, looking, reading and thinking" (1969b, 29). Schwab said that "we have left [students] ignorant of the complex structure of knowledge, innocent of the exacting work involved in the responsible concern for truth, and undisciplined in the discrimination of meaning and the estimation of possibility" (1969b, 21). Indeed, Schwab held that "most of these competence deficiencies and satisfaction deficiencies point unmistakably and in the most conventional sense to deficiencies of curriculum" (1969b, 29). Education as it had been presently constituted had no exchange value.

Schwab felt that as education presently existed, for those engaged in the educational process, "It is not obvious and not irrelevant that knowledge is a consumable goods—in a specific and urgent sense. Problems are solved by applying new practices and policies. These practices and policies derive from knowledge currently in hand. It is precisely these solutions—these policies and practices,—which give rise to the next generation of problems, for new practices divert the old streams of events; some things are different now from what they were; new connections were established and new interactions have occurred" (1969b, 268-9). For Schwab, education ought to help people solve problems in the application of new practices and policies (1969b, 268). These practices and policies must derive from knowledge presently in hand, but may not be found within that knowledge; that discovery is wholly dependent on context and how present knowledge might be transformed—translated into practice by intelligence. "It is not only more knowledge of the kind we already know which is required but new forms of knowledge, stemming from new kinds of questions and problems, new principles of enquiry, which reach out for new kinds of facts and interpret them in new ways" (1969b, 269). At present, Schwab complained, the classroom was blind to the future. Speaking specifically of the college general education curriculum, but applicable even moreso to the work of the public school, Schwab said that "the majority of these required general courses and core-requirement fulfillments are of another kind [of knowledge]: surveys of knowledge, instillation of 'principles' abstracted from their meaning—conferring structure, or intensive drills in fundamental facts without the framework which confers their significance on them" (1969b, 201). In this system of exchange, students are offered worthless merchandise: either what they do not need or that for which they have no practicable use. In exchange for such knowledge, students offer up their lives.

A BRIEF EXCURSUS

In American educational history, sometimes the nature of the exchange has been clear though not necessarily certain. When the Yale faculty (in Willis et al., 1994, 26-37) argued that a liberal arts college curriculum ought to lay the foundation of a future education, they were addressing the upper classes of society whose privileges included the luxury of not having to labor for their survival while they attended school where they studied the intentionally not-practical liberal arts curriculum. The Yale faculty had argued that the purpose of the liberal arts education was to discipline the mind (faculty psychology) and to furnish that mind—the seat of a yet unmeasured intelligence—with the best materials human kind had produced. In this educational encounter, in exchange for enrollment in schooling a student would develop his mental powers and acquire a well-furnished and powerful mind. But, that education would not necessarily enable a student to know how to do anything, at least not in a practical way.

The Yale faculty had argued in 1828 that, indeed, the liberal arts curriculum ought to have no practical function. As Aristotle had argued more than a few years earlier, anything but a liberal education would deform the growth and form of the individual. Clearly the ideal nature of this education was suited only those for whom education was no sacrifice and could be claimed only by those for whom work could be postponed or altogether avoided. Clearly, these privileged graduates were understood to be marked as future social leaders, and the education they acquired at school ought to prepare them to assume leadership roles in the variety of professions and social positions available to them. In exchange for payment for a Yale education, and for the investment in time and effort such endeavor demanded, students would acquire intellectual acumen to pursue further education and to eventually assume roles central to social functioning. In exchange for time and effort, students would be given the tools of power.

With the invention of the common school in the nineteenth century, (I have neither time nor inclination to discuss the political and/or social motivations for educational agendas here) and attendance in it by the lower and middle classes, this liberal arts curriculum came under attack for being exactly what it was meant to be—impractical. Students in the common school had intention to spend but a few (often, forced) years in education before they went necessarily out into the world of vocations.

Often, these children were sent to school by parents who did not know what else to do with their charges during the daylight hours in the off-seasons of farm life. Nor did the vast majority of the social world of vocations require education as a necessity. Even middle-class students did not find much need for even a high school experience before embarking on a life of work and the daily essay of life. But with the growth of mandatory educational laws, the questions concerning the value of that formal education of which the school curriculum consisted remained: what was exchanged in such an educational system, and what could one acquire in it? Schwab (1978, 137) wrote that traditionally "The task of the school was to provide the verbal arts, some taste and experience of the fine arts and literature, a modicum of mathematics, a great deal of history and a larger and more heterogeneous society than that afforded by the home environment—this last to provide experience of men and of the manners and morals of leadership." But, Schwab continued, for most students in the latter part of the twentieth century, to employ Marx's terms, what could be acquired in school had veritably no use value, and for the vast majority of the population, little could be exchanged for engagement in that education. For the most part, school was an irrelevant luxury—and it was the luxurious social classes that received whatever social benefits might derive from formal education. These privileged students continued to occupy professions of power. And while they feasted on the best that Western culture had to offer, the rest of the population, as do the little ones in the folk song, "The Fox," "chewed on the bones." Schwab insisted that if students were to be given bones upon which to chew, then there must be meat upon those bones.

Despite the ideal hopes of the advocates of the Common school movement, education did not become the social equalizer its advocates hoped it would be. Horace Mann had idealistically looked to education as the quintessential institution of democracy. In 1848 he had written, "Education . . . beyond all other devices of human origin, is the great equalizer of the conditions of men—the balance wheel of the social machinery" (in Cremin, 1957, 87). The common school, where all social classes (but not necessarily genders, and certainly not all races!) attended school *in common*, would ensure democratic development and equal opportunity. The meritocracy that Mann and his colleagues envisioned never materialized; perhaps it was always a narrow sighted vision. The educational meritocracy assumed by Mann, presumed a society of equal access and opportunity, where exchange was governed by principles that ensured some sense of fairness and justice. But that society has always been—and and continues to be—a far cry from reality. Scholarship monies notwithstanding, academic success has less to do with effort than with social support which includes, but is not limited to, financial means. For example, Gerald Bracey (2002) reports that though all students regress during summer vacations (hence the argument for year-round school), children in inner cities regress more in Math and Reading during those summer vacations than do children in middle-class suburban communities. Clearly, in the latter communities, opportunities to continue reading are plentiful and well supported by and in the social structures, whereas in the former environments support for this learning is visibly detracted, unavailable, or simply missing.

Clark Kerr, an advocate of the concept of meritocracy, said, "The great university is of necessity elitist—the elite of merit—but it operates in an environment dedicated to an egalitarian philosophy. How may the contribution of the elite be made clear to the egalitarians, and how may an aristocracy of intellect justify itself to all men?" (in Lemann, 1999, 139). Kerr was perhaps speaking from desire and hope, but certainly he was not expressing a social reality. Kerr imagined educational environments wholly isolated from outside influence. Even access to the great universities was not equal nor based equally on merit; much less so was the availability of social resources and support. Nor did the work of this "aristocracy of merit" offer a just society in exchange to those whose effort supported that aristocracy. Even today, though the Wisconsin Educators Association declares, "Every kid deserves a great school," we cannot even agree upon the definition of a great school, much less allocate the resources to establish one. George W. Bush's charge that "no child be left behind" does not include social programs to ensure that each child has even the physical sustenance to maintain the social pace the schools support, advocate, and demand. Nor included in Bush's cry is the assurance that the schools themselves will have adequate resources to ensure that each child is at peace and on pace. Though we have no lack of standards, we assume that their existence is sufficient to effect proper learning and leave no child behind. In this view, schools are assumed to be islands of equality floating undisturbed in oceans of inequality. Nor have we established a society—my suspicion is that a democracy could never do so—that uniformly supports the work of an agreed-upon definition of a great school. Nor will brilliant teachers and a dynamic curriculum comfort a hungry or abused child. Nor will cared for and physically healthy children in a "great school" be necessarily academically or even socially successful. Hence the tragedy exemplified in Littleton, Colorado. Students in our schools have little sense of for what their effort is to be exchanged. Certainly, if they do not know what it is that they acquire, they have little sense of a value of education. Use value and exchange value are problematic when it comes to education.

As Schwab argued, education divorced from the lives of its students is a meaningless enterprise and has no value. For such education, there is no perceived use, nor can it be exchanged for anything that could be deemed valuable. Perhaps in this case, it does not even deserve the name, "education." Nothing is acquired. The classically oriented liberal arts curriculum proved irrelevant to children for whom liberal arts held no meaning. Whatever it could be exchanged for was neither valued nor evident. But, Schwab would argue, those liberal arts are not intrinsically without significance and value but were rendered meaningless by the curriculum in which they were embedded. The measures of exchange established in the schools were senseless, or false, or unfair. Students who had no intent to go on in school beyond the primary years were engaged in subjects that were not presented as having meaning to their daily lives. Curriculum was totally disassociated from the actual lives of the students. Schools were perceived as totally impractical. Useless. Irrelevant. Perhaps they even were.

Hence, arose a call for a practical education, for a meaningful education, a socially efficient education that would suit each citizen to an appropriate social position and adjust the vast majority of average citizens to life, ah, life. In exchange for the time and effort and behavioral cooperation necessary to succeed in school, students would acquire viable skills that would ensure not only their vocational success, but their life adjustment. In the world created by science, where the whole is comprised of the sum of its parts, each citizen functioning appropriately would yield a society efficiently operating in truly democratic fashion. Vocational education was advocated for all but the socially and financially elite—an education that would certainly be socially efficient in both its aims and its use of resources.[1] Eventually, and sooner rather than later, these students would require vocational

[1] A judge in a recent case (Gehring, 2002) in New York wrote that the State was responsible only for educating a child until the eighth grade and providing that child with the skills and values to enable him/her to be gainfully employed.

skills, and schools were the opportune environment for that training. Exchange should be precise, material, and obvious. For whatever time the children spent in school—whether by law or by choice—that time should be practically spent—preparing children for their hopefully long adulthood rather than for their brief and passing childhood. And since work was required by all, or since social roles—such as housekeepers—were prefigured, then let those functional skills and knowledges be the foundation of the curriculum. In this manner, the nature of education altered, and the idea of intelligence became tied to the capacities to learn ideal subjects in an ideal atmosphere. Smart was not what schools produced, but what they already required. Curriculum became a tool of social planning, and the pawns of its strategy soon knew how little agency they finally possessed.

The question of curriculum and its functions never abated. Following World War II, James Conant and the Harvard committee advocated a general education for all—not unlike the call of the earlier Committee of Ten in 1893, chaired as well by a president of Harvard, Charles Eliot. The latter had argued that education for college was equivalent to an education for life. The Committee of Ten had held that for as long as they remained in school, students would be heterogeneously grouped into classes in a slightly elective curriculum structure. But by 1945, this democratic ideal had changed. The Harvard committee argued that "The ideal of commonness must therefore, show itself chiefly in a common requirement rather than in a common way of carrying it out. There must be courses of different difficulty and different method in each of the three spheres of education, and the criterion for membership in these should be neither a student's intention in life nor his background nor the kind of diploma for which he is aiming, but simply whether or not a given course is the best for him—which is to say, his criterion of ability" (in Willis et al., 1994, 329). Everyone would learn the same things but at different levels of complexity and difficulty. Ah, if schools could only function so independent of the social fabric, and if ability existed independent of its social definition. Ah, if courses could be addressed not to their ends but to their means.

The nature of these spheres of existence defined by the committee, "the physical world," "man's corporate life," and "his inner visions and standards," were to consume those concerned with constructing and delivering curriculum and with its exactly defined use values.

These spheres had to be exactly defined, and their use values had to be eminently quantifiable and quantified. The separation of educational objectives into smaller and smaller units—Ralph Tyler's Basic Principles of Curriculum and Instruction, and Benjamin Bloom's Taxonomy of Educational Objectives and Madelyn Hunter's Eight Steps to Lesson Design—allowed the definition of the exchange values to become more and more focused. Whatever was taught in school must have visible accountability both inside and outside of it. Insistence on immediate accountability and practicality demanded clear measures of outcomes. Everything had to be defined by its exact purpose, even those courses that represented remnants of the liberal arts curriculum. In the consistent hierarchy of educational objectives, citizenry depended upon knowledge of grammar and the cultural canon, and hence a modicum of the liberal arts curriculum was *de rigueur* for all. But in reality, how students were taught tended to alienate most students because the curriculum addressed them according to perceived ability and according to practical concerns and future life paths. Exchange was based not on fairness but the social planning of the elite. The curriculum offered skills; it sought to make students practicable rather than smart. Schwab decried this development, an education based in "professorial recital, memorization, and re-recital" (1969b, 20). But alas, as Eliot Eisner noted (1984, 205) and as the present advocacy of national standards attest, we are today no closer to Schwab's vision.

The point, however, Schwab might argue, is this: As long as schools are understood as institutions that prepare students for a specific place in society, then the curriculum that schools offer, of necessity, must direct students into that place and the curricular focus turns to training and not education. Or, rather, education becomes defined as training and the character of exchange defined as skills for time. Even upper- and middle class students are taught that forms of education have different value and that engagement in education directs each to a specific life roles. Recall Brian, in *The Breakfast Club*, whose belief that enrollment in shop class is an easy "A." That is, for Brian, manual labor—work that directly addresses vocational skills—lacks the rigor of academic courses, and can be exchanged for an easy "A" which will increase overall average academic score, which, in turn, increases the possibility of admission to a prestigious university. These vocational courses *because they address vocational skills* are of no value except as grade inflators for those who will not do manual labor for a living. The learning in this classroom is meaningless except as easy grades because there is nothing of value exchanged. The work itself is meaningless. When Bender asks pointedly why Brian considers the work "easy," Brian offers no response. Perhaps it is that he can now recognize the prejudices explicit in his statement; perhaps for the first time he was confronted with the prejudice explicit in his statement.

But for Brian, and the millions of Brians throughout the United States, school does serve as a classifying machine for a stratified society of the haves (the academically successful—social elites) and the have-nots, (academic inadequates—the workers). Schools did not function to expand ability by educating students but, rather, schools worked to efficiently train an ability already defined, and then to prepare each student for his/her role in the social structure. Schools did not enhance intelligence so much as work with "it"; whatever "it" was had previously been socially defined. Hence, students graduated with trained abilities to accomplish the tasks to which they had been directed by the curriculums in which they had engaged, but remained, in terms employed by Joseph Schwab, woefully inadequate to deal with life, the task for which schools ought to have been designed. Schools were divorced from life and the curriculum of those schools, though potentially viable, was without meaning. Schools did not make people smart. What students acquired from their school educational experience had little or no value.

THE IDENTITY OF KNOWLEDGE

Joseph Schwab (1969b, 29) held that the substance of education was inadequate because the "practical competences of deliberation are not . . . traditional obligations of the academic curriculum." Students never learn that "well-developed (intellectual) competences are a major source of human satisfaction"(1969b, 29). In too many of our classrooms, students do not so much acquire as they must relinquish. For the most part, students are required in the end to return all materials to the teacher, and students generally leave class empty handed and empty headed. Students are too often expected to give back to the teacher—in the form of tests founded upon imposed standards—what has been offered during the class. Students acquire, as it were, nothing. The complaint perennially made—and made pointedly by Joseph Schwab (1969b) is that education is useless—it has no exchange value.

Karl Marx had written (1967, 46) that "exchange-value is the only form in which the value of commodities can manifest itself or be expressed." But in schools, in exchange for their time and effort, students acquired little of value. As Schwab complained, if education has no exchange value, then it could be deemed useless and dismissed as irrelevant. Schwab complained that as presently constituted, schools were ineffective because students acquired little of value in the schools. "Students are irresponsible about facts and what they mean, about words and their reference, about ideas and their relationship to facts, *because we have left them ignorant of the complex structure of knowledge, innocent of the exacting work involved in a responsible concern for truth, and undisciplined in the discrimination of meaning and estimation of probability*" (1969b, 21, italics added). In the educational system, what students were offered not only had no currency—could be exchanged for little—but was, in fact, often completely worthless. Engaged in the educational effort, in fact, students acquired nothing.

Joseph Schwab believed that schools ought to make students smart; students should learn in school how decisions were made and, therefore, how to make decisions. In this endeavor, traditional knowledge of the structure of the disciplines might be necessary though not sufficient. Schwab's advocacy of discipline learning was qualified. Schwab believed that it was learning *in the disciplines* and not the disciplines themselves that should constitute curriculum. For Schwab, the disciplines themselves were always incomplete; the disciplines themselves were the *product* of knowledge rather than the mere *repository* of it. Schwab stated unequivocally, "Who knows the structure of the disciplines? The answer is *Nobody*" (1978, 243). The disciplines themselves existed because of a prior act of *meshikhah,* a term I will soon address in greater detail, but which the Rabbis defined as an act of physically pulling an object toward the one who wishes to acquire it. Schwab argued that "A given conclusion in science is therefore about a taken something, not an objectively given something; the conclusion is true only of that something as it is, and it seems, in its incompleteness and distortion, out of connection with much that would normally alter and affect it" (1978, 133). Schwab held that the knowledge of the disciplines must be understood as merely subject matter, "convenient groupings of things and events, groupings designed to facilitate their study in a disciplined way" (1978, 267). The disciplines, rather than being natural, were an artificial but convenient fiction.[2] In this perspective, Schwab's statement concerning the disciplines reminds me of William James' comment (1907/1970, 66) about the weather: "The low thermometer today," James wrote, "is supposed to come from something called the 'climate.' Climate is really only the name for a certain group of days, but it is treated as if it lay behind the day, and in general, we place the name, as it were a being, behind the facts it is the name of." The disciplines are not real, though in schools we act as if they had real existence.

Schwab said that a discipline was a *useful* fiction, but a fiction nonetheless; if students were to become smart, then the identity of the discipline as a fiction ought to be highlighted, and the means by which that particular fiction might be translated into the practical situation in the actual life of the student must be made clear. The problem with a curriculum organized by the discipline structures was that it was not practical; rather, "it was *virtually* practical [but] not *actually* so" (1978, 267, emphasis in original). The structures of the disciplines dealt ideally with the world in artificially organized systems, whereas "practical problems have the nasty habit of arising on one or another of quite different grouping of things and events." Problems were, in fact, not neatly discipline specific, but messy and interdisciplinary, as it were. Education as traditionally organized into and by the disciplines could have little currency or circulation. Such education could have little use in the world in which the student lived. Rather, education must at best employ the disciplines to inspire education. "One major purpose of this recommended procedure is to introduce the child early to the experience of successfully solving problems, to provide him, through an external, objective element of experience in the school, with the inner experience of his own competence, his own ability to master and control a fragment of the world" (1978, 272). Schwab believed that curriculum required not division into disciplines, but the arts of joining those disciplines into a heuristic, what the Woods Hole conference would pejoratively refer to as "a nonrigorous method of achieving solutions in problems" (Bruner, 1960/1977, 61).

---

[2]Perhaps this could be best compared to the work of Phillip Phenix, who argued in *Realms of Meaning* (1964, 5) that "*general education is the process of engendering essential meanings*" (italics in the original). Schwab advocated meaning making as the work of education, but did not believe in "essential meanings."

Schwab's advocacy of deliberation seems to me modeled on the method of Talmudic discourse: "By way of associations, loose connections and indirect allusions, the Talmudic sugiya (a unit of discussion in the Talmud) drifts away" from its original subject to a variety of subjects, ranging from profound theological observations to folk tales and from intricate legal discourse to magic, science, and demonology . . . . [the discussions] preserve and clarify the wealth and multiplicity of approaches to the problem at hand" (Halbertal & Halbertal, 1998, 460). Schwab held that despite the artificiality of schools, perhaps even because of it, in deliberation students could there acquire not merely the *matter* of knowledge but the *process* of intelligence.

Schwab acknowledged that a solution to any problem was always an artificial answer and represented an "incomplete view." What Schwab called for in an earlier essay by the term, *engineering*, "a correlative semi-discipline [whose] task is to establish lines of connection between practical problems as they arise and are recognized with the disciplines whose substance contains the virtual solutions of these problems" (1978, 267), he would refer later to as *arts of the eclectic.* These arts are concerned with the particulars of the practical omitted by theory. "There are eclectic arts concerned with the incompleteness of each subject of the behavioral sciences" (1971, 503). Schwab advocated for the necessity of "the eclectic, of arts by which a usable focus on a common body of problems is effected among theories which lack theoretical connection" (1969a, 10). Schwab argued that "scholars, as such, are incompetent to translate scholarly material into curriculum" (1973, 501), a line I think as bold as Schwab's earlier accusation that the field of curriculum is moribund. Schwab acknowledged that no single subject of the social sciences was adequate to either explain reality or to consider it. "There is no foreseeable hope of a unified theory in the immediate or middle future, nor of a meta-theory which will tell us how to put those subjects together or order them in a fixed hierarchy of importance to the problems of curriculum. What remains as a viable alternative is the unsystematic, uneasy, pragmatic, and uncertain unions and connections which can be effected in an eclectic" (1969a, 10). Furthermore, these connections are always changing and, therefore, they require always different orderings of separate theories. Education was an active process of grasping and pulling towards. Solutions to real problems required an eclectic method that could approach a specific problem using a variety of perspectives drawn *from* the disciplines. Smart was not embedded in knowledge of the disciplines, but the ability to draw from them the means to solve a problem. Becoming smart was an active process of pulling toward. What ought one to pull, and for what might that merchandise be exchanged? How to effect a system of fair exchange in the classroom was problematic. But, then, Schwab was arguing from a Talmudic perspective.

Chapter Three

What Is Jewish about Joseph Schwab

This is not a biography of Joseph Schwab, and so I do not intend to situate him in his Jewish life. I do not know if Joseph Schwab engaged in an observant Jewish life; for my purposes here, this participation is not relevant. Nor is it my intention to "out" Joseph Schwab as a Hebrew dressed in Greco-Christian clothing, though in the project of this book I intend to make clear that Schwab's Jewishness was central to his work in curriculum. In fact, my intention is not so much an outing as an embedding. I would like to suggest that Schwab's work can be best understood—indeed, may only be fully understood—when it is situated in Jewish discursive traditions. I think that Schwab worked in an environment implicitly anti-Semitic and with texts that wholly ignored and/or completely misunderstood Jewish wisdom. He was constrained to speak a strange language in a strange land. As such, he may not have been properly heard.

In education, our knowledge stems from the texts we read, but those texts are riven with silences and prejudices. If Schwab's work is misunderstood, misrepresented, and misread, if his work has had minimal influence on American education, perhaps this condition results from the necessity of translating his thought into a language and tradition that of necessity would distort it. In a magnificent essay on Joyce's *Ulysses*, Leslie Fiedler comes to understand that "I was Bloom, a comic, earthbound father who is also an Apostle to the Gentiles; which is to say, I have discovered at long last that I am a Hebrew of the Hebrews and a Pharisee of the Pharisees who, try as he will to be all things to all men, cannot resist, from time to time, still kicking against the pricks" (1991, 46). Perhaps the same may be said of Schwab: In the attempt to speak to all men, he of necessity misrepresented his thought—even, perhaps, misrepresented it to himself. But in his strong criticism of education—no, in his strong condemnation of it—Schwab was a Hebrew of the Hebrews and a Pharisee of the Pharisees, still kicking against the pricks. I do not here intend to give voice to Joseph Schwab; I think his voice is eloquent enough. My intention is to suggest that Schwab's work is rooted solidly in Jewish practice and wisdom, and that to appreciate Schwab's remarkable achievements in curriculum requires situating him in that Jewish tradition. The discourses of American education have avoided almost completely any reference to Jewish educational practices; implicit in this virtual silence is a denial of any influences. I would like to speak here from the place if that silence.

THE SILENCES OF JOSEPH SCHWAB

There was this conference. Held January 8-10, 1973 at the Ohio State University, it was entitled "Applying Jewish Scholarship to Contemporary Programs of Education." The conference was sponsored by the Melton Research Center for Jewish Education and the Jewish Studies Program of The Ohio State University. The Melton Center is the research arm of the Jewish Theological Seminary of America's total education program, and the conference was meant, in the words of Chancellor Gerson Cohen, to "enlist the scholars to interpret the tradition, and work with educators and others to mediate their interpretations and translate their research into school curricula at various levels" (in Fox & Rosenfield, 1977, ix-x). This conference was part of the Melton Center's total educational program and strove to facilitate the translation of theory—mere texts—into practice—curriculum. The conference was part of an ongoing project, said Cohen, to "achieve a modern Jewish *paideia*, which would once again make of Torah the pervasive force that it has always been in great periods of Jewish creativity. Such a *paideia* would include not only knowledge of classical texts in the original language, but a total ethos that would reflect a Jewish response to modernity and a Jewish articulation of genuine modernity" (in Fox & Rosenfield, 1977, x). The achievement of such a project "will not create a perfect society or a scintillating system of Jewish education . . . [but] . . . it can . . . help us to define our problems in all their complexity and to focus on genuine diagnoses and solutions." Such an education, Chancellor Cohen argued, "requires not only mastery of the great Jewish texts, but the transformation of the texts' essential philosophy into life forces" (in Fox & Rosenfield, 1977, xv). What was sought was a translation into curriculum.

This project seemed based in the complaint uttered several years earlier by Schwab when he declared the field of public school curriculum moribund, no longer able to continue its work. More recently, David Purpel has written about a similar moral and spiritual crisis pervading contemporary public secular education. In language that recalls Chancellor Cohen's charge to the conference participants, Purpel (1989, 3) speaks about curriculum's "evasion or neglect of larger, more critical topics and the stress put on technical rather than on social, political, and moral issues." It is a similar sterility in Jewish education to which Fox and Cohen referred. Schwab, sensitive to the barrenness of curriculum and the ineffectiveness of the public schools, called for the renaissance of both. Identifying a similar vacuity in Jewish education, the conferees called upon Schwab to address this crisis of principle, and Schwab spoke in the language he had earlier used in his addresses to the public schools. Schwab recognized the similarity of issues and needs. Interestingly enough, Ralph Tyler, another conference participant, distinguished between the work of this conference as it might effect the American Jewish educational condition and the applicability of the conferees' effort to the American public school and its work. Tyler apparently saw a distinction between a public school classroom and that of a Jewish schoolroom. "We know that you are people who have the kinds of intellectual interest and concern that are likely to be significant in the context of the American Jewish situation, and particularly, the American Jewish classroom" (1977, 100). But for Tyler, what might be good for the gander was not also good for the goose.

I appreciate the modesty yet urgency of these albeit, parochial curricular concerns with which the conference was to deal: it had been but a few years earlier that Joseph Schwab (1969a, 6) had declared the general curriculum field moribund and had described the crisis in curriculum as one where "the principles are exhausted—when the questions they permit have all been asked and answered—or when the efforts at enquiry instigated by the principles have at last exhibited their inadequacy to the subject matter and the problems which they were designed to attack." Schwab had argued that without a revitalization of curriculum, education would be not merely irrelevant, but tragic. Schwab, too, had spoken of a moral and spiritual crisis of enormous proportions. This 1973 conference to which I refer was meant to address from within a Jewish framework the effeteness of contemporary Jewish education. It would be, it would seem, a quite radical approach to Jewish education—that was the word used by Chancellor Cohen—an opportunity to employ discourses heretofore ignored to address issues of curriculum. It was a project akin to that which Schwab had charged the public curriculum field: How to recover curriculum from its death throes strangled as it was by its emphasis on theory. It required nothing less, declared Seymour Fox (Fox & Rosenfield, 1977, xvi), than "an educational approach which calls for the merging of many and diverse talents." Curriculum for Jewish education in America needed translation from theory to practice, from the sterile presentation of the authoritative voice of texts to a policy of textual interrogation and integration. This was, for these Jewish educators, a challenge of principles.

Appropriately enough, it was Joseph Schwab who was invited to "open the conference with a discussion of the many problems related to the application of the fruits of scholarship and research to elementary and secondary curricula" (Fox & Rosenfield, 1977, xvii). After all, it was Joseph Schwab who "had made a major contribution to the scholar-curriculum problem in general education, and had worked in this area with the Melton Faculty seminar" (Fox & Rosenfield, 1977, xvi). Schwab was invited to address issues concerning the revitalization of Jewish education by engaging the discourses he had earlier articulated in his attempt to examine and regenerate secular education. His charge was to assist in the translation of Jewish tradition into curriculum, a project not unlike that which Schwab had, not a few years earlier, described as so essential for the renaissance of the secular curriculum world. But Schwab was not the first Jew to practice or, in the view of some, perfect, the art of translating theory into practice. Indeed, Jewish Talmudic discourses—or perhaps, in a more postmodern spirit, certain veins of Jewish discourses—might similarly be understood as ***already*** the translation of theory into practice, of the scholar to the classroom. That is, I suggest that there is already intrinsic in Judaism a tradition of the practical—a translation to curriculum. I believe that this event—this translation—might be already part of the tradition of which Schwab had knowledge. As I have said, Schwab was Jewish and had been for some time active in educational programs within the Jewish communities. Schwab had been integral to the development of curricula for Ramah summer camps—and so it might be to Judaism to which we might look for the origins of the now well-known "practical." This knowledge might, finally, offer some insight into the work of Joseph Schwab that has at various times been called oblique and frustratingly dense.

Indeed, Schwab's "translation" might be already situated within the discourses of the Rabbinic Judaism that produced and redacted the Talmud in the early centuries of the present millennium. Perhaps an acknowledgment of, and an introduction to such methodology of these texts and practices to curriculum practice might today add to the richness of curriculum discourse and translation, as Schwab might have advocated. The purpose here is not mean to proselytize; rather, I mean to enrich the discourses of curriculum engaging other sets of languages and lenses heretofore disregarded and to continue to add to what Joseph Schwab would call a polyfocal conspectus, "an alternation of mastery of a view-affording doctrine with thorough going involvement in bringing the doctrine to bear as a revealing lens on real, simulated, or reported instances of its subject matter" (1971, 516). Polyfocal conspectus—as both means and ends—is the employment of a variety of lenses and discourses to effect practice. A polyfocal conspectus—deliberation—might be also understood as the method of Talmudic discourse in which the intricacies and problems of everyday life were interrogated and discussed in public discourse. The end of these deliberations using a variety of rhetorical and textual strategies was life in the practically mundane.

A RELIGION OF DEEDS: THE PRACTICAL

Judaism might be understood fundamentally as a religion of deeds. As Martin Buber once wrote, Christian thinking tends to focus on identifying the correct beliefs to hold, whereas Jewish thinking tends to focus on "doing the right things." Abraham Joshua Heschel (1955, 292), the great Jewish philosopher, says that for Judaism "Every deed is a problem; there is a unique task at every moment. All of life at all moments is the problem and the task." That is, Judaism is a religion of events: Attachment to the text represents the attachment of the Jew to events. Heschel writes that "In the Torah, nothing is said about books [the patriarchs or matriarchs] wrote or ideas they innovated. Instead, we are told tales of their adventures, their deeds . . . . Hence we learn the purpose of Jewish existence: we are obligated to live lives that will become Torah, lives that are Torah" (1996, 67). Heschel reminds us that for Judaism a good deed performed with impure motives is yet a good deed. "Judaism," says Heschel, "is not a science of nature but a science of what man ought to do with nature . . . . It takes deeds more seriously than things." Robert Brody (1998, 283) says that "Classical Judaism placed very little emphasis on dogma . . . [Judaism] was much more a religion of 'works' than of 'faith,' and that one's membership in good standing in the religious community depended on practical observance rather than on formal assertions of belief." We might understand Judaism as situated in the immediate; learning occurs in the doing. Heschel writes (1996, 136) that "When Moses recounted to the people the laws of the covenant with God, the people responded, 'We will do and we will hear.' This statement was interpreted to mean: *In doing we perceive.*"

At its core, then, Judaism seems to be akin to the Schwabian translation of theory into the practical. If, for Schwab, the eclectic arts are "concerned with *bringing a principle to its case*" (1971, 504), then the eclectic rests at the heart of Judaism; it is the search for how to be a holy people in the daily act of being alive. Judaism might be the search for the specific in the general. Schwab says about curriculum: "The road we drive on has bends and potholes not included on the map. We teach not literature, but this novel and that. The child with whom we work is both more and less than the percentile ranks, social class, and personality type into which she falls" (1971, 496). Schwab's particularity, his practicality, might have its beginnings in the Jewish attachment to Torah.

It is to the text—the Torah—that the Jew looks for the knowledge that "life without commitment is not worth living; that thinking without roots will bear flowers but no fruit" (Heschel, 1996, 16). That text, however, always requires enquiry. Enquiry is the commitment Schwab insists is required to effect the deliberation which rests at the core of the practical. Enquiry is the ends and means of education. Schwab writes: "'Problem' has here its usual two senses. It stands for something we complain about or ought to complain about: a handicap, an undesirable, a vice. It also stands for the query by means of which we begin to seek correction of the vice complained of" (1971, 505). Talmud is the eclectic and far-roaming enquiry concerning Mishnah—the third-century written redaction of the centuries-old oral law. But unlike any other law text, Talmud represents the arts of the practical and the eclectic: No subject of interest to the ancient rabbis failed to find its way into this immense body of teaching, and for that reason no question arising in later centuries was deemed outside the range that Talmudic teaching might legitimately claim to resolve. Talmud represents a polyfocal conspectus. And as in Talmud, Schwab's "problem" is discovered by asking questions. Schwab says that problems may be discovered by the "examination of the various symptoms and the generation of alternative responses or treatments of these problems." I love to read Talmud for its method; two of the most common questions I find in Talmudic discourses are: "Why did the rabbis say this?" and "Where did this idea come from?" The doctors of the Talmud discuss issues and feel no compulsion to come to conclusion. Indeed, many opinions are offered though few are disclaimed.

Enquiry has always been at the center of Jewish practice. The opening portion of the *Pirke Avot* (1:2) declares that "Upon three things the world exists: upon the Torah, upon the temple service, and upon the practice of charity." The Temple service disappeared in 70 C.E. with the destruction of the Temple, and study replaced the sacrifice and service performed there. Study for Rabbinic Judaism was situated in the practice of questioning and answering: It was in the institution of this process that the Rabbis saved Judaism after the destruction of the Temple and the end of sacrifice. The study of texts replaced the sacrifice, and the study of texts was accomplished by asking questions. "Study consists of thinking everything that is thinkable in a question, thoroughly, at all costs" (in Ouaknin, 1995, 62). Thus, for Rabbinic Judaism, text—its study and an ethics that is implicit to and derives from the study of that text—sustains the world.

But textual study only reaps value in practice. It cannot be sterile conversation. There is a story in *Ketubot*, a tractate of Talmud, about Rav Yehudah, a great scholar. Yehudah would study Torah until twilight six days a week, but he would return every Shabbat to his wife and, in the celebration of the day, engage in marital relations with her. When he walked home each Shabbat the people would see before him a column of fire. One day, Yehudah became so engrossed in study that he failed to return home. The story continues: "Because they didn't see this sign, Rabbi Yannai said to them, 'Overturn his bed, for if Yehudah were alive he would not cancel his marital obligation . . . .' Indeed, it was on that day that Yehuda died." By failing to translate text to action, Yehudah had abandoned life. Here is an exemplar of a curriculum from which to learn and to heal. In this Talmudic story, we might discover a rich source of Schwab's translation.

TRANSLATION INTO CURRICULUM

Schwab's presentation at this conference was the now-recognized third installment of the practical: translation into curriculum. But that translation remained unclear because Schwab would not, or could not, acknowledge the sources of the discourse. As a result, perhaps, he remains thoroughly misunderstood. Seymour Fox (1985, 64), writing in *Curriculum Inquiry*, says that "From his earliest writings, Schwab has been searching for the appropriate role which theory can play in education." But I believe Schwab at the outset understood a relationship between theory and practice, but could not give voice to it using the Greco-Christian discourse prevalent in education. As a result, he was constrained to speak in a foreign tongue. Ralph Tyler's response to Schwab's "The Practical 4" was a reflection concerning how Schwab's work supports Tyler's own efforts, which date from the latter's experience as the Director of Evaluation of the Eight-Year Study. Something for curriculum professors to do results, says Tyler, in the construction of objectives. "As I read *Practical 4*, I found myself continually relating it to my own experience and seeking to judge Schwab's paper in practical terms. My judgment is that this is a very comprehensive overview of desirable curriculum practices. In terms of my experience, it is a sound, comprehensive, and coherent explanation of the bases of effective curricula" (1984, 102). But the preparation of objectives was not what Schwab had in mind in the Practical. Rather, Schwab meant that curriculum should be organized by the deliberative: Deliberation requires consideration of the widest possible variety of alternatives if it is to be most effective. "Each alternative must be viewed in the widest variety of lights" (Schwab, 1978, 319). What Schwab argues as the manner of curriculum planning ought to be also the matter of curriculum. This, as I will later show, is Talmudic practice.

Others, Wankowski and Reid (1982), for example, argued that Schwab was so obvious or "reasonable" as to be absolutely invisible and therefore, ineffectual. No doubt Schwab's influence on curriculum is dilettantish—professors of curriculum are familiar with him, but it remains John Dewey, Ralph Tyler, Madeleine Hunter, Henry Giroux, Paolo Freire, and Maxine Greene who sit so easily on the tongues of so many teachers. Declaring Schwab's approach to curriculum as "reasonable," Janek Wankowski indicates to me a thorough misunderstanding of Schwab's entire method. Though he acknowledges that, in Reid's words (127), Schwab "talks about the necessity of all those who are going to be involved in the consequences of a decision, making a contribution to it," Wankowski does not acknowledge—nor seems to recognize—that this pedagogical method is steeped already in a Rabbinic Judaism whose method has little to do with Greek dialogue. Nor does Wankowski appreciate the subtlety and complexity of Schwab's methods of enquiry, based as they are in Talmudic practice. David Kraemer (1990, 189) writes that "The Bavli makes the imperfect and imperfectible pursuit of truth the very center of its enterprise. It concerns itself and its students with multiple interpretations of scripture, with multiple opinions in the law, that is, with multiple approaches (but only approaches) to the truth" (Kraemer, 1990. 190). In Talmud, the conversation is paramount: "The text is the initial conversation which expands and develops by dialogue with it. Re-enactment is not a repetition: the student introduces a new interpretation, a novella or a *chidush* (a new way of approaching a problem)" (Halbertal & Halbertal, 461). Robert Goldenberg comments (1989, 105): "The well-known Talmudic penchant for hair-splitting dialectics reflects the rabbis' concern that each of these sets of teachings be internally consistent on the one hand and significantly different from any other such set on the other. Hence the frequency with which the Talmud records the chains of transmission by which individual sayings were passed on. Hence the steadily growing integration of teachings from widely disparate fields of law into a single web, and the often forced effort to find unifying principles behind teachings that seem to have nothing to do with one another." Or, as Steinsaltz (1976, 99) notes, in Talmud, "[a]ny subject under the sun may be related to another matter by internal association." Such is the thrust of Schwab's prescriptions for curriculum.

For Schwab, discourse and the process of argumentation remained paramount. Schwab's polyfocal conspectus is prefigured and defined by Talmudic method. Exploring principles of enquiry which Schwab advocated as the only basis of curriculum, Schwab (1969b, 86) offered method:

> Given two or three related enquiries, students can proceed by contrast and comparison to identify differences of terms, distinctions, data, interpretation. They are often able to reconstruct the questions being asked with sufficient precision to show the similarities and differences among them. Occasionally, it is possible to follow the trail back to a formulation of the principle itself.
>
> Depending on the clarity and coherence of the paper under study, the harvest of such an enterprise will be at least the discovery that the papers are not contradictions of one another; it will usually identify the perspective from which the enquirer has viewed the subject matter and what of it is visible from such a perspective: occasionally, it will permit the student to see when and under what circumstances of practice and application one view is preferable to another, what each can do that the other cannot.

Schwab's deliberation is based in Talmudic argumentation. This curriculum for Rabbinic Judaism which arose about 200-600 C.E. lies at the very center of a significant body of contemporary Judaic practice. I would say this curriculum had influence. In Talmud, we find origins of Schwab's arts of the practical and eclectic. But where is Schwab's influence? Schwab acknowledged that the issues of curriculum are particular and rest in the immediate task—the deed. Commitment is deed. Commitment is practice in the immediate. "Theories of curriculum and of teaching and learning cannot, alone, tell us what and how to teach, because questions of what and how to teach arise in concrete situations loaded with concrete particular of time, place, person and circumstance," says Joseph Schwab (1971, 494). Rather, the practical is always marked by the particular. That is, curriculum is always the activity of the classroom in which learning will occur. What that learning may be is situated in the practical via the arts of the eclectic. The practical is the translation of the theoretical—always insufficient—to the practical—necessarily imminent. Curriculum is not ***what is to be learned;*** rather, curriculum is ***what is learned.*** In his essay "The Practical: A Language for Curriculum," Schwab (1969a, 11-12) argues that

> The materials of a concrete curriculum will not consist merely of portions of "science," of "literature," of "process." On the contrary, their constituents will be particular assertions about selected matters couched in a particular vocabulary, syntax, and rhetoric. They will be particular novels, short stories, or lyric poems . . . . They will be particular acts upon particular matters in a given sequence . . . . The curriculum will be brought to bear not in some archetypical classroom but in a particular locus in time and space with smells, shadows, seats and conditions outside its walls which may have much to do with what is achieved inside. Above all, the supposed beneficiary is not the generic child, not even a class or kind of child out of the psychological or sociological literature pertaining to the child. The beneficiaries will consists of very local kinds of children and, within the local kinds, individual children. The same diversity holds with respect to teachers and what they do.

Curriculum is deed. And Judaism, as Schwab might have known, is a practice of deeds.

THE TRANSLATION FROM THEORY TO PRACTICE: THE ARTS OF THE ECLECTIC

The achievement of curriculum, Schwab (1978, 148) says, rests both in the use of materials that reflect enquiry and the "treatment of them

[that] must constitute a second enquiry." Literacy—the end of curriculum-is inquisitive; for Schwab, education is immersion in and development of what may have come to be called a cultural literacy. Abraham Heschel argues that the problem with our schools is that we teach children to weigh but not to wonder; this was Purpel's (1989) complaint as well. Schwab, too, was concerned with the education of wonder, and it is possible to assert that Schwab's work in total—and his specific talk at this conference—may have finally discussed not Jewish education but what might be already Jewish about education. Ironically enough, this love—of text, of study, of interpretation—will be what Schwab refers to elsewhere as the Platonic Eros (see, Schwab, 1978, 109). Schwab says in this early essay that education should function by eros, the energy of wanting—a pre-postmodern version of "desire." "Eros, the energy of wanting, is as much the energy source in the pursuit of truth as it is in the motion toward pleasure, friendship, fame, or power. Any means or method of education taps this energy source to the extent that the method is at all effective." The object of education is to link eros to enduring objects, to master the arts or skills or methods necessary to their pursuit, and to digest the knowledge which bases these arts and skills. In "The Impossible Role of the Teacher in Progressive Education" Schwab (1978/182) argues that "Only as the teacher uses the classroom as the occasion and the means to reflect upon education as a whole (ends as well as means), as the laboratory in which to translate reflections into actions and thus to test reflections, actions and outcomes against many criteria." This is not, however, Socratic dialogue. This is not the Platonic search for Truth: This is the "radical revision of curriculum materials" in both the "form of its materials and its way of treating them. The materials, says Schwab, (1978, 148), "must reflect enquiry, and treatment of them must constitute a second enquiry, engaged in by student and teacher alike, aimed at practicing the arts of enquiry and at grasp of that full meaning of a body of knowledge only the enquiry which produced it can supply." This, to my mind, is the method and purpose of Talmud.

Discussion leads not necessarily to truth, but to further deliberation. Outlining the functions of discussion, Schwab lists three criteria by which the instructor may judge the efficacy of a proposed plan or query. The *substantive* seeks whether the discussion is an efficient means of arriving at a specific planned goal; the *exemplary* asks whether it is a defensible instance of movement toward that kind of understanding; and the *stimulative* functions asks if the discussion is to produce any movement on the part of the students (1978, 126). Aristotelean though this sounds, it has its real roots in Talmud. But the Rabbis do not distinguish functions of discussion; rather, they engage in it. Yet, as Aristotelian as Schwab may sound, he is cautious to distance himself from Socratic dialogue where, "The end is reached in the allotted time, as a rule, and the student *seems* to move and grasp the conception, theory, or view which the instructor had in mind. It will be found, however, that at best the student moves from one carefully fashioned query to the next in much the same way a woman in high heels uses stepping-stones across a brook: the far shore is arrived at with a sigh of relief. The goal is reached, but no cognitive map of the route persists in the mind of the student" (1978, 127). Nonetheless, Schwab does not acknowledge his relationship to Talmudic discourse, where the circuitous and often cryptic discussion about so many details is clue that what is sought is the practical, the particular based in theory. It is how *to be* that is the subject of Talmud.

Schwab argued that curriculum should instill and develop this eros in the student. "The outcome of a liberal curriculum is *actively* intelligent people" (1978, 109). And this activity is realized in the act of enquiry; curriculum must teach and facilitate the process of enquiry. This clichéd truism is, of course, an issue for many curriculum theorists and not a few practitioners as well: Indeed, might we not acknowledge that it is this quest that is endemic to curriculum theorists—certainly to reading specialists—to create critical thinkers. Perhaps the translation of theory to practice is to be discovered in Jewish intellectual traditions.

REVIVING CURRICULUM

This conference, *Applying Jewish Scholarship to Education*, then, intended to examine curriculum theory and classroom practice with the hope of developing a renewed and renewable education system—to make a better world—and it meant to do so within the framework of Judaism. I think that Judaic discourses should lie at the center of curriculum discourse today and might be originally reflected in the work of Joseph Schwab. At the center of Judaism is the love and study of text—of Torah. This study is not theoretical but practical, reverential but critical: At the center of Judaism is practical study. Heschel (1996, 191) says, "Humans are never alone before God; the Torah and Israel are always with him . . . . What are the acts and moments in which man becomes attached to God. To the Jew, the Torah is the answer." That is, the only purpose of textual study is behavioral change. The end of Judaism is not mere textual exegesis but behavior; it is the text that stands always with the Jew; it is the text that always requires translation into practice. It is deeds in the text and not the idea of the text which sits at the heart of rabbinic Judaism. Opposed to the Greek cosmos, the Jew offers text—Torah: not idea, but event. Heschel (1996, 191) says that "Jewish existence is not only the adherence to particular doctrines and observances but primarily the living in the spiritual order of the Jewish people, living in the Jews of the past and with the Jews of the present." Judaism is the attachment to events. It is the Torah that situates the Jew in past, present, and future. Emmanuel Levinas argues that it is not God we have in this world—the world is too cruel and too mean to think of God within it—but rather, it is Torah that we possess. Levinas (1990a, 144) says that "the link between God and man is not an emotional communion that takes place within the love of a God incarnate, but a spiritual or intellectual [esprits] relationship which takes place through an education in the Torah. It is precisely a word, not incarnate, from God that ensures a living God among us. Confidence in a God Who is not made manifest through any worldly authority can rely only on internal evidence and the values of an education." The study of this text—the study of texts—became the center of Jewish practice after the destruction of the second Temple in 70 C.E. Thus, textual study is the center of rabbinic Judaism: The love of God's Torah surpasses the love of God. The Torah is the practical—it is deed. Its study—textual study—is the means of translation of the theoretical to the practical.

Schwab's practical might have its foundation in rabbinic Judaism. Curriculum must offer students not the meaning of texts, but the variety of possible meanings of texts and the opportunities to try the several meanings as several different ways of looking on the problem. Perhaps his embeddedness in Socratic education prevented Schwab from giving voice to Talmudic language. But I think it may be possible to understand Joseph Schwab's deliberation as developing from his own immersion in Jewish intellectual culture and tradition. That is, for Schwab, as for the Rabbis, curriculum should result in a functional and structural literacy based in textual study. "The problem of pragmatic rhetoric is to move men [sic] to an informed and reflective practice" (Schwab, 1978, 170). Curriculum should be so constructed as to facilitate this practice. The development and enactment of curriculum must be founded in deliberation.

Deliberation, says Schwab,

> treats both ends and means and must treat them as mutually determining one another . . . must try to identify, with respect to both, what facts may be relevant . . . must try to ascertain the relevant facts in the concrete case . . . must try to identify the desiderata in the case . . . must generate alternative solutions . . . must make every effort to trace the branching pathways of consequences which may flow from each alternative and affect desiderata . . . must then weigh alternatives and their costs and consequences against one another and choose, not the right alternative, for there is no such thing but he best one . . . . (1969a, 20-21).

This, as the chapters that follow will show, is the practice of the Talmudic scholars. That is, Talmudic discussion does not arrive at a final and definitive decision, so much as explore the alternative positions presented. Any discussion of Talmud is not conclusive because alternative points are always presented—the opposite opinions always remain open. In "Enquiry and the Reading Process," Schwab argues that the activity of reading ought to be understood as made possible by enquiry. "The process of initiating the student into participative rhetorical and dialectical interpretation must also be a process of initiating him into the existence of enquiry, of exhibiting to him the extent to which organized knowledge depends on terms chosen and subjects defined, and of showing him how he can identify these terms and definitions and trace their effects upon the knowledge which embodies them" (1978, 158). It is the function of reading instruction to focus not merely upon the subject matter, but upon the means by which the argument has been constructed. It is the study of enquiry by enjoining enquiry as method. This, again, is Talmudic practice.

Of course, all answers to the questions 'What knowledge is of most worth?" and "Whose knowledge is of most worth?" are the attempt to prepare our children to succeed in the world they must inherit whether by choice or by imposition. And of course, our methods are always part of the answer to these overarching questions; our methods are always intimately tied to the substance of the answers. Now, if subject matter alone is our focus, it is not a fulfilled life but the successful test that will assess our children's learning; if subject matter alone is our focus, it is error and not eros we seek. But arguing against the focus on educational and behavioral objectives, Schwab (1969a, 9) will say that learners are "not only minds or knowers but bundles of affects, individuals, personalities, earners of living. They are not only group interactors but possessors of private lives." No theory, says Schwab, will ever account for everything that must be accounted for in considering the learners. Schwab intended to produce learners: "a curriculum is not complete which does not move the Eros, as well as the mind of the young, from where it is to where it might better be" (1978, 109). This is not a description of levels, but of the achievement of process: It is the ability of students to at least have capacities to reflect on actions and consequences and to have knowledge organized as tested ends and means. It is to achieve a practical ethics. In the early essay, "Eros and Education" (1978/1954), Schwab argues that the only way to inspire and direct Eros is to engage in the practical, a situation—an event. That event must lead from and to enquiry. For the Jew, Torah study is not abstract but immediate, not theoretical but practical. Thus, this Greek eros might be better understood as the Hebrew *ma'aseh*.[1]

That work of textual study is consistent with the entire framework of Rabbinic Judaism that developed in the first centuries of the Common Era. It is a pedagogy alternative to the developing curricula in Platonic and Neo-Platonic Christian world; it is an alternative discourse absent from present pedagogical discourses insistent on a curriculum based in national standards. The rabbinic method of Torah study that is redacted in the Talmud represents a translation from scholar to curriculum. Not a Socratic monologue, Talmudic discourse is critical inquiry often digressing far from the original topic. "The unique conversational structure of education in the Yeshiva and its attempt at maximizing cross-generational exchange aims at shaping the study of the text of Torah as a communal experience. Moreover, study is institutionalized in the Beit Midrash as a performative act carried out by the students' participation. In such a discursive mode, students are not passive spectators in a reality shaped by teachers. A *Beit Midrash*[2] is a learning space shaped by the intensity and quality of the ongoing exchange of its students" (Halbertal & Halbertal, 1998, 459). But acknowledging need for deliberation in education as it might have been epitomized in the Beit Midrash, Schwab, did not, perhaps even could not, acknowledge that his advocacy for this especial engagement in the deliberative process is based in the process canonized by rabbinic Judaism in the very texts they

[1]*Ma'aseh* is an action, or deed, and is based on the verb that means "doing."
[2]Literally, this Hebrew phrase means "house of study."

produced and from which the learning institution of the Yeshivah derived.

That is, the Talmud, compiled between 200 C.E. and 600 C.E. is already an extended and often digressive discussion of phrases and words in the attempt to particularize the Mishnah, or the Code of Law; this practice sits at the center of a Jewish scholarly tradition and derives from a dominant form of Jewish scholarship. The goal of this eros is to make a holy people. That is, already Talmud represents the translation of scholarship into curriculum and seems to me finally the model of Schwab's deliberation. Schwab's work seems to me immersed in an unvoiced Jewish pedagogy, and the series of papers he produced between 1969 and 1984 seem to me steeped in an unnamed Talmudic discourse. Translation into curriculum might have been better served had Schwab named this discourse, for Talmud is the translation of theory into practice that Schwab insisted was required if the field of curriculum was to be revived. Arguing against the possibility of a single theory, arguing against the possibility of the establishment of a fixed hierarchy of pedagogical materials and skills, and arguing against the possibility of a single approach to curricular problems, solutions pervasive in curricular history, Schwab calls for a specific and radical means for addressing curriculum issues in a practical way. In the absence of theoretical certainty but with the necessity of vision, in the acknowledgment that curriculum must deal with real children and real situations, real acts and real teachers, with "things richer and different from their theoretical representations," Schwab (1969a, 12) argues that "What remains as a viable alternative is the unsystematic, uneasy, pragmatic, and uncertain unions and connections which can be effected in an eclectic. And I must add, anticipating our discussion of the practical, that *changing* connections and *differing* orderings at different times of these separate theories, will characterize a sound eclectic." The model for this eclectic is Talmud.

This eclectic may be traced to Talmudic discourse where the issues of the intricacies of daily life—how to be an ethical people—are singularly addressed in an eclectic manner. No subject of interest did not find its way into Talmud and, thereby, precedent was set for a wide ranging series of practices that Talmud might address. Discussion of particularissues draws upon a disparate body of holy texts: Issues of labor relations might be addressed by the love poems in Psalms. There is in *Berakhot*, a tractate of the Babylonian Talmud, a story the Rabbis tell about Moses. The great prophet approaches God, who is writing the Torah, and asks God why it is necessary to add crowns to the letters of the Torah. God responds to Moses that there will come a man who will interpret these strokes brilliantly and from them will produce heaps and heaps of rulings. Moses asks to see this man and God shows him Akiba. Sitting in the back of Akiba's classroom, Moses does not understand anything that Akiba says, but is reassured when he hears Akiba say that his words derive from the Torah given to Moses. *Interpretation is all.* Textual exegesis is at the center of Talmud, and it is a deliberative and eclectic process that is eminently practical. Schwab argues consistently against the idea of subject matter as central to curriculum and toward what in 1969 he would call the practical: the means of translating the theoretical to the practical. Of course, this is a problem for Talmud as well—to take the Torah and make it useful so that we might live in the world. David Kraemer (1990) reminds us that there is in rabbinic Judaism no canon other than the whole Torah. It requires interpretation. Thus, in *Bava Metzia*, a tractate of Talmud, we read that "If a man sees people running after a lost article [an injured stag or after unfledged pigeons], and says 'My field acquires for me,' it does acquire possessions for him. But if the stag runs normally, or the pigeons fly [naturally] and he says 'My field acquires for me,' there is nothing in what he says." This ruling concerns the acquisition of unowned property. Who has the rights to it? And where do the rabbis go to justify this law. Of course, to the Torah, and in this case, to Deuteronomy—and the subject of gleanings. And I think that they go there because Biblical law requires that gleanings be left for the poor and the widow and the proselyte: Acquisition of unowned property is founded on an ethical principle of charity and community.

Curriculum for Schwab was always a process—before Pinar's *currere* Schwab talked about the necessity in curriculum for "deliberation." In Judaism, learning is the process of attachment to the events and it is achieved through development of literacy. In "Eros and Education," Schwab argues for the centrality of deliberation as a curricular basis. "Discussion is, therefore, in one sense only a systematization, a conscious and controlled development, of what every good teacher tends to do and what he would want to do, had he only the appropriate climate in which to function and a curriculum which provided the necessary raw material of discussion—problems to be solved, dignified occasions for deliberation on policy and action, and unsentimental accessions for apprehension of works of art" (1978, 124). Talmud is only deliberation: Each particular phrase of the Mishnah is discussed, analyzed, and applied for as long as the editors of the Talmud have materials to supply; when materials are exhausted (sometimes after very long and quite wide-ranging digressions), the discussion simply moves on to the next phrase or paragraph. In the process of study, the process of study is highlighted. Talmud is Schwab's translation; or, rather, Schwab discovers the model for his translation in Talmud. And remarkably enough, it is what Schwab advocates for curriculum and methods. The issues of Talmud are the substance of daily life. That is, as Levinas (1990, 4) says the Talmud "governs the daily and ritual life, as well as the thought, of Jews confessing Judaism . . . but these rules of ritual, social and economic life, as well as the personal status of the faithful . . . have a philosophic extension often concealed beneath questions of 'acts to do' and 'acts not to do' which were seemingly of immediate interest to the sages." Levinas argues that Talmudic discourse concerns fundamental ideas concerning how to live. If Greek philosophy is the search for the meaning of ideas, the search for the abstract idea, then Jewish philosophy is the search for meaning in events. Jewish philosophy derives its sources from the daily activity of the world. An "event" is a singular and particular happening and may not be recreated; like Schwab's curriculum, revelation is rooted in the practical. No theory can explain all of it. "The root of Jewish faith," says Abraham Heschel lies not in a "comprehension of abstract principles but an inner *attachment to those events*; to believe is to remember, not merely to accept the truth of a set of dogmas" (1996, 13, italics in the original). That is, the root of Jewish faith lies not in the mere celebration of events, but in the renewed—and renewable—participation in the event for which the celebration stands. This enactment is, of course, the translation into curriculum.

Schwab's entire presentation at this conference makes mention of Jewish tradition not once, though he acknowledges that the translation of the theoretical into the practical (through the arts of the eclectic) requires knowledge of the "congregational community, the particular grouping of the religious, class or ethnic genus" (1977, 4). Nonetheless, his talk is a continuation of the work he had begun from the early part of his published work: an attempt to radically alter curriculum practice by founding it not on product but on practice. Obvious as this may seem, this focus is often attributed to John Dewey; but I would like to suggest that it is an emphasis that has its origins in Talmudic ethics and discourses, and that Schwab's work may be reexamined and better understood with these lexicons and lenses. The Talmud, Levinas (1990, 4-5) says, "is intellectual struggle and courageous opening unto even the most irritating questions. The commentator must carve out a path toward them without letting himself be deceived by what appear to be Byzantine discussions . . . . The pages of the Talmud, mischievous, laconic in their ironic formulations . . . [and] seek contradiction and expect of a reader freedom, invention, and boldness." David Kraemer (1996, 12) notes that "The Talmud is replete with ellipses and other gaps, its arguments often build on unstated logical associations or contrasts, and it routinely addresses the reader directly." It is to this tradition to which we must harken if we are to properly understand Schwab's important work. Schwab's style, obscure though it may appear, may be better appreciated if placed within the Talmudic tradition. The reading of Schwab by Eisner and others, however, occurred within the Greco-Christian tradition, and therefore, Schwab's work appeared to be somewhat "exasperating," or "opaque," or even, "common." I believe, however, it is not Schwab's style that is exasperating; rather, we might look at the lack of familiarity with Jewish discourses that present readers with difficulty with Schwab's work. I think Schwab's work is steeped in Talmudic discourse.

Chapter Four

Gold Acquires Silver

The Nature of Exchange

What is or, at least, ought to be the nature of exchange in our classrooms? Without doubt something ought to be gained from the effort that transpires there, but the identity of that acquisition remains unclear. Not only *what* ought to be acquired remains uncertain, but by what effort ought that acquisition to be accomplished? What should be the substance of classroom events that what occurs there may be categorized as education? It might appear that I am here assuming a positivist character to knowledge, though I will argue that this is not so. On the one hand, I am suggesting that education may be categorized as a material exchange: one item for another. On the other hand, I will show that for the Rabbis of the Talmud, and as I believe it was for Joseph Schwab, it is the *character* of the exchange rather than the *substance* of it that is paramount. That is, the Rabbis place primary emphasis on the process of exchange rather than the extrinsic value of the material to be acquired. The Rabbis argue that if one wishes to acquire an object, one must physically and materially draw that object (or something which may act as a symbol of the object to be acquired) into one's possession. In the process of that acquisition, money may be exchanged, though such payment does not itself finalize acquisition. And in Talmud, there are other means of acquisition than the exchange of money for merchandise: For example, barter may effect exchange. However, regardless of means, a physical act of drawing the object into possession must be still performed to complete the acquisition. That act of drawing is referred to by the Rabbis as *meshikhah* and must be accomplished in all cases to legitimize and complete the transaction.

It is often argued that what students acquire in schools can be readily evaluated by an increasingly complex system of standardized tests. What a student acquires may be precisely measured. What a student acquires may be exactly identified. For much of the twentieth century, the pervasive ideology argued that knowledge is quantifiable; knowledge must have, therefore, a material reality. E. L. Thorndike had argued that if something existed, it could be measured. But it would seem that contemporary practice of quantification seems not so much an act of pulling towards—*meshikhah*—as one of pushing away. In this system of exchange, if acquisition is effected, students have little sense of acquiring; rather, students wonder, "Did I give you the correct answer?" Smart, now identified by good grades, is measured not by what was acquired but what could be returned and, too often, unscathed by human use.

These test scores legitimize the ideology that intelligence (smartness) not only may be measured, but measurably exists. Intelligence quotients determined the measurable capacity to learn, and argued that knowledge was itself quantifiable—that the amount of knowledge—potential and actual—available to an individual could be measurably determined. Stephen Jay Gould (1983, 24) said that "Once intelligence becomes an entity, standard procedures of science virtually dictate that a location and physical substrate be sought for it." Twentieth century educational science has continued to seek for a more accurate topography and measure of that intelligence. School practices were, and yet are, established on these beliefs, and smart became defined by the measured quantities of bits of information recovered from the student during isolated testing procedures. The mapping of the human genome means to discover the biological source and potential of intelligence. In this positivistic educational demand, exchange in the classroom becomes a spurious enterprise; students are promised an education for their effort, but in the end, they have no notion of acquiring anything for that effort. Nor, usually, will students dedicate more than the minimal effort to that acquisition. Schwab held that "learning is active participation in the pragmatic rhetoric—the recovery and test of meaning. Hence, the effective learning situation is not the one which leads by the quickest, most comfortable route to mastered habit and attitude, used precept and applied knowledge, but the one which is provocative of reflection, experiment and revision" (1977, 173). In today's classrooms, however, meaning is not constructed, nor discovered, nor recovered, and then tested. Rather, meaning is imposed. There is no participation in meaning's creation; children remain uncommitted to their effort; they have no part in what they do and what they know. If they acquire, they remain ignorant of their acquisition. Smart, argued Schwab, was the ability to make and test meaning in the world in order to live in it more satisfactorily. The classroom must offer the student the world to be grasped and pulled toward him and her.

It is now commonly held that a material reality must be materially translatable outside of the classroom. That is, knowledge acquired within the classroom should allow students to do something specifically outside of it, else what's a heaven for! From this rubric stems the plethora of practical and applied courses, the preponderance of behavioral objectives as the organizing principles of curriculum theory and practice, and the constant measurement of America's competitive power vis à vis elementary and secondary educational test scores. Schwab, however, believed that for the time they invest in the classroom, students ought to receive intellectual challenge that would develop their capacities to think; students should acquire in schools an awareness of how decisions were made and, thus, develop the ability to make informed decisions. I believe that the Rabbis in the Talmud offer us a method and a madness to such education. For them, the basis and process of argument is paramount; the manner of their discourse is as significant as the matter of that discourse. In the complex exercise of Talmudic debate, it is not the end but the means that is the matter. In Talmudic debate, there is, in fact, rarely an end; there is always another answer. I am certain Schwab would have approved of such practice. I am certain this Talmudic debate—its method and often its substance—exists as a rich source of the Schwabian practical.

CURRICULUM AND EXCHANGE

Education is a social event occurring in mannered fashion in classrooms established for the purposes of education and overseen by a professional. What should occur in a classroom so that what transpires within it can be deemed education? If to become educated is to become "smart," then what does one acquire in becoming "smart." As I have said, I believe that education concerns a matter of exchange and value. Questions of curriculum concern what is to be acquired in the classrooms and what are the processes that effect legitimate acquisition there. Constructivism notwithstanding, students must have something in the classroom that they can actually acquire so that they might construct meaning. How might exchange in the classroom be made fair and honest and ethical so that it might be understood as education by all engaged in it? To answer some of these questions would go a small way to the consideration of curriculum issues.

These were Joseph Schwab's concerns: he complained (1969b, 9) that in the educational world students

> may have some idea of what he will learn *about* in a given course, but not much of *what* he will learn about it. He cannot know what disciplines are required by the problems of the course. He has no way to know what disciplines he will acquire or forever miss. He does not know whether he wants them, whether he ought to want them, or what they will do to him. Yet there the electives are, and elect he must. The election thus becomes a repeated exercise in blind choice, submission to scuttlebutt, or control by the equivalent of broker's tips.

Such educational practices in Schwab's perspective may not be characterized as exchange but as indoctrination. In too many of our public schools, even this much choice does not exist, and students are even less able to participate in the curriculum process and have less sense of honest exchange and acquisition. Education in this arrangement is training and not exchange. Indeed, such may not even be deemed education. Students engaged in the classroom ought not to be organized by givens—strict written behavioral objectives that students must accept and not willingly acquire. Rather, Schwab held, in their classrooms students should actively acquire real and practical knowledge, what Schwab would describe as the essence of smart. Schwab did not mean that students ought to be given knowledge; rather, in the best constructivist fashion, he believed that students should build their knowledge. Schwab wrote: "To 'learn by doing' was neither to learn only by doing nor to learn only how to do. Doing was to go hand in hand with reading, reflecting, and remembering. And these intelligent activities were to eventuate in something more than efficient coping with the bread-and-butter problems of existence. They were to yield the capacity for rewarding experience, a doing and undergoing not merely for the sake of the material outcome . . . but for the satisfaction of the work itself" (1978, 182). Exchange in the classroom should be not only a material matter of the delivery of measurable standards and objectives, but must be an erotic concern as well.

Education should satisfy a desire to know, and it should offer means to make knowing possible. Schwab wrote: "Eros, the energy of wanting, is as much the energy source in the pursuit of truth as it is in the motion toward pleasure, friendship, fame, or power. Any means or method of education taps this energy source to the extent that the method is at all effective . . . . not only the means, however, but also the ends of liberal education involve the Eros. For the end includes not only knowledge gained but knowledge desired and knowledge sought" (1978, 109). Students must acquire something real for the real desire they bring to the classroom. Schwab wrote that the method of the practical "is, then, not at all a linear affair proceeding step-by-step, but rather a complex, fluid, transactional discipline aimed at identification of the desirable, and at either *attainment* of the desired or at an alternation of desires" (1978, 291, emphasis added). If students bring something to exchange, then in schools there must be something to acquire.

Joseph Schwab believed the classroom must be alive with practical exchange. Schwab had complained that the schools had ceased serving their necessary function: the development of intelligence. Schwab boldly declared (1969a, 1) that the "the field of curriculum is moribund, unable by its present methods and principles to continue its work. . . ." For Schwab, schooling ought not to be designed to prepare people to function in the world in the commonly held sense of preparing them, to achieve "easily . . . familiar goals [achieved] . . . by familiar means." Rather, Schwab believed that schools ought to function practically by having available for students the means by which they might develop the capacities to consider a variety of choices and to make decisions from those choices that are "defensible, and not merely theoretically sound." In exchange for engagement in curriculum, students should expect to develop expertise in the ability to engage intelligently in life. In this orientation, schools would have use-value *if* they taught students the complexities of thought so that decision making would reflect pragmatic (not utilitarian) reality. Learning in schools should enhance the possibilities of living, and living, in becoming valuable, should involve understanding and meaning-making. Learning occurs in the activity of living; the purpose of learning is to acquire the confidence and competence to assert some active control over the small and indeterminate section of the individual's life. Schwab held that because our whole past life determined how we would experience the present, then schools ought to structure experience to empower insight into our lives where none before had been possible. "In short, it is our *past* experience as well as present external events which determine our present experience. What we are, what we know, how we have been bent, and what we remember, determine what we experience in the present. It follows, then, that with proper preparation, experience may arise for a child from participation in present events which, on the surface, appear to be without childish significance" (1978, 272). That is, what each student might draw into her/his possession could not be predetermined; terms would have to be negotiated, and the culmination of the process must be accomplished in a physical act of *meshikhah.* The purposes of school should enable a child to develop the inner experiences for dealing successfully in mastering and controlling a fragment of the external world.

As it was presently constituted, Schwab accused, the curriculum was sterile, offered an education that was vacuous, and failed to prepare students for actual existence. The problem with curriculum was that it was effete, separated from the life and world of students. Either students did not see any smartness in curriculum—or else the smartness in it was removed from their lives. Curriculum to them served no purpose, and for them curriculum offered nothing that they cared to acquire. That is, Schwab charged, as presently constituted, the subjects themselves and the argument for their being required were opaque (Schwab's term); if there was relevance in the subject matter, students could not know it. But, Schwab believed, the purpose curriculum should serve was to enable participants immersed in it to increase their capacities to make decisions in their present lives.

When Schwab named the vices of curriculum, each was tied to the lack of instruction in decision making. First, he complained, student government was rendered irrelevant because the decisions made by it were subject to administrative approval. Hence, decisions made were either meaningless or easily ignored. Making decisions and being responsible for those decisions was not made a significant aspect of schooling for students. Second, Schwab condemned the plethora of "electives" whose "names and catalog descriptions [were] opaque as far as students are concerned" (1969b, 8). Course descriptions, he held, are about subject matter and not disciplinary thought; the electives were about transmission of knowledge rather than immersion in the disciplinary matter itself. "What is required, especially on the subjective side, [is] the side of knowing what it *feels* like to submit to and to be master of the disciplines . . ." (1969ba, 10). Third, Schwab complained that the insistence on declaring a major early on in a student's educational life was anathema to education. Rather than permit students to learn about their own tastes and talents, and rather than offer them the opportunity to sample the variety of academic fields each with its various methods of inquiry, students were taught early-on to close off their possibilities and restrict their thought to a single direction and view. Today, school-to-work transitions begin in sixth grade!

Last, Schwab complained (1969b, 8), the "neatness and air of inevitability with which we invest our accounts of science in textbooks and lectures of the evidences which lead to current theory" are devoid of the process of contention and discovery and decision-making that make one theory viable and another not so. Education had no use value. There was nothing of value intrinsic to education worthy of exchange; its ends could not be practically used to facilitate the continual enhancement of the quality of life. There was little to acquire, and students acquired very little. Schwab cautioned: "I would take care to follow an old rule: when children are given bones to chew on, let there be meat on them and let them chew as if for the meat—not as if for the tempering of their teeth" (1978, 270). That is, education must provide sustenance and not mere exercise. Little ones must do more than chew on the bones.

Joseph Schwab believed that schools should enable the growth of intelligence—in schools students should acquire the means of becoming smart. He naively, but perhaps bravely, blamed student protest in the 1960s on the poverty of the curriculum. Appalled, I believe, not by the student protest movement but by the nature of its complaints, Schwab (1969b, 7) asserted that students "do not know who makes decisions" and they "do not know how decisions are made well. They have only foggy and incomplete knowledge of the number and variety of considerations which go into the making of good decisions." Though he declared that a few of the student protestors might be "really sick paranoids," the rest, he averred, were just poorly educated. For Schwab, poorly educated meant to be left unaware of the decision-making processes and, therefore, to be incapable of making informed decisions. Schwab (1969b, 7) asserted, "They [students] do not know because, on the one hand, we have not taught them and because, on the other hand, we have mistaught them by making them on occasion both witness and victim of bad decisions badly made." Not only within the schools do we have examples of bad decision making, but the school itself (and by extension, society) exemplifies and even glorifies bad decision making.

Schwab held that a proper education ought to enable wise decision making and to permit an understanding of how decision making had led to present conditions. Education should show how present conditions had been the product of decision making. In exchange for engagement in the educational process, students should receive the ability to live pragmatically. "The general character of the sweeping curricular change by our diagnoses is clear enough. Its purpose is to return to the curriculum an intellectual challenge to students and the fullest possible opportunity to develop the arts of recovery, enquiry, and criticism appropriate to each discipline. . . . [T]he foundation of the whole effort is extensive grounding of all programs and all courses . . . in materials which contain structured meaning and reward for the search for it" (1969b, 183). Students should have materials they wish to acquire and the means by which to effect acquisition. There must be meat on the bones on which students are to chew.

Therefore, Schwab's prescriptions for curriculum were intended to make students smart—smart, that is, for living. And Schwab seemed to have a very clear definition of what that curriculum should consist: "It is clear, I submit," Schwab (1969a, 9) boldly declared, "that defensible curriculum or plan of curriculum must be one which somehow takes account of all these subjects which pertain to man." It was not the subject matters that were central to curriculum, but what was done with and to that matter. Education, Schwab held, is for living, which states a pragmatism if I ever heard one. And Schwab's pragmatism, as I will show, is Talmudic.

Education might be understood in Schwab's terms as a matter of exchange. One social entity offered something that was called "education" in exchange for an investment of time and effort by the recipient of that education. We might hear even in the conservative ideology of *A Nation at Risk* the idea that education is a matter of exchange. They admonished the youth of America that "You forfeit your chance for life at its fullest when you withhold your best effort in learning. When you *give* only the minimum in learning, you *receive* only the minimum in return. . . . When you *work* to your full capacity, you can hope *to attain* the knowledge and skills that will enable you to create your future and control your destiny (in Willis et al., 1994, 412, *emphasis added*). The language here is clear: Give us your time and energies, and in return you will receive "knowledge and skills" that are practically usable in and for the future. These skills are directly knowable and transferred over to students. These knowledges and skills are understood, in common educational parlance, as standards and educational objectives: what students ought to know and, therefore, what teachers ought to teach. According to *A Nation at Risk*, knowledge is not something to be taken but, rather, something that must be accepted. Requisite and predetermined knowledge are offered; the student rejects such learning at her/his own risk.

But I am clear that Schwab's curriculum prescriptions eschew such certainty. "It should be noted in advance that the suggested alternatives to doctrinaire instruction may each contribute to somewhat different outcomes. . . . It is not at all clear which of these possible outcomes, *if any*, is the most desirable for prospective educators" (1971, 506, (emphasis added)). And so, in questions concerning education, issues of exchange are central to Schwab's work: what should one expect in the process of exchange, and what gives evidence of having acquired an education. And Schwab seemed consistently clear that an education should make one smart: "[T]hese intelligent activities were to yield the capacity for rewarding existence, a doing and undergoing not merely for the sake of the material outcome; often not for the outcome at all, but for the satisfaction of the work itself. Here lies the region which involves enjoyment—of problems and of work, of art, and of our relations with out friends and neighbors" (1978, 182). Education must be for life.

Schwab argued that direct instruction—whether it be by teacher or textbook or instructional materials—led to a sterile curriculum and could result only in ignorance. "Our students are almost entirely deprived of proper curricular occasions, especially sufficiently early occasions, for discovery, assay and exercise of their competences with respect to form and structure, coherence and cogency, evidence and argument, recovery and formulation and meaning" (1969b, 40). That is, students are not learning—because they are not being taught—how to think. In exchange for their time, they receive empty and useless knowledge. Students, Schwab complained, "are unaware of the extent to which the immediate representations to consciousness of wanting and not wanting are unreliable: that the midnight 'wanting' of a peanut butter sandwich can go unappeased by the eating of the sandwich; that our impulses are often dark and obscure; that they are often seen only in the mask with which our inexperience clothes them; that they require, if life is not to be entirely short and brutish enough of suspense, of temporary check, to permit examination of them and reflection upon them" (1969b, 13). Schwab spoke here of desire, and of the ultimate unknowability of its origins or even directions, but he affirmed the life affirming quest that education ought to be; education should seek out not simply the object of desire but the sources of it as well. Education should acquire that which sustains life.

Schwab argued for a curriculum based in the practical in which, in the classrooms, a variety of theories are discovered and engaged and significant inquiries are made of each theory. "What remains as a viable alternative is the unsystematic uneasy, pragmatic and uncertain unions and connections which can be effected in an eclectic" (1969a, 10). Schwab proposed a curriculum that could deal with the messy techniques of negotiating life rather than one that offered isolated bits of knowledge for which no purpose could be discerned. I think Schwab was very much concerned with exchange when he spoke of curriculum and education. I would like to pursue his method in order to pursue his prescription. What is exchange and what are its terms?

I would like to explore Schwab's notion of curriculum and of education using a small section of the Babylonian Talmud, *Bava Metzia* (44a-b). Schwab was very much concerned with the nature of the exchange in the classroom. The nature of this exchange remains today a crucial issue in educational discourses. Schwab complained that the present curriculum lacked intellectual content, lacked a substantial and mature practical component, constructed a community that excluded students, and alienated students from potential entry into that society (1969b, 35); and that these privations created a student population of tolerated aliens who "feel deeply and reset their alienation" (1969b, 41). Exchange systems were grossly unethical in the educational settings. And I think this Talmudic *sugya* offers a typical Schwabian perspective concerning and rectifying this issue. In *Bava Metzia* (44a), a tractate of the Babylonian Talmud, the Mishnah[1] states, "Gold acquires silver, but silver does not acquire gold; copper acquires silver, but silver does not acquire copper; cancelled coins acquire current ones, but current ones do not acquire cancelled coins; uncoined metal acquires coined, but coined metal does not acquire uncoined metal; movables acquire coins, but coins do not acquire movables" (*Bava Metzia*, 44a). This Mishnah is about exchange, use value and acquisition, and I think that it has much to suggest about the matter and conditions of exchange in the classroom. The Rabbis are here concerned with the character of exchange; the Rabbis are here concerned with the processes and execution of honest

[1]The Mishnah is a body of law codified by Rabbi Judah Ha-Nasi in the third century of the common era. The Talmud consists of Mishnah (the law) and the far-reaching rabbinic commentary on that law. A *sugya* is a unit of Talmud under discussion.

exchange. The Rabbis are concerned with issues of what exactly are the means and processes by which one acquires in an exchange.

A MATTER OF EXCHANGE

Rabbi Adin Steinsaltz (1990, 1), a Talmudic scholar, says about the nature of exchange: "One of the general questions arising in connection with the laws of acquisition is how and when acquisition takes place—i.e., at precisely what point does the transfer of ownership take effect when property is purchased." That is, when is it possible for a purchaser to say that she has actually and legally acquired an object she desires. In schools there are similar concerns: At what point can we say that education has taken place—that an honest exchange that might be called education has occurred. Education, as I have said, may be considered a matter of acquisition, and the question here raised concerns the identity of the substance(s) that are to be exchanged in the process of education. The question concerns the manner of that process of exchange.

The Rabbis are concerned with the issue of what constitutes fair exchange and at what point that exchange may be said to be honestly completed. According to Jewish law, merely the commitment to enter into exchange does not finalize any transaction. Saying I will purchase a house or car or piece of clothing does not commit me to actually complete the purchase. Of course, as we know, and as Schwab bemoaned, neither does enrollment nor tacit attendance at school guarantee the acquisition of an education. Nor, say the Rabbis, does payment of money alone make final the exchange, as we in schools must also acknowledge that turning in all assignments does not effect an education. Something else must occur for education to be acquired. Unlike acceptable procedures in our contemporary economy, for the Rabbis not merely the agreement to purchase, nor the down payment on purchase, nor physical proximity to the item of purchase completes acquisition. Rather, Steinsaltz says, "for the agreement to become legally enforceable, a formal act of acquisition must be performed" (1991, 3) Some formal and physical act must be accomplished concluding the acquisition. Exchange must be more than theoretical. There must be some personal and physical activity.

Schwab believed that exchange was integral to the work of the classroom: "I can anticipate that the much which may this time be demanded from me will be returned on another occasion from the much expended by another. . . . the cost in expenditure of means to a possible goal is a factor in the estimate of the value of the goal; on the other hand, the value of a possible goal helps determine the approximate expenditure" (1969b, 27). And, Schwab insisted, the work of the classroom must be practical; that is, it must take account of the practical world. "But curriculum in action treats real things: real acts, real teachers, real children, things richer and different from their theoretical representations. Curriculum will deal badly with its real things if it treats them merely as replicas of their theoretic representations" (1969a, 12). Engaged in education, one learns what one wants to learn and learns to learn what one did not know could be learned. Education fulfills and increases desire, but what must be acquired in the classroom, and by what means, and under what terms that acquisition takes place remain yet a question. The Rabbis engage in spirited discourse concerning the issue of what constitutes the means of fair and open exchange. They begin: Gold acquires silver but silver does not acquire gold.

These are Schwab's concerns. He averred that education had failed to educate, and that students suffered from what he called "privations of competences.' During the educational process, either they had acquired nothing or what they had acquired was of no use. Most students, Schwab complained, had not been very well educated. "The practical competences of deliberation are not . . . traditional obligations of the academic curriculum. . . . Our students are almost entirely deprived of proper curricular occasions, especially sufficiently early occasions, for discovery, assay, and exercise of their competences with respect to form and structure, coherence and cogency, evidence and argument, recovery and formulation of meaning" (1969b, 29, 41). But those competences that Schwab argued students must acquire in school are exactly the method of Talmud. David Kraemer (1990, 170) writes: "Virtually every page of the Bavli[2] records arguments that have no conclusion, or contrary opinions that are equally well-defended. Nearly every deliberation includes manipulations of tradition and reason wherein the latter transforms the former." Talmud represents a technique of translating theory into practice and creating practice out of theory. Schwab's practical accomplishes a similar purpose by similar techniques.

[2]The Babylonian Talmud.

> "These arts are concerned with *bringing a principle to its case.* This is achieved not by bringing one to the other, but by mutual accommodation. The principal (theory) must be selected and adapted to the case. But the case become a case of (an instance of) this theory or another only as it is made to be so. We carve it from the situation in a fashion which makes it so; we select from facts of the situation which we shall treat as relevant facts of the forming case; then we divide the relevant facts into those we shall entertain as alterable and those we shall treat as fixed (Schwab, 1971, 504, emphasis in the original).

Theory informs practice and practice informs theory: What is acquired is the knowledge of *how* knowledge is produced and the pragmatic uses of that knowledge. To be smart is to know not only a subject matter, but to know how that subject matter has come to be defined and to "select among, adjust, and sometimes combine the incomplete views" that make up the bulk of theories.

MESHIKHAH

According to Biblical law, mere payment of money is not considered a valid mode of acquisition; a further act is required. One such physical act is called *meshikhah,* "an act of drawing the article into the physical possession of the buyer." One of the objects in an exchange—the merchandise—had to be "drawn" into the possession of the purchaser. In the varied and multiple economies in existence during the Rabbinic period, different coins of different values were always in circulation, and since coins that were less valuable could be exchanged for ones of greater value and, as we will see, vice versa, then in order to effect acquisition it was necessary to determine which coin could be counted as money and which was considered to be merchandise. The Rabbis' question concerns which coin *had to be drawn* into the buyer's possession to complete exchange.

The first thing of interest here is the idea that, for the Rabbis, in order to acquire an object in an exchange, a physical act of "drawing" must be performed *on the object to be acquired.* Acquisition could not be accomplished passively. In another discussion in *Bava Metzia*, the Rabbis argue that the acquisition of an *unowned object* is "contingent upon the activity within a space" and not merely on occupation of the space itself. power, and not by our mere presence in the same space as the ownerless object (see, Block, 1999-2000, 25). Similarly in the present Mishnah, the Rabbis insist that ownership in an exchange transaction occurs by a physical act of drawing the object to be acquired toward us rather than entering into a verbal agreement or mere payment of money. In Schwabian terms, perhaps we might think of these latter methods as too theoretical. "Theory achieves its theoretical character, its order, system, economy, and above all, its very generality only by absorption from such particulars [of time, place, person and circumstance], by omitting much of them" (Schwab, 1971, 494). In schools presently, students do not have to draw much of anything into their possession; rather, they are required to passively absorb. "In the ordinary curriculum, [materials] are 'assignments,' not challenges. . . . they are designed to be learned, and they are presented as official doctrine to be submitted to" (1969b, 52). Students needs not draw anything into their possession; rather, material is placed with the student for later return. Perhaps in our classroom we first must offer for acquisition what is shown to have value, what students acknowledge they desire, or what enlarges the capacity for desire. And then, we must create conditions whereby that knowledge can be acquired by a physical act of *meshikhah*. Acquiring is the practice of education, and, I wonder, what in our classrooms could constitute an act of *meshikhah*—an act of drawing—and how can the items offered in payment be identified? How might we identity the merchandise—knowledge—that must be drawn by the purchaser, and how might we recognize the act of *meshikhah* by which the merchandise is drawn and acquired. Finally, I wonder for what monies must that merchandise be exchanged?

I am convinced that test taking cannot constitute an act of *meshikhah*; indeed, for the most part this exercise is not a drawing toward but a pushing away. Nor can work sheets or formulaic homework responding to pre-written questions with set answers constitute an act of drawing. Indeed, these too must be understood as acts rather of pushing away. And standards, because they are, as I will suggest, so current, must always be recognized as money and therefore, by law, cannot complete a transaction.

I think that Joseph Schwab sought answers to similar questions. In his 1959 essay, "The Teacher in Progressive Education" (1978, 181), Schwab wrote: "To live is to do. . . . Education . . . must occur through and for concrete doing and making. There is no place in it for the inactive, the abstract, the verbal; education ought not to offer academic "thought" and "logic" not focused on a concrete problem to be solved, an existent need to be filled." Schwab insisted that education must consist of real exchange and that it be physical and active. "The child with whom we work is both more and less than the percentile ranks, social class, and personality type into which she falls . . . we will . . . teach 'Tilda well only as we take account of conditions . . . which are not included in the theories which describe [her] as learning child. . . . We must take notice of these conditions, make some estimate of the relevance of each to the task in hand, and devise some means by which to cope with them" (1971, 496). An act of *meshikhah* must be performed to complete the transaction, and it is 'Tilda who must do the drawing. And 'Tilda must desire the object she will draw toward her.

Not only must education consist of active doing, but it must also be acknowledged that the very substance of education already consists of a drawing. To study anything, Schwab held, is to have always-already performed an act of *meshikhah*, to pull it out of its context so that it can be studied at all. This primary act of *meshikhah* confirms the subject of study as always partial and necessarily restricted. Schwab argued that "A given conclusion in science is therefore about a *taken* something, not an objectively *given* something; the conclusion is true only of that something as it is, and it seems, in its incompleteness and distortion, out of connection with much that would normally alter and affect it" (1978, 133). Education must be constituted not only by an act of *meshikhah*, but must also make clear that education occurs at all because of an act of *meshikhah*. Only in this way will the complexities of knowledge be revealed. "If a theory is to be known as a showing-forth of some aspect of the world, we must also teach what the theory is a theory of and what about that subject is and is not incorporated in the theory" (1978, 134). That act of *meshikhah* must be open and conscious. When we study we must actively pursue—to draw toward us—not only what is under study but the context in which and from which that study has been drawn. And the principles of exchange that legitimate that acquisition must be understood.

THE ETHICAL

Merchandise that is to be acquired must be physically drawn; neither mere verbal agreement nor simple payment of money effects a sale. But for the Rabbis, though exchange is an economic relationship, it isoriginally based in the ethical. For the Rabbis, life was infused with a spiritual existence, and exchange between parties was more than a material transaction: There was always-already a spiritual component implicit in exchange. Leviticus 25:14 says, "When you make a sale to your fellow or make a purchase from the hand of your fellow, do not aggrieve one another." And so in this Mishnah under discussion, the question addressed concerns about what it means to treat your brother fairly in these business matters. What is referred to here concerns equitable dealings in matters of simple exchange; principles of exchange value and the mechanics of sale derive from relations between people. On the one hand, we are engaging in simple exchange for which prescriptions are necessary: gold acquires silver but silver does not acquire gold. Which item must be pulled—which item is money and which is merchandise? But on the other hand, we are attempting to deal with Biblical injunctions. If Leviticus 19:22 states, "I am Holy therefore you shall be holy," then the laws of exchange are part of the process toward holiness. "When you make a sale to your fellow or make a purchase from the hand of your fellow, do not aggrieve one another." So, too, in the classroom, what is to be acquired there must be finalized in a proper manner—the merchandise must be pulled toward the purchased, and the exchange process must be grounded in an ethic: Do not aggrieve one another.

Exchange is, therefore, based in an ethic greater than cumulative acquisition. The accumulation of great quantities of money acquired abusing another is unlawful; mean and miserly possessiveness is also illicit. Education, too, must be based on an ethic greater than cumulative acquisition. For Schwab, of course, education pursued truth, varied though it may be. "[T]hese intelligent activities [of reading, reflecting, and remembering] were to eventuate in something more than efficient coping with the bread and butter problems of existence. They were to yield the capacity for rewarding experience, a doing and undergoing not merely for the sake of the material outcome; often, not for that outcome at all, but for the satisfaction of the work itself. Here lies the region which involves enjoyment—of problems and of work, of art, and of our relations with our friends and neighbors" (1978, 182). The purpose of education is to discover how we might, in the words of Abraham Joshua Heschel, "outdo ourselves, to go beyond ones deeds and illumine the world" (1959, 185). Heschel writes, "The child becomes human, not by discovering the environment which includes things and other selves, but by becoming sensitive to the interests of other selves."

Schwab complained that education had failed because "we have left [our children] ignorant of the complex structure of knowledge, innocent of the exacting work involved in a responsible concern for truth, and undisciplined in the discrimination of meaning and the estimation of probability (1969b, 21). The accumulation in classrooms of great quantities of knowledge acquired abusing another is as unlawful as the mean and miserly possessiveness of wealth.

In the classroom, such ethics are often too absent. With the heavy imposition of strict academic standards, classrooms are carefully structured and controlled spaces for the transference of information to supposedly empty and awaiting vessels. What else but such an arrangement could justify the idea that underlies cultural literacy and the identity of the academic canon? Grateful is what we desire our students to be rather than inquisitive. Indeed, aggrieving another seems too often the basis of our classroom ethics. I have elsewhere argued that study is the equivalent of prayer and that the classroom must be considered a sacred place. For the Rabbis, study must be related to the practical—to the continued striving for a holiness that can only be realized in our daily lives in this world. Heschel writes (1959, 82) that "It is in *deeds* that man becomes aware of what his life really is, of his power to harm and to hurt, to wreck and to ruin; of his ability to derive joy and to bestow it upon others; to relieve and to increase his own people's tensions. . . . In his deeds, man exposes his immanent as well as his suppressed desires. The deed is the test, the trail and the risk." Perhaps until we understand this, we cannot establish the economy of the classroom as a place of fair and ethical exchange.

Schwab said that "if most species of listening, looking, reading, and thinking are tedious to students who are potentially competent at listening, looking, reading, and thinking, it is because we have not discovered to them the existence of their competences or contributed to their sufficient development" (1969b, 29). Indeed, exchange in the classroom might be considered unjust: it offers nothing of practical value. Schwab again: "Our systems of lectures, lecture notes, prescribed readings, and examination must make room for some experience of deliberation and reasonable choice, of mutual criticism, of a pooling of diversities of experience and insights—and do so frequently enough and effectively enough to constitute them as sources of durable satisfaction" (1969b, 29). One must learn in school how to live outside of it, where conditions and experiences are definitely not similar to those of the school. A story: Once a very learned man came to see the Rabbi. Though the man was a scholar, he had never before been to the Rabbi, and so the Rabbi asked him, "And what have you been doing all of your life?" The man answered, "I have gone through the Talmud three times." And the Rabbi answered, "Ah, and how many times has the Talmud gone through you?"

Study is central, but it must be practical as well, and its practice must lead only to ethical living. Heschel writes (1996, 59), "Judaism teaches that beauty which is acquired at the cost of justice is an abomination and should be rejected for its loathsomeness." The same is true for study. Schwab wrote that "An undergraduate curriculum which is a mere inculcation of what I have elsewhere called a rhetoric of conclusions and of a body of rote methods for solving rote problems is the excluding wall [leading] to protest and resentment . . . [and] . . . noneducation" (1969b, 19). Such practice must be rejected. School must make people smart: "The need is for a curriculum which, through and through, requires competences of looking, listening, and reading with respect to form and structure, coherence and cogency; which provides adequate occasions for the development of these competences; which rewards their development" (1969b, 48). Exchange in the classroom is, at present, characterized by aggrievement.

THE ROAD TAKEN

According to the law, a percentage of everything in one's possession must be given to help support the social structure and its functioning. These obligations consisted of priestly dues, terumah,[3] and the first tithe, which were the contributions by the people to the Levites, who were forbidden by Torah to own land. This first tithe, then, was given by each farmer for the maintenance of these landless people, the Levites, who served the public and had to be maintained by that public. After these obligations had been fulfilled, a whole social economy was possible with the produce and merchandise remaining, and the exchange procedures established had to ensure fairness—when you make a sale to

---

[3]*Terumah* is the heave offering given from the yields of the yearly harvests, from certain sacrifices, and from the *shekels* collected in a special chamber of the Temple. The quantity of terumah offered varied with the generosity of the giver.

your fellow or make a purchase from the hand of your fellow, do not aggrieve one another.

Torah teaches that after these original tithing social obligations are met, an additional tithe was to be imposed in the first, second, fourth, and fifth years of the seven-year Sabbatical cycle.[4] Directions for the use of this second tithe are given in *Deuteronomy* 14:22-26. There the Israelites are commanded to "tithe the entire crop of your planting, the produce of the field, year by year. And you shall eat before God, in the place that God will choose to rest God's name—the tithe of your grain, your wine, and your oil, and the firstborn of your cattle and your flocks, so that you will learn to fear God, all the days." This tithe, called the Second Tithe, had to be taken up by its owners to Jerusalem to be enjoyed. Produce central to physical maintenance also has spiritual value and must be carried to "the place where God chooses to rest God's name, to be consumed!!" The substance of our daily lives is infused with a spirituality which is enacted. But *Deuteronomy* continues: "If the road will be too long for you, so that you cannot carry it, because the place that God will choose to place God's name there is far from you, for God will have blessed you, then you may exchange it for money, wrap the money in your hand, and go to the place that God will choose. You may spend the money for whatever your heart desires—for cattle, for flocks, for wine, for alcoholic beverage, or anything that your soul wishes; you shall eat it there before God, and rejoice." Thus, that the tithe might be enjoyed, and to ensure the fulfillment of this spiritual mission, that tithe might be exchanged for coin to facilitate its transport. Fifty silver coins is easier to transport than five hundred bushels of wheat, ten oxen, and fifty sheep; and one gold coin is easier to carry than fifty silver coins. However, since exchange is only effected by an act of *meshikhah,* in the exchange of coins, one must know which coin counts as money and which counts as merchandise. Suddenly, the issue concerning exchange is no longer merely academic—it concerns fulfillment of the spiritual quest.

I have dealt elsewhere with the spiritual nature of study (Block, 2001). Education," I said, "is a private engagement in a public world for the redemption of both" (37). Engagement in the classroom must ensure that the inner as well as the material life of the student be developed. I

[4]In the third and the sixth years, the tithe was left for the poor.

argued that, "Education should address not the isolated intellect, as the advocates of standards suggest it ought, but the hopes and dreams of the self of which intellect—the complex, reflective self—is merely a part" (Block, 2001, 36-7). Students must acquire in the classroom; in the classroom there must be real exchange that has both physical purchase and spiritual purpose in the world. Upon what merchandise must the act of *meshikhah* be performed in the classroom? Gold acquires silver but silver does not acquire gold. The definitions of money and merchandise are of concern here because acquisition occurs only when the merchandise is pulled—what is counted as merchandise and what is counted as money is of primary importance.

WHY NOT STANDARDS?

Gold acquires silver, but silver does not acquire gold: In an exchange of coins, silver is the money and gold is the merchandise. Now, the payment of the money, silver, as I have said, does not finalize the transaction: first, the merchandise, the gold, must be drawn by the buyer into her/his possession to complete the transaction. Similarly, the Mishnah reads, "Copper acquires silver, but silver does not acquire copper." In an exchange of copper coins for silver ones, the latter are considered money and the former merchandise; in this transaction it is the copper that must be drawn by the buyer to effect acquisition. The principle of exchange appears relatively simple: What counts as money seems dependent not on intrinsic value—gold is certainly more valuable than silver—but on currency. That which circulates more easily is considered money, and the other item is considered merchandise—it is this merchandise which must be drawn to finalize the exchange.

In educational markets, we might consider money as what is current—today what is current is referred to as standards. In the Rabbis' formulations, these standards may be used *for* purchase in the classroom, but may not themselves be acquired. That is, standards are currency payment for merchandise, but it is the merchandise that must be drawn by an act of *meshikhah* in order to complete the transaction. It is this *merchandise* that must be carried to Jerusalem and there be redeemed to be enjoyed. Ironically, then, if we see our academic standards as current, as monies, then by the present focus on the achievement of standards, we have made acquisition in the school impossible because, according to the Rabbis, money cannot acquire. And if what we have offered in exchange is current—monies or silver—then it is we, the teachers and administrators, who acquire by pulling merchandise toward us. Perhaps in this act of *meshikhah* we have perverted the whole purpose of the educational enterprise. Perhaps, in this act of *meshikhah* what we acquire is our children but, then, I recall, Torah forbids us to aggrieve our brother in a transaction, and in such an educational arrangement, in this act of *meshikhah*, our children are surely aggrieved. In this exchange, the students acquire nothing that they desire and are required to do nothing to finalize acquisition. Rather, students are themselves acquired—trained, in educational terms. The entire transaction is unethical. If gold acquires silver, we have purchased from our children their lives.

I think we might understand educational merchandise as equivalent to the merchandise that was to be carried to Jerusalem to be enjoyed. That is, what is learned—what is drawn in the act of exchange—must directly and knowingly improve the whole of our lives. Schwab knew that the purpose of education was to enhance living: "A good education aims to develop whatever potentials each individual may possess. It identifies and then nurtures to maximum growth the uniqueness of each child. . . . Ultimately, the goal of education can only be to provide means for adjustment to the environment" (1978, 181). But unlike Franklin Bobbitt and the social efficiency theorists, and unlike the life adjustment theorists of the post-World War II generation of educational workers, Schwab knew that such adjustment did not mean accommodation to given conditions but to "take notice of these conditions, make some estimate of the relevance of each to the task at hand, and devise some means by which to cope with them" (1978, 324). That is, education should not *adjust* anyone to life but should offer resources by which each individual might *make adjustment* to his and her lives. "With respect to goals, this means that proximate goals are hit upon by searching out and rehearsing a wide variety of possible goals to find the one or ones that yield to the greatest degree the diverse goods needed and sought by the diverse interests represented" (1969b, 26). Education must be accomplished by an act of *meshikhah*, and what must be pulled is not the money but the merchandise. This merchandise must satisfy not only the individual but the greater society to which that individual belongs. This merchandise must be taken and carried on the road to Jerusalem.

GOLD ACQUIRES SILVER

The notion that gold acquires silver but silver does not acquire gold establishes the basic principle that in an act of exchange of coins one item must count as money and the other must be identified as the merchandise. The discussion might be brief and obvious—except for the complicating factor that the entire hierarchy is a reversal of a former decision. The Gemara[5] begins: "Rabbi (Judah Ha-Nasi) taught his son R. Shimon: Gold acquires silver. Said he (Shimon) to him (Ha-Nasi): 'Master, in your youth you did teach us, Silver acquires gold; now advanced in age, you reverse it and teach, Gold acquires silver." The Rabbis wonder what reasoning dominated Ha-Nasi's earlier ruling and what reasoning inspired the change of opinion. The Rabbis are not seeking the right answer; rather, they wonder what Ha-Nasi was thinking.

There is for the Rabbis no question that in either situation—whether gold acquires silver or silver acquires gold—Ha-Nasi's thinking was based in both the practical and the ethical. How could it not be? Nor do the Rabbis dispute the present law as presented in the Mishnah that had been redacted by Ha-Nasi; rather, the Rabbis mean merely to understand it. In Schwabian terms, the Rabbis seek the context. If education is intended to make people smart, then Schwab (1971, 515) offers a meaning of smart, and it mirrors the Rabbis' method. "From such analyses, reconstruction, and comparisons there arise, first vivid awareness of some of the alternative attacks available to the family of enquiries under scrutiny and perception of the differing consequences of different patterns of attack on the character and content of the knowledge which accrues. There comes, second, increasing mastery of the critical competences which disclose these structures of inquiry." That is, from the classroom students would learn how decisions are made and, therefore, how to make decisions. Knowledge presented as complete is always false. Knowledge is always theoretical because it exists unaffected by the daily and mundane world of experience. "All theories, even the best of them in the simplest sciences, necessarily neglect some aspects and facets of the facts of the case. A theory covers and formulates the *regularities* among the things and events it subsumes. It leaves behind the

---

[5]The Gemara is the Rabbinic discussion of the law. It is the recorded discussion of numerous sages talking over centuries.

nonuniformities, the particularities, which characterize each instance of the facts subsumed. Moreover, in the process of idealization, theoretical enquiry may often leave out of consideration conspicuous facts of *all* cases because its substantive principles of enquiry or its methods cannot handle them" (1969a, 11). To be smart requires that something be done to knowledge to make it practically useful. "If, then theory is to be used well in the determination of curricular practice, it requires a supplement It requires arts which bring a theory to its application, first, arts which identify the disparities between real thing and theoretic representation; second, arts which modify the theory, in the course of its application, in the light of the discrepancies; and third, arts which devise ways of taking account of the many aspects of the real thing which the theory does not take into account" (1969a, 12). Schwab is describing the method obvious in Talmudic discourse. Schwab says that "The old knowledge may require extensive reformulation. Extensive re-education and sweeping rewriting of textbooks and monographs may need be done." Schwab would approve of Talmudic discourse.

The Rabbis offer an explanation for Ha-Nasi's earlier reasoning: In his youth, Ha-Nasi had earlier held that the more valuable metal—gold—served as money, but later, Ha-Nasi reasoned that the coin in *greater circulation* and not the one most valuable ought to be considered money in matters of exchange and acquisition. Perhaps in our youths we always imagine that value is intrinsic to the material. But in his old age, Ha-Nasi reasoned that since the less valuable silver was more apt to be possessed by the greater number of people, then it ought to serve as money because it had greater circulation. Perhaps Ha-Nasi also understood that the plurality and diversity of the population precluded a single standard of exchange based merely in extrinsic value. Ha-Nasi understood that principles of exchange must serve the citizens; exchange must be practical. As money is a means of purchase, then the identity of money must take account for what people might actually have in their possession that may practically circulate.

It is not true, of course, that gold is never money; upon this fact the Rabbis agree. There will be times when incontrovertibly gold is money. For example, Torah sets the redemption fee for a first-born male at five shekels, and five shekels were equal to five silver denarim. If the father gives the priest a gold coin for the redemption fee, the value of that coin must be absolute or the priest will not know how much change must be returned to the father. If gold were merchandise, then the amount of gold a family offers for redemption would vary according to its present value and therefore, the redemption fee would, depending on the market and trade in gold, be at times inconsistent with Torah. Torah forbids as well the collection of interest: If gold is merchandise and not money, then it might increase in value from one day to the next and its use in exchange might be compromised. Thus, it is obvious from the Rabbis' discussion that it is in relation to silver coins that gold is merchandise, and, therefore, when coins are gold and silver coins are to be exchanged, it is on the gold that an act of *meshikhah* must be performed to finalize acquisition.

But reasoning is the issue for the Rabbis. What is important for them is the process by which decisions are considered and reached. For example, it appears to Rabbi Ashi that Ha-Nasi's youthful opinion—in which the more valuable metal, gold, acts as money—must be the more appropriate one because that earlier opinion appears to be consistent with the principle in our present mishnah (law) that states that copper acquires silver: In an exchange of copper and silver, the latter counts as money and the former is considered merchandise. Ashi reasons that in the present case the more valuable silver may purchase copper, as in Ha-Nasi's earlier opinion that the more valuable gold may purchase silver. Ashi seeks a syntactic consistency. Rav Ashi argues that Ha-Nasi's earlier opinion, that silver acquires gold, makes more sense because it seems consistent with the next clause in the present mishnah: "copper acquires silver." Ashi reasons: as the first clause in the law establishes the principle of value, then in his youth Ha-Nasi argued that silver was produce in relationship to the more valuable gold. Therefore, the second clause in our present mishnah, that copper acquires silver, teaches with similar reasoning that in relation to copper, the more valuable silver is money. Thus, reasons Ashi, the principle is established: the more valuable metal is money. In this view, all would be consistent and clear.

But, argues Ashi, if we accept Ha-Nasi's later opinion stating that gold acquires silver, that silver is money in relation to gold, then the second clause in the present Mishnah, that "copper acquires silver," seems redundant, adds nothing to the issue, and need not be stated at all. If because silver circulates more easily than gold, it serves as money, then the additional principle "copper acquires silver" is obvious since silver is *both* more valuable and more current. Obviously, Ashi claims, if silver acts as money in relation to gold, which is more valuable, then certainly, in relation to copper, silver would be money. If silver is money with regard to a metal more valuable that itself, silver is certainly considered money with regard to a metal less valuable than itself. Thus, since this redundancy exists and ought not to do so, Ashi argues that Ha-Nasi's earlier opinion must be valid and the redundancy ceases to be so.

However, other Rabbis respond to Ashi and address what he interprets as contradictions and redundancies: evidences of obfuscation, bad scholarship, and false reasoning. *However,* the Rabbis see apparent variances and redundancies and contradictions not as a means to invalidate opinions, but as an opportunity to engage in considered thought. Because the Rabbis are scholars, and because it is processes of thought which intrigue them—they trouble each notion. Redundancies must be accounted for and contradictions explained. In the absence of the Temple and the decline of the priestly caste, in the diaspora where authority rested in scholarship rather than cultic ritual, the Rabbis must have been concerned to establish principle and law to establish and maintain the identity of the Jewish people. Contradictions might invalidate the basic structures, and so they had to be explained. Unlike Socrates who held that contradictions are evidence of false reasoning and must be corrected, the Rabbis held that contradictions must be explained and not invalidated. Multiplicity of opinion is the hallmark of Rabbinic thought in Talmud; the explanation of contradictions reveals such diversity. Ashi never acknowledges that the Rabbis' alternative opinions invalidates his arguments.

Schwab held that such cognitive processes, indeed, ought to be the substance of education. He argued (1969a, 10), "What remains as a viable alternative is the unsystematic, uneasy, pragmatic, and uncertain unions and connections which can be effected in an eclectic. And I must add, anticipating our discussion of the practical, that *changing* connections and differing orderings at different times of these disparate theories, will characterize a sound eclectic." Not the theory itself but the context in which the theory arises is the matter of education. All theories, Schwab acknowledged, have their gaps, their disputants, and alternatives.

Other Rabbis respond to Ashi. They argue not necessarily with the principles of the law, but with its specificities. Or, as Schwab argues, "We need therefore, to add to grammar, syntax, and rhetoric, a fourth level of interpretation in which a whole discourse is 'placed' as providing such-and-such a treatment, in *these* but not *those*, of a certain part of a large subject disjoined from other parts, and providing a solution to this but not that problem involved in the subject" (1978, 153). The Rabbis say that even if we accept Ha-Nasi's later opinion, that gold acquires silver, the second verse is not redundant but rather, teaches a new principle. It suggests that just as gold in relation to silver is merchandise, so too, in relation to copper, silver is considered money. Since in the first clause it is circulation that determines the identity of the merchandise, one might expect that, since copper ought to be more available to circulate than silver, in an exchange copper ought to be identified as money and silver be declared the merchandise. Were the reasoning to be such, then Ashi would be correct. But, the Gemara states, the statement copper acquires silver "is necessary [for] you might have thought to say: these copper coins in the place where they circulate are more current than silver, [So you might] say they are money. [Hence] it tells us: Since there is a place in which they do not circulate, they are merchandise" (*Bava Metzia,* 44B). That is, the second clause establishes the new principle that even though there are places where copper coins do circulate and because of their value circulate more easily than silver and therefore, by the principle established in the first clause, *ought to be money*, since there are places where copper coins do not circulate, they must not ever be counted as money because their value cannot be guaranteed. The conclusion at which the Rabbis arrive seems wonderful: Silver is money because it is generally current and not because it has intrinsic value. It may be used to acquire, but it may not itself complete a transaction. Another act must be performed on the merchandise.

Exchange is relative and must be fluid. In this discussion the Rabbis explore not just the technical aspects of Ha-Nasi's communication—what was precisely spoken—but the entire context of its import. They say that the reasoning suggested in the latter opinion assumes that because gold is so very valuable and expensive, few could acquire enough of it to constitute an exchange; money must be silver so that it can be used. Were gold to be considered money exchange would be necessarily rare, and the social order would suffer. People would want. Furthermore, if gold is money with regard to silver, then it would be rare that a person would ever have enough silver coins to exchange for gold coins so that the journey to Jerusalem might be made. Thus, one would postpone the journey. Therefore, as in the later opinion, silver, which is more easily accessible, must be considered money in relation to gold: silver acquires gold and the act of *meshikhah* must be accomplished on the merchandise, gold. The latter must be pulled by the purchaser to finalize acquisition. The principle established suggests that that which is more readily available and exchangeable must count as money. Of course, others disagree—Bet Hillel argues that even if a person could not acquire enough silver to exchange for gold coins, they would still not postpone their journey to Jerusalem. Bet Hillel has a rather wonderfully high opinion of the human sense of moral responsibility. Gold is money—but it is so not absolutely by virtue of its intrinsic value but, rather, is so relatively with regard to its currency. Its currency must serve practical but ethical function—it must get us to Jerusalem and its use in exchange must not aggrieve its neighbor. What the Rabbis seek is explanation based on pragmatics and ethics

NOT A CONCLUSION

But of course, that is the issue: The spiritual journey to Jerusalem to fulfill God's command may occur because a system of exchange to facilitate that pilgrimage has been established. In the absence of money markets and coin collection, what other purpose for the exchange of coins could exist except to make possible this travel. Exchange here is practical and ethical. It must enable the spiritual quest of fulfilling God's law and of getting to Jerusalem. It is in this sense that I think the Rabbis' discussion is immediately relevant to issues concerning contemporary education and very much central to Schwab's thinking. The Rabbis argue from the perspective that law should enable life and social interaction rather than restrict it. Their argument that the identity of money is relative and dependent on what is current ensures that no one suffer and that all may yet get to Jerusalem. Such exchange must involve real *activity—meshikhah*—and, since money cannot effect an exchange, the identity of the merchandise in the transaction must be firmly established.

What a student will acquire in the classroom must be actively drawn by her in the exchange, and what is acquired must be in the service of getting to Jerusalem. As the exchange of coins enables a spiritual life and is based on ethical principles, so, too, must the activity of the classroom be spiritually and ethically based. Students ought not to be given a life, but must be educated to actively construct one. For this end—for this journey—specific objectives are not only inappropriate, but inadequate as well. Schwab said (1983, 240): "Ends or objectives can be defensibly selected only in the light of consideration of available or obtainable means, materials, and teaching skills; nor can ends chosen lead to means and materials which yield only the ends for which they were chosen."

Exchange in education must aggrieve neither brother nor sister, and exchange must facilitate the journey to Jerusalem—fulfillment of a spiritual and spiritually dedicated life. Schwab cautioned that curriculum must account for the actual lives of students and for their hope for the future: "These features [of their present life] will determine the exemplifications of adulthood and of a desirable life which students encounter and which determine, in some part, what they will expect from schooling and upon what they are most willing to devote their energies" (1983, 242). These are not the strictures of the social efficiency theorists. Schwab argued that "[C]urriculum reflection must take place in a back-and-forth manner between ends and means. A linear movement from ends to means is absurd" (1983, 241). We must not set the same curriculum for all, and we must not plan for each their Jerusalem. Getting to Jerusalem—fulfilling the spiritual quest is too important: "We cannot impose a single norm on all individual," Schwab asserted (1978, 180). That would be unethical. Rather, Schwab desired that everyone acquire for themselves the means to get to Jerusalem. The Rabbis tell us that the manna the Israelites gathered in the wilderness tasted to each according to her/his particular need: "To young men it tasted like bread, to the elderly it tasted like wafers made with honey, to sucklings it tasted like milk from their mother's breast, to the sick it tasted like fine flour mingled with honey, while for the heathen it tasted as bitter as linseed." According to need—each must know how they will get to Jerusalem—to fulfill the spiritual life; each must gather the manna that is offered, and for each it will taste differently though it may look the same; education is only acquired when it is identified as merchandise and pulled toward the purchaser by an act of *meshikhah.* We must make available an education that would taste according to the needs of each individual.

Chapter Five

"They Pelt Him With Stones"

Standards, High-Stakes Testing, and Culpability

"My Stomach Hurts"

I sustain a powerful memory. It is of a Peanuts cartoon that I encountered many years ago, when, for reasons I no longer remember, I purchased and read over several days time about a dozen volumes of paperback anthologies of Charles Schultz's comic series. The books now have vanished, the actual cartoon strips physically displaced in one move or another, and the memories a bit faded. But, there is one episode that stays lodged in my memory and of which through the years I have always been particularly fond, though, alas, its precise details, along with the books themselves, have been lost. In this one particular strip, Charlie Brown stands proudly on the pitcher's mound at the start of a new season. Atop his head solidly sits his baseball cap, resting only slightly askew. Charlie Brown's arms hang by his side; on his left hand, he wears his baseball glove, and in his right he clutches the baseball. In the strip's first two frames, Charlie Brown declares, "Ah, the start of a new season. I love the smell of the fresh grass, and of the newly oiled leather of the glove. I love to see my players waiting expectantly for the first pitch." But in the third frame, comes the harsh voice of Lucy van Pelt who occupies some undefined outfield position: "Throw the ball you knucklehead. I've got better things to do." In the final frame, Charlie stands dejectedly on the mound with his arms dangling by his side. "I have a stomach ache," he says.

This story of Charlie Brown calls to mind the terrible discomfort I have repeatedly experienced during the sixty-odd semesters and twelve hundred weeks I have spent as an educator in the public schools. At the end of each quarter or semester, teachers—of whom I am one—tote up the various numbered and letter grades in their grading books and assign a mark of evaluation upon the student. The "A" may be royal or scarlet, but it is a brand nonetheless. At the end of each quarter or semester, teachers define who is a student and who is not, who shall live and who shall die, who shall perish by fire and who by water, who by hunger and who by thirst, who will live in harmony and who will be harried, who will enjoy tranquility and who will suffer, who will be impoverished and who will be enriched, who will be degraded and who will be exalted.[1] It is an awesome responsibility, which, I suppose, accounts for the enormous salaries awarded to the teachers in our public schools. Subverting all of my hopes and desires in the classroom, this dangerous fault line, on which only precarious relationships with learners can develop, threatens the very purpose of the classroom and transforms what should be its play into a dangerous and treacherous business. "Throw the ball you knucklehead. I've got better things to do!" At the end of every semester, I develop horrible stomach pains.

A story is told of Rabbi Elazar.:

> One day a certain laundryman called Rabbi Elazar "Vinegar, son of wine." [Elazar] said: "Since he is so impudent, infer from this that he is a wicked man." [Elazar] said to the soldiers: "Arrest him," [and] they arrested him. After his mind was calmed, Elazar went after the laundry man to redeem him, but he was unable [to do so]. He said of him: "He who guards his mouth and his tongue guards his soul from troubles." They hanged him. [Elazar] stood under the gallows and wept. Elazar's students said to him: "Master, let it not be grievous in your sight, for that man and his son had intercourse with a betrothed maiden on the Day of Atonement." Elazar laid his hand on his belly [and] said: "Rejoice, my belly, rejoice." But even so, he was not at rest. They gave Elazar a sleeping potion to drink and brought him into a house of marble, and tore open his abdomen. They removed from him basketfuls of fat and placed [them] in the sun in Tammuz and Av, but it did not decay.
> But no fat decays!.
>
> No fat decays, [but if it contains] red streaks, [it] does decay. Here, even though there were red streaks, it did not decay. Elazar said of himself: "My flesh too will dwell in safety" (*Bava Metzia*, 83B-87B).

This is an interesting, though admittedly, bizarre story. Some background may offer some insight: Elazar had previously devised a method for accurately distinguishing those in the kingdom who were wicked from those who were righteous. To those who studied with him, Elazar had announced: "Come and I will teach you what you should do.

---

[1]These are the words of a central piece of liturgy for the Holy days of Rosh Hashanah and Yom Kippur. The prayer is the *Usanaeh Tokef.*

Go at the fourth hour to a tavern. If you see a man drinking wine and holding a glass in his hand and dozing, ask about him. If he is a Rabbinic scholar and is dozing, he rose early for his studies. If he is a worker, he rose early [and] did his work. And if his work is [done] at night, he was stretching [metal wires]. And if [he is] not [one of these], he is a thief, so arrest him." This method so appealed to the king that by his order, Elazar had been given license to employ his methods. Elazar was hired as gatekeeper, as it were, to the kingdom. It was Elazar who would oversee the maintenance of the high standards of moral integrity in the king's domain. It would be Elazar who would be responsible for carrying out evaluation on the relative worth of each individual. It was Elazar who would discern the good from the bad, the honest from the dishonest, and the worthy from the unworthy. It is, I think, an awesome power to ascribe to a frail humanity. And it will lead, as I will show, to severe stomach aches.

The story above, however, recounts how Elazar caused the arrest of someone not for being in the tavern at the wrong hour, so to speak, but for personally offending him. The man had called Elazar a name: "Vinegar, son of wine." There is some sense in the story that the vituperative remark directed at Elazar refers to his newly appointed position as a government official charged with arresting fellow Jews. Once power is proffered, as we well know—even of that to arrest—it is not suffered lightly or without condemnation by those subject to it. Certainly it does not endear Elazar to this particular laundryman. Nor is power proffered—as we well know—exercised ideally in a cultural and personal vacuum immune from even irrelevant forces. Nevertheless, such proffered power, as we well know, may be exercised too often with relative impunity. Woe to the administrator who trifles with the teacher's assignment of grades. Woe to the parent who makes active inquiry regarding their child's failures. Woe to the child who voices complaint of a teacher's fairness. Despite some real limitations, and despite propaganda to the contrary, teachers possess an enormous amount of power. They assign grades; they determine futures; they often determine who shall live and who shall die, who by fire and who by water, and etc., etc. Elazar, offended by this certain laundryman, took recourse made available to him by the methods he had himself established, to redress the calumny he has personally suffered. Elazar assigned this man a failing grade, and the arrested man was condemned to death. Elazar experiences a terrible stomachache.

Despite assurances from others of the man's wickedness, and having had time to reflect upon the incident—perhaps even honest enough to appreciate the role his personal motives may have played in his arresting order—Elazar expresses doubt concerning the laundryman's guilt and pleads for his release. But the king refuses to relent, and Elazar quickly acquiesces. Then, to justify the fate of the accused, and to absolve himself of responsibility, Elazar quotes Proverbs 21:23: "One who guards his mouth and his tongue guards his soul from troubles." The man was careless with his tongue and now suffers justifiably for his reckless abandon. The man brought this fate on himself—were he of better character, he would not have spoken so irreverently. He would have had more respect for my position and my responsibility. Elazar, we come to appreciate, demands a strict and unwavering standard of behavior. Perhaps Elazar assumes that a student engaged in constant Torah study will act with the same righteousness that ought to derive from that study; Elazar expects, as well, that an assiduous worker would also have no time nor inclination to engage in such vituperation. I think Elazar imagines a more perfect world than the one in which I live. Only the student and the worker have tenable justification for their presence in the tavern; the thief has no excuse to be asleep in the tavern at this hour! It would seem that Elazar acknowledges that it is not in the specific ***performance*** of set standards by which men are judged —after all, in the tavern the student and the laborer and the thief are each asleep. Rather, one is measured by the direction of his/her life. It is not specifically ***what*** the student knows but ***that*** the student knows that becomes the standard Elazar would promote; study is a lifelong activity and the student is known by his engagement in that study rather than from the standards set for the evaluation at its end. The student's efforts have tired him. He dozes in the tavern. A person's life requires evaluation more so than the quantified measure of his specific engagement in study.

VINEGAR, SON OF WINE

We don't always like our students, nor do they always speak well of us. The official power by which we are licensed permits us to condemn not a few. I do not doubt that I have sentenced several because they referred to me as "Vinegar, Son of Wine." Of course, Elazar assures me of the correctness of my judgement: If they would have guarded their tongue, then no judgement would have fallen upon them. On the other hand, the verse in proverbs suggests that insisting I am right, in fact, defines my own evil. Proverbs suggests that the good do not boast; they are too busy studying. If this is so, then my evaluation of students is not only superfluous but vain. The grades I assign are for all intents and purposes inviolable. And wasteful. Teachers inevitably complain that the evaluative process often shrinks the time that might be spend learning. Proverbs suggest that the trust the wise inspire—teachers are meant to be wise—comes not from their words, but from their restraint. Grades are an excess of presumption.

Perhaps it is not that the wise are silent, but that they are humble. Because study is interminable, then any moment is an inappropriate one to make a summative evaluation or judgement; *the wise refrain from completion.* Teachers who assign evaluative grades in this sense might be identified with the impudent and wicked. For Elazar, the sluggard who is incapable of disciplining him or herself, or practicing restraint is slavishly subject to her/his will. He is easily distracted and is capable of neither study nor work. That person is a thief. And what does this teacher steal, I wonder. The value of life? Certainly, in the process of evaluation we rob students of their lives. Teachers often accuse recalcitrant students of robbing the teacher's time. These thieves require judgement, we aver. Elazar suggests that arrest is appropriate; in schools, where teachers have power, albeit limited, that death sentence, as it were, arrives in the form of grades.

The grades that we assign are, indeed, as permanent as any death sentence. Narissa Wilnes, a ninth grader I taught many years ago but who I can not yet forget, came to me one beautiful autumn afternoon sobbing. "Narissa," I asked, "what's the matter?" "I got a "C" on this paper," she said through her tears. Indeed, she had done so; I had given her that "C." "But, Narissa," I responded, "its only October; your grades will change as you learn more and as your writing improves." What must I have been thinking about back then? Was it Narissa who had earned that "C," or was it her previous teachers to whom that grade should have been assigned? Was it I who had so poorly prepared her to complete the assignment? What could that "C" have meant so early in the school year of her first year in high school? That Narissa had much to learn? Didn't I already know that? Obviously Narissa didn't know that yet—she presently concerned with some vague distance goal. She wailed, "But how will I get into law school?"

Rather than worrying about the sentence that grade had rendered, Narissa could have been learning the beautiful endlessness of study. Narissa was distracted from learning by my evaluation of it. Wasn't that "C" a *non sequitur*? It interjected absurdly in a situation to which it added nothing. What could that grade announce about Narissa's anticipated learning? If everyone knew that Narissa was in school to learn, then what purpose was served to assign her that "C" so early in the year. Or ever, in fact,? What could that grade have meant?

What does any grade signify? Grades are only meaningful as a means of comparison. My "C" has meaning only when compared to his "A" and to her "D." Or my "C" measures my approximation to the achievement of standards previously and objectively established to which I would urge Narissa to aspire. But then those grades are founded in competition and of themselves say nothing at all about Narissa's learning in this particular classroom. Conversely, if everyone receives an "A" ***because*** they learn, *and everyone learns something in the classroom,* then what is the standard that is measured by that "A"? I was hoisted on my own petard. And so I joked: "Narissa, if this "C" is a hindrance to your admittance to law school, you come back and I'll change it." It was a crude and insensitive remark. What I think I actually communicated to Narissa was that the "C I had assigned her contained no meaning. At least for me. She, on the other hand, was devastated by it. I felt like Vinegar, Son of Wine.

Elazar responds humanly—with original anger at the slight—and then with regret at his impulsiveness. But the established powers render his contrition ineffective. He is too late. Our judgements sometimes have consequences over which we lose control. No wonder Elazar suffers stomach troubles.

And this disquisition on evaluation does begin to address the trouble with the plethora of scores found on student records from the standardized tests that like cancer cells, multiply uncontrollably. They are killing our children.

I am always disturbed by grades. I dread the end of the term when I am responsible for grading. My stomach begins to hurt. Indeed, isn't Elazar's stomach exactly his problem, and isn't his affliction tied to his summative evaluation of the laundryman? It is my responsibility to measure up a student's semester with a single letter grade. I am overwhelmed by the act: on any single day every student earns an "A" and on any single day every student earns an "F." Which day shall I evaluate? Are we all merely the sum of our averages? I am thoroughly inadequate to the task. Or perhaps such evaluation itself is a meaningless task of which adequacy is no measure. I know what the advocates of standards argue; Diane Ravitch (1995, 12) writes: "Curriculum standards describe what teachers are supposed to teach and students are expected to learn. . . . Performance standards describe what kind of performance represents inadequate, acceptable, or outstanding accomplishment." John Benson, former Superintendent of the Department of Public Instruction in Wisconsin, writes: "Standards should indicate what students should know and be able to do, what they might be asked to do to give evidence of meeting the standards, and how well they should be able to do it" (1998, vii). And all this learning in the sterile atmosphere of the classroom divorced from the actual life for which that learning is meant and in which it should have meaning. Oh, I know what the standards advocates desire: I just don't believe them. And if standards include multiple performance levels, then of what value is standards?

Wisconsin's Department of Public Instruction has required the revision of teacher education programs to a performance-based approach to licensing. Rather than counting on the fact that students in college completed the requisite course work, the Department demands that there be a measure of performance to substantiate that the candidates for a license had the knowledge and skills needed to succeed. What a fascinating paradox! The Department of Public Instruction has moved to a performance-based approach to licensing and insists that certain knowledge and skills be required in order to be licensed. And those performance standards will be assessed not in performance but by a standardized test. It is a closed system where the knowledge base is static. Nothing enters; nothing leaves. Entropy. Standardized tests, we are informed, approved by the state superintendent will be used to assess content knowledge. Well, as soon as we find out what material is on the approved tests, we will know what knowledge and skills are required for licensure, and then those rules and regulations that are declared by the Department of Public Instruction as the bane of individuals and colleges will return with a vengeance. Standardized tests are standardly marked—usually and at least, in large part, by some machine. Will the scholar with a 74 be denied license and the scholar with a 75 be so granted? What is the difference between the scholar earning a 74 and the one earning a 75? I wonder if the Narissa Wilnes to whom I gave a "C" is a good lawyer and a good person. My grade accounts for neither.

SKATING STANDARDS AND PERFORMANCE MEASUREMENT

Emma came home last night from ice skating sobbing. Emma, my daughter, has been skating for several years now. Every Wednesday during the long Wisconsin winter months, she has taken lessons offered by the Recreation Department in the university town in which we reside, and as a student she has moved steadily and slowly through the various skill levels. She loved to skate. This night she was in tears. "What happened, darling?" I asked as she came running into the room, threw her arms about my waist and burrowed her face into my chest. "I failed. I didn't pass Basic 6. Kelly said I didn't even come close to achieving mastery of the things I had to do to pass. I hate Kelly." I didn't know what to say. She had called her teacher, Vinegar, Son of Wine!!

But I am being specious; actually, I responded immediately.

I said, "Emma, if Kelly said what you said she said then she is not a very good teacher. No teacher would ever speak so rudely to a student." Of course, that is true, though I am familiar with not a few teachers who speak even more harshly about their students and do so even to their faces. But finally, Kelly is not a teacher; rather, she knows how to ice skate better than my daughter. I assume Kelly has passed at least Basic 6 level. She has passed the standards that are set for content area knowledge, I suppose. I do not think there is a pedagogical component required by the recreation department for those who will teach ice skating to the children. More is the pity, I say. Kelly may know how to skate, but from her behavior it is clear she knows little about children and teaching. She does not know how to help Emma achieve the learning that would identify a Basic 6 level of skating. She may have even evaluated correctly, but perhaps not very well. Of course, except for evidences of truly bizarre behaviors, everyday personalities and peccadilloes are not a legitimate criteria for granting or denying licenses to teachers, and many are licensed who have not the character for teaching.

Emma does not want to be an Olympic skater. She wants to skate. Kelly's designation of her failure got in the way of Emma's skating.

And even that isn't really the issue right now and right here. What are the standards that Kelly looked with and for when she judged my daughter's achievements? I assume that there is some level of expertise which marks requisite learning for Basic 6, but I cannot for my life fathom what they might be in *this* community program or how they could be so objectively assessed. Oh, we have watched enough Olympic competitions to understand the point ratings, and we accept almost without question the judgement of the judges, though it appears from the more recent Olympic Games that even these ratings are not very objectively determined. I listen impatiently to the sportscasters sitting safely in their booths point out the imperfections I cannot see in the performance. Finally, however, I do not care who wins or loses, who will wear the gold and the silver medal. The skaters are for me interchangeable, which is to say, that she/he who wins today will lose tomorrow, and vice versa. What all of the skaters have in common, however, is that they all—first- and second-place finishers—return to the practice arena—the study, as it were—the day following the performance. By the standards of sports they are professional because they earn money as a result of their performance, but by my standards they are professional because they are always studying. Of course they improve!

Emma skates once or twice a week. She is yet a child and remains relatively unfocused in her interests and desires. And to my untrained eye, she skates rather adeptly. She is nine years old and she is not Michelle Kwan. But then, she has no desire nor need at this time to be so. She is, rather, competent and content on the ice.

Did Kelly wonder if Emma had stolen her time? And even by Olympian standards, what exactly is the difference between a total score of 46.9 and a 47.1? And does it really matter? Is it really true that a sprinter who runs a hundred-yard dash in 9.9 seconds is qualitatively better than a sprinter who runs it in 10.0 seconds. Why? Wouldn't tomorrow's race yield, perhaps, a different result with the same times? How could my daughter who skated at least twice every week not come even close to achieving mastery of the things necessary to pass? How could she have come that far and be yet so ignorant or remain so silent concerning her inabilities? What can be said of her teachers?

But perhaps Narissa was correct. How can I know that this meaningless "C" did not stop her from going to law school? Or that Emma's failure to pass Basic 6 will keep her off the ice again? Or diminish slightly the smile she wears when she skates? Then how will I justify the evaluation. My stomach will hurt.

Ah, I wonder: what if our standards are not appropriate ones? What if we are wrong? How, indeed, can we believe so highly in our certainty? "Standards must be rigorous and world-class, reflecting perspectives in

Wisconsin, across our nation, and around the world." I truly wonder, what is at stake that we could break the heart of a little girl who loves to ice skate for the achievement of a set of standards? Or to a child whose report writing is preparation to the writing of briefs. Albert Speer fulfilled and surpassed all the standards set for the study of architecture. Look what he designed. Richard Milhous Nixon satisfied all the standards in his curriculum.. Bill Clinton was a Fulbright Scholar. Newt Gingrich performed satisfactorily all the standards necessary to become a teacher. But in his practice he wasn't very ethical. None of the above were. George Bush, the President of the United States, proudly displays his mediocre academic record. Indeed, his schools might have received failing scores because of his lack of achievement there. Of what service did the standards accomplish?

A MORAL TALE AND A TALE OF MORALITY: ANOTHER FAILURE

Rabbi Elazar is unable to relieve his sense of culpability and assumes full responsibility for his part in the execution of the condemned man.

> And even so Rabbi Elazar the son of Rabbi Shimon did not rely on his [own] opinion, [and] he accepted upon himself afflictions. In the evening they would spread for him sixty felt mattresses, [and] in the morning they would draw from under him sixty basins of blood and pus. The next day his wife would prepare for him sixty kinds of food made from figs, and he ate them and recovered. But his wife would not allow him to go out to the study hall, so that the Rabbis would not push [and hurt] him. In the evening he would say to them [his afflictions]: Come, my brethren and my friends." In the morning he would say to them: "Go, because of neglect of Torah." (*Bava Metzia,* 84b).

Poor Rabbi Elazar can't seem to get over his own doubts; every evening he makes space for the suffering he must endure because he condemned a man to death. Perhaps Elazar is emblematic of all of us who would be certain in our roles as teacher, parent, or lover but cannot, alas, be so. We are oppressed by our doubts. Despite the assurances of his students that the man whom he condemned to death, who, you will recall, referred to Elazar as "Vinegar, Son of Wine," was, indeed, a wicked man who had had intercourse with a betrothed maiden on Yom Kippur, Elazar cannot put himself at peace with the role he played in the man's execution. For despite the fact that Elazar's fat did not decay in the hot summer's sun despite signs of blood marbling throughout it—a sign of his purity—despite even some suggestion that the Elazar's judgement contains a modicum of validity, he remains haunted by the consequences of his accusation. He nightly assumes suffering for his actions. I am awed by his degree of personal responsibility and sense of culpability.

Yet every morning, he wills the suffering away so that he might continue to study. Perhaps there would be some benefit to giving up the power that accrues to evaluation in order that the process of teaching might be enhanced; would we could put away our grade books that we might facilitate learning.

Another story: Once there was a student. A young boy, this student loved to play and hated to work. School was, to him, work. Though he would sit in class, he was always in motion. Of so much energy was that child comprised that his pen could never stay long on the paper, and though it would start ably enough, by the middle of the line that pen had moved into flight and the sentence never reached its destination. But then, the boy was young and did not care about the future or about getting his thoughts down articulately on paper. And yet his teacher was obsessed by it. Terrified that without constant vigilance the teacher would despoil the future by his failure to properly prepare its intended inhabitants for its momentous arrival, the teacher would conscientiously pull the boy through the curriculum as one might pull a young child into the bathroom to wash hands and face.

But the boy smiled so beautifully that his teacher loved him. In that smile, the teacher saw an innocence that he cherished in the world, even saw the innocence he would seriously stain. When the student would not study for the quizzes and the tests the teacher prepared in order to evaluate the quantity of material the student had retained, the teacher would give this student a failing grade; and he would smile at the student with concerned affection. He would gently admonish the student with words of love, even employing the vocabulary words the student had yet to learn. When the student failed to turn in his writing lessons, the teacher would keep him after school and sit next to him and help push the pen across the paper. The teacher hoped that his concern for this student evidenced in the proffered smiles and failing grades would seduce the student to greater effort, and then the student would succeed. The teacher hoped that his own passion would become the beacon that the student might use to steer safely to shore.

But the student remained, as it were, happily afloat at sea. He sensed no danger. And so the teacher caused winds to blow and waves to pound about the student. He sent home warning notices and called parents in for conferences. After class, he would hail the student to the front of the room to urge him to make greater effort. And the student would smile and assure the teacher that, yes, he would do so.

But the future remained too far away, and the teacher's urgings remained unheeded; the boy continued unenthralled by the books and words with which the teacher meant to seduce the student. The student did not heed the teacher's beacon. The student did not believe the teacher when he warned of the consequences of his inactions, as it were. Nor did the student fall in love with either the teacher or the subject matter. Or perhaps the teacher could not recognize the love of his student because he could not see the student through the filter of the teacher's own image. And so at the end of the year the teacher failed the student with a grade point average of fifty-seven. Sixty was a passing score.

And the student went to summer school for the three points.

This morality tale has no moral. But its persistence in my memory suggests the doubts I still retain concerning my behavior almost thirty years ago. This remains for me a very painful memory, but I think it serves me well in the present. Academic suicide is an option in my classes, but not so execution. I think for me now the issue concerns not the matter of the three points: had I been wiser I would not have failed the student. But the three points seem symptomatic of a larger concern and perhaps illumine a somewhat different issue. If a grade is assigned based on a computed average of a body of quantitatively assessed work, then in the assignment of grades a teacher ought to consider a fifty-seven as inviolable. And whether the computed average is one point or three points or thirty points from passing, it ought to remain a failure. Perhaps few teachers would fail a student with a fifty-seven, except perhaps Mr. Feeny on *Boy Meets World.* Most of us, I believe, would assign a passing grade based in some subjective assessment—effort made, attendance, extra-credit assignments, compassion. But, as soon as I adjust these numerical computations (often via numerical assessments of subjective qualities) then I have delegitimized any final evaluation based in these numbers. If these computed averages are by nature uncertain and their meanings so ambiguous that they can be subjectivity adjusted, then how can we ever depend on any computed average for a permanent assignment of final grades? If my subjective assessment can adjust the objective evaluation, then of what value is the objective assessment? If my subjective assessment can alter the outcomes of the objective evaluation, then what role does my subjectivity play in the construction in what we think of as objective assessment? Is a "B+" an 87 or an 88? If I cannot tell the difference between a "C" and a "C+," then how can I tell the difference between an "A" and a "C"? And if I can't be assured of the difference, then how can I sentence anyone to either grade?

And finally, I know that in a basketball game three points might mean the difference between winning and losing, but in the classroom, where the final buzzer will not sound for years if at all save at death, could three points have any value whatsoever?

OF WHAT USE IS EVALUATION?

Joseph Schwab decried the practice of testing and evaluation in the schools. Schwab held that if the purpose of education was to make people smart, and smart has something to do with a successful and ethical engagement in life, then no test could be written which would with any validity measure the accomplishment of any student. Schwab (1978, 277) wrote that if the purpose of a general education has "something to do with a good and happy life for the men and women our students will become," then our complete lack of agreement of what that good and happy life might be constituted makes an evaluation of an education designed to achieve that life an absurdity. In the absence of certain knowledge of the definition of a "good and happy life," Schwab wrote, we are always only "partly right." Yet our summative, absolute evaluations in schools condemn not a few.

Furthermore, regardless of the actual validity of the material our tests purport to measure, that "true" measure itself remains false. Schwab claimed that education should enable an informed life, but that life occurred in complex contexts. Tests whose validity derive from their "one-to-one correspondence" with specific operations in a specific discipline, are, by definition, invalid because the very operations that they test are pulled out of a living context, are "concrete" and "absolute" and not real and functional. Thus, Schwab argued, our examinations and evaluation procedures are reduced to being mere "shadows of a shadow of a shadow" (1978, 279). These tests are then, substantively, irrelevant. By ***smart***, Schwab meant that a person so deemed should have experienced a curriculum that would develop his/her capacities for infinite adaptability to the infinite situations tht life entails. "What is needed is a body of knowledge which can enable a leadership to comprehend and to exercise its judgment upon the specialized component which will be present in almost all its problems. Since the specialized components will be numerous, various, and recondite, the task of supplying such a body of knowledge appears to be insuperable" (1978, 139). Life is always more complex than are our tests, which purport to evaluate the knowledge acquired from engagement in curriculum that itself has been especially designed to enable us to successfully negotiate that life. Any test that claims validity must be erroneous because it would only measure phantoms. Furthermore, we are humanly limited in our capacity for knowing. "As curriculum makers, we are more often wrong or incomplete than right about the nature of our subject matter" (1978, 279). If our tests are meant to evaluate knowledge that students have acquired, that knowledge is always "wrong and incomplete," and therefore, our tests are always wrong and incomplete. And yet, the products of these tests—grades—like the blood libel leveled at Jews, permit heinous attacks on the lives of our children.

It was not that Schwab felt that tests might serve no purpose; indeed, Schwab averred that "education at large would benefit much more from a campaign of validation directed conjointly at the teaching process, the curriculum, the principles of curriculum construction, and tests, than it now profits from a campaign which treats only the test as a variable in the system of education factors" (1978, 275). Of course, what Schwab sought was a test which would evaluate not only that students learned, but that what they learned always had practical application and was presently true. What Schwab desired was a testing program that would evaluate not the students but the entire educational process. For Joseph Schwab, it was not the students who required evaluation; it was not the student who must be held accountable for the material that was offered to them as education. Rather, Schwab believed, it was the very substance of education that was to be held accountable. Such a system, always in revision, should itself condemn no students.

Joseph Schwab decried the practice of testing and evaluation in the schools. Well, he did not condemn it in so many words. But what he did say was this: As it is the purpose of a general education—ostensibly the ***raison d'être*** of the curriculum of the public school—to prepare a person to be a good citizen, and since the definition of that citizen is subject to "radically different answers," then to produce a "valid" test of success in general education "would have to proceed by measuring the extent to which each graduate was a good man and a good citizen" (1978, 277). Because there could be no single criteria by which judgement could be made, such a test, Schwab argued, was a "palpable absurdity." Aside from the fact that grades would have to be assigned *ex post facto*, the character of knowledge required for and the definition of a good citizen would have changed over the intervening years between education and practice, thereby, invalidating assignment of reliable grades. The entire process of grading was not only useless but impossible. The idea that a "valid" test could ever assess the extent of an education was an absurdity. Indeed, says Schwab, only that test THAT "would disclose the unknown and unanticipated consequences (in addition to those intended) of the curriculum would be a valid instrument, but clearly such test would be non-valid in the normal sense of validity (1978, 277). I think Schwab labored in curriculum to make examinations and testing irrelevant. "We have proposed a curriculum and a climate in which the faculty member is a possessor and imparter of disciplines in quite another sense: mentor, guide and model; ally of the student against ignorance; participant with the student in high adventures into the worlds of intellect and sensibility" (1969b, 20). I think Schwab struggled courageously to ensure that education be a successful venture for all involved in it and that none participating in it would fail. Education should serve nobler purposes.

THEY PELT HIM WITH STONES

Deuteronomy 21:18-21 says, "*When a man has a son, a stubborn-one and a rebel—he does not hearken to the voice of his father or to the voice of his mother—and they discipline him, but he (still) does not hearken to them, his father and his mother are to seize him and are to bring him out to the elders of his town, to the gate of his place; then they are to say to the elders of his town: Our son, this-one, is a stubborn-one and a rebel—he does not hearken to our voice—a glutton and a drunkard! Then all the men of the town are to pelt him with stones, so that he dies.*" Now, these are very harsh terms; indeed, we might declare them cruel and unusual punishment. But in their interpretation of the law (Sandhedrin, 68b-71b), the Rabbis have made it veritably impossible that the sentence ever be carried out. No, not veritably impossible, but absolutely so. By the time the Rabbis' exegesis is complete, no child could ever be subject to such punishment. What the Rabbis accomplish in their search for culpability is the exemption of all children from summative judgement. Rather than condemn the "stubborn and rebellious child," the Rabbis have made the assignment of that label to any individual impossible. According to the Rabbis' beliefs, no one would be ever condemned. Every child would pass the test. To assume the perspective of the Rabbis, education—learning—would be forever redemptive: It would execute no one. Ah, would we be so careful in the schools with regard to the executions we practice by our tests and grading procedures. Though I think that Schwab augured for such an exemption: "My personal inclination," he said, "is to do away entirely with the *terminal* examination and return to the very old-fashioned, unscientific, unobjective business of judging a student on the basis of his day-to-day contribution to the course—oral contributions as well as written" (1969b, 223). I think what Schwab offered was an ethic of life in school rather than an instrument to measure that life. And I think a study of the Rabbis' thought offers a perspective on the present practice of grading and suggests a different ethic upon which education ought to be founded.

ONLY A MAN, NOT A SON; ONLY A SON, NOT A DAUGHTER

The first exemption the Rabbis make derives from the identity of the accused. Using the very language of the law, they find cavernous spaces for exemptions. The law mandates that "If a father has a son" who is stubborn and rebellious, and who does not listen to the voices of his parents, then this son must be brought to the elders of the community for evaluation and judgment. The Rabbis reason that this son must be a minor or the text would no longer identify him as the son of a father. Rather, he would be known primarily in the greater role, as a father. And, the Rabbis had declared much earlier that minors should not ever be held responsible for fulfillment of the commandments. Thus, this "son", albeit difficult, even stubborn and rebellious, is exempt from the judgment of the law. In Jewish practice, that moment of the assumption of adult responsibility for the laws occurs when a child reaches bar or bat mitzvah, at the age of thirteen years. Thus, by this ruling, the Rabbis have ensured that a child prior to age thirteen could not be held liable for stubbornness or rebelliousness. And since the verse in Deuteronomy says, "When a man has a ***son***," the Rabbis establish another severely limiting restrictions—the suspected child must be a "son." A daughter may be not held liable.

Thus, I think the Rabbis have drawn a severe fence about this supposed culprit—the designation of this child as "a son" suggests to the Rabbis that he is a minor and, therefore, may not be held liable. However, once the child is no longer a minor, then by law he also can not be held liable because as a *man* he can no longer be identified as a stubborn and rebellious *son*. Secondly, this child may not be female. Methinks there are few who would not be, thus, exempt from accusation and execution..

Perhaps we might understand grades and standards in a similar perspective. Who is culpable for the imposition of grades. This definition hinges on the identity of the student. Certainly, if the goal of the schools is to prepare lifelong learners—a cliché present in so many mission statements of the public schools—then we are all always students. Logically, then, as we are all students, then who may cast judgement? Or, if a student is someone who has much to learn, then we are, again, by definition and by joy, all always students. No one ought to be condemned for lack of ultimate and final knowledge. If a student is any-one who learns, then, again, we are all students, and the monopoly of the adult hierarchy —the mothers and fathers of the school system—for grade assignment bespeaks an original injustice. If a student is one who asks questions and challenges the knowledge and even authority of the teacher, and if it is the purpose of education to offer the pedagogy of such challenge, judgement of this behavior is hypocritical and the exercise of power jealously maintained by the assignment of those grades must be judged unreasonable. If, as Schwab held, the makers of curriculum—and its practitioners—are more often wrong than right, then our standards are finally false and no one should be condemned for the lack of knowledge of planners and implementers of curriculum. The Rabbis insist that a child who cannot be held responsible ought not to be subject to execution; a student who does not know cannot be failed. Once the child is no longer a student—does not learn—then obviously, he ought no longer to be held responsible. The Rabbis mean to fail no one by exempting everyone; underlying our educational practice ought to be not the execution of the rebellious—or the separation of our youths into discrete, measured, and condemnatory categories—but the continued invitation to engage in the wonder of study. If one hour of return is worth the whole life to come, then the student must be forever offered that hour to return.

Some Rabbis express doubt about the exemption of the minor: They wonder that, if there is no where else in law that a minor may be held responsible for the commandments, then why is it now necessary to explicitly exempt the minor here in the present Talmudic discussion. The Rabbis assume that there must be more meant by this particular exemption. One scholar argues that judgement on the stubborn and rebellious son is effected not so much for his actual iniquity, but "on account of his ultimate end," that is, to prevent future rebellious behavior (*Sanhedrin,* 68b). Thus, by these premises, the execution of a minor might be justified. But such an act seems absurd, even to the Rabbis. They apparently dismiss the culpability of the minor without question.

Of course, this is not the ideology in our places of education: The purpose of school is to prepare for the future, and grades are a measure of an assessment of movement towards that goal. The intent of grades is to make judgment on the student's effort in the endeavors society has assigned to the school in preparation for a future. The Department of Public Instruction of the state of Wisconsin claims that *Model Academic Standards* "set high goals and expectations for all students . . . [they] reflect the collective values of our citizens and are intended to prepare our young people for opportunities that exist in Wisconsin, the nation and the world." Standards are a definition of the future, and the grades assigned in school judge the competence of a student to succeed in that future. Grades are assigned "not so much on his actual iniquity," but "on account of his ultimate end." According to school ideology, successful achievement of the standards should lead ***quid pro quo*** to a successful future. And vice versa: Failure in school prepares for failure in life. To prevent the latter, failing grades for failure to achieve standards are mandated. Judgement must be made "on account of his ultimate end." But the Rabbis are bent on preventing execution of such judgement and exempt seemingly all from it. And we all know how absurd the claim that there exists a relationship between school grades and success in life. Obviously, then, the expressed exemption of the minor here must have other meaning.

HOW LONG, BROTHER, HOW LONG?

The Rabbis continue their discussion concerning exemptions based in the identity of the accused. They acknowledge that a minor is obviously not liable, and neither could a father—regardless of that father's age—be held liable for execution as a stubborn and rebellious child. That is, because the law states that "if a man have a son," then the son must be only a son and not also a father. The Rabbis do acknowledge—Rab Judah to be exact—that the proximity of the word "son" to the word "man" in the exact language of the text—"if a man have a son"—suggests that that son must be at least *near to the age of manhood*, and therefore, some culpability is acknowledged in even a son who is clearly not a minor but yet not also a man. That son, the Rabbis reason, might be condemned as a stubborn and rebellious son and be liable for execution. After all, the Rabbis reason, the text of Torah, though perfect, must yet be recovered. Someone must be liable!! The Rabbis wonder, for what period of time exactly might that son be held accountable? The Rabbis answer: "From the time that he produces two hairs until he grows a beard right round (by which is meant the hair of the genitals not that of the face)" (*Sanhedrin* 68b). The reference is not to facial but genital hair growth, and Hiyya further specifies that this refers to growth about the penile shaft and not about the testicles, which, the Rabbis say, occurs much later. Before there has been this growth, the minor is exempt, but after this hair growth has occurred, then the child is no longer liable for he is no longer a son—rather, he is known as a man and, by the language of the law, no longer held accountable. According to the Rabbis, this period of genital hair growth lasts for a period of approximately three months. It is only within this time period that the son may be held liable.

In Wisconsin we have instituted standardized tests to be administered in the fourth, eighth, and tenth grades. The national government suggests that students ought to be tested yearly throughout grades three through eight. Eleventh and twelfth graders are subject to the PSAT (Preliminary Scholastic Assessment Test), the SAT (Scholastic Assessment Test) or the ACT (American College Tests), and Regents Examinations. There are admission exams to some public schools and exit exams from all public schools. There are intelligence tests and personality tests and projective interests instruments. There is a steady barrage of tests from the moment a child enters the fray until he/she is privileged to leave it. There is, in fact, no cessation of liability in our educational system. Unlike the Rabbis, not only have we have exempted none from judgment but, rather, we have extended the period of liability until veritably all must be subject to some form of execution. It would seem to me that the Rabbis struggle to dramatically minimize a period of culpability in order to prevent execution of judgement; I think the Rabbis have absolutely no interest in carrying out judgment on anyone. Rather, they have reasoned from an ethic of caring and hope. We, on the other hand, have ensured such judgement, and have reasoned from an ethic of competition, fear, and distrust.

We might learn much from the Rabbis' desire to avoid having ever to enact the law.

But the Rabbis are not finished with their exemptions—it is as if they are committed to ensure that no one is ever subject to this judgment. The Rabbis would not ascribe to anyone the condemnatory charge of a stubborn and rebellious child—all can learn and effect return. The Rabbis continue: Since the verse in Deuteronomy reads "if a man have a son," then the son of a minor may not be held liable: it is a *man* who must have a son. Furthermore, since Torah states *if a man have a son*, the Rabbis reason that if that son is ***also*** a father, then that individual is no longer culpable because he is more than a son. I like the literalness of their interpretation. We all become many characters in the course of a daily life; we all enact many characters in our lives in schools. Judgement on any one character is to misrepresent and misunderstand the complexity of the child. Thus, when a child in our classes learns even one thing—even if it is not what we have taught—that child ought not be liable for the label of a failing student.[2] And besides, that child might have learned something somewhere else and thus, may no longer be condemned as a failing student.

---

[2]There is a joke: The star quarterback had failed the final exam in mathematics and was ineligible for the big game. The professor was coerced by the administration to give the student a make-up test. He told the player, "I am going to ask you two questions. You must get at least one of them correct to achieve a passing grade. Here is the first: What is the sum of the angles of a right triangle?" And the quarterback quickly answered, "45." The Professor frowned. "No, I'm sorry. Now be careful, Here is the second question. What is the product of twelve times twelve." The student thought and thought, and finally, sweating profusely, threw up his hands. "I don't know," he cried. "Ah, very good," said the Professor, "you have correctly answered that question. You've passed the test with a 50%."

NOT THE STUDENT SHOULD BE FAILED, BUT THE FAILURE SHOULD BE FAILED

The Rabbis continue: If a person, regardless of his age, impregnates a woman, then that child is no longer a son but a father and again, he is no longer liable to law of the stubborn and rebellious son. Even if a minor be responsible for the pregnancy, since gestation of the fetus takes nine months, and the law concerning a stubborn and rebellious child operates only between the time when the child produces two hairs about his penis until he grows a beard around his testicles, it is clear that the male responsible can be no longer liable to the judgement since by the time the child is born this three-month period of culpability will have passed. The Rabbis reason that by the time the baby is born, the son, having now become a father, may no longer be held liable. Since the law reads that it must be the son of a man, children of minors are not culpable.

Actually, the Rabbis argue, minors do not even have the capability of producing children and, therefore, the entire discussion is irrelevant. To accomplish this exemption, the Rabbis resort to the exegesis of the Hebrew word, *ya'zid.* This word is used in Exodus 21:14, and refers to capital murder: "if a man came presumptuously (*ya'zid*) upon his neighbor to slay him." This word *ya'zid* is derived from the word *zeed*, which means to seethe and boil—a term used in reference to the excitation and emission of semen. Therefore, since the phrase reads, "If a ***man*** came presumptuously . . ." and since the adverb derives from a word that refers to sexual ejaculation, the Rabbis reason that clearly the Torah suggests that only men and not minors can emit semen. Though they might be capable of intercourse, their semen is "like the seed of cereals less than a third grown," incapable of growth. Thus, since, minors ar never responsible for fulfilling the commandments, and since minors could never be fathers, and since fathers cannot also be rebellious sons, and since full-grown men may not be also sons, it would follow that no male child could realistically be held liable to the law applicable to the rebellious and stubborn son of a "man."

Perhaps this exegesis might be taken into account when we plan for the execution of our children in the schools. For according to, the Rabbis' reasoning, as a male child may be exempted from the law's judgement by the identity of his father—only the rebellious son *of a man* could be liable for execution—so could a student be exempted by the identity of the teacher. If only a son of a man is liable to judgment, then only a child of a "teacher" is liable for failure. If a man become identified by his generativity, then so, too, a teacher might be known by his/her generativity. I believe that a teacher ought not to be defined by the quantity of her/his knowledge, but by her/his ability to engage the child in learning. And a child learns always what the child desires to learn. Martin Buber writes that (1999, 141) the teacher must be she/he who cleaves "to him who needs me, so soon as his need arises . . . to be where one is needed and to be according to the character of the need." John Dewey held that the teacher must guide the child from that place where she/he already participates in the disciplines to that place in the disciplines where the child might go with the assistance of the teacher. It is the guidance by which a teacher is defined and not the destination. Thus, it ought to be the teacher who is liable for judgment and not the student. But, since all teachers are, by definition, students, then, again, all children ought to be exempt from the execution that grades effect since students may not execute judgement.

Indeed, the hierarchy on which grades are based and on which they must be assigned, distracts the teacher from her/his true work by establishing a false standard of achievement as a measurement of learning. Grades and national standards ignore the means for the end. Grades confuse the acquisition of wisdom for its measurement. Learning ought to be for the sake of living, and that can only be measured in actual life. Rabbi David says that though the eyes are important, "they are not the most important things about a man. The important thing is what the eyes seek to see when they exercise their power of vision. And that is not determined by the eyes" (Buber, 1999, 130). Neither ought knowledge be determined by its measurement in the assignment of grades. But because desire is not easily identifiable and certainly not quantifiable, in schools we measure only what the eyes see and not what the eyes seek to see. The Yehudi says that the device of the Evil Spirit is to "show to each the high levels he can reach and lets him reach them. Then is that man's mind fixed upon the levels; then he is no longer devoted to God alone, even though he thinks he is. The power which alone he does not perceive to be either delusion or fraud comes in the end to be himself and his striving from level to level" (Buber, 1999, 216). The quest for levels assumes a hierarchy based in measurement in which the focus is on self-aggrandizement and not learning. The Rabbis would condemn no one whose teacher has taught him and her to aspire to levels and not to learnings. The Yehudi says that such a student must "go out into the lonely forest and stand there and cry out until the levels and grades are taken from him again" (1999, 216). Perhaps this is an argument for the presence of recess in our curricular plans, but, alas, schools are ending recess because, it is claimed, it detracts from learning. And besides, recess cannot be evaluated.

I love these exclusions made by the Rabbis. They reduce my stomach pains. If a student fails a test . . . and what is a student but one who acknowledges that she/he does not know. By this definition, such a one must be exempt from failure. When does a person become a student and when does that appellation cease to apply? As learning is a lifelong process, we are all always students and therefore, all exempt from the execution that results from the administration of tests and grades. Can a child fail a test if she has no teacher? Or if that teacher focuses on the standards as the definition of knowledge? The circumscription that the Rabbis draw around the law renders it unenforceable. The Rabbis ensure here that no one may ever be executed.

DEFINING FAILURE RIGHT OUT OF POSSIBILITY

No student in my class ought to be ever liable for execution; I am immeasurably relieved. And the Rabbis offer my travails in the academy even more relief. Having reduced culpability to an absurd three-month time span and ensured that the recalcitrant son be defined by the identity of the father, the Rabbis now move even further to prevent the execution of even a single culprit. The Rabbis wonder what does it could mean to be a "stubborn and rebellious child." This is not an uninteresting question: There have been students who not only did not attempt to accomplish the prescribed work, but who, while classes were in session, even absented themselves from felicity a while. Ah, there are students who referred to me as "Vinegar, Son of Wine." What does it mean to be a stubborn and rebellious child? Indeed, the fate of my very children rests on this decision, though they be both girl-children. The Mishnah (law) declares that one becomes a stubborn and rebellious son "When he eats a tartemar of meat and drinks half a log of Italian wine" (*Sanhedrin,* 70a). There is, as I have come to expect, some disagreement regarding the actual measure. Rabbi Jose said that the son becomes liable when he eats a *mina* of flesh and drinks a *log* of wine. Actually, it is more than a disagreement—the problem is definition and no one can exactly define the quantity stipulated: "Rabbi Zera said: "I do not know what is this *tartemar*; but since Rabbi Jose doubled the measure of wine, he must have doubled that of the meat too; hence, the conclusion is drawn: the *tartemar* is half a *mind*' (*Sanhedrin,* 70a). The Rabbis declare that since the verses in Deuteronomy states that the accusation against the son describes him as drunken and a glutton, then it is only for the acts of eating and drinking for which the son might be liable. The Rabbis have severely limited the behaviors for which execution might be justified.

Finally, however, I do not think that it is quantity with which the Rabbis are concerned: Regardless of the quantity consumed there are, ah, some exemptions. Rather, the Rabbis concern themselves with the context—the motives—in which eating and drinking are done. Rabbi Hana ben Moladah said, quoting Rabbi Huna, that the son is not liable unless he purchases the meat and wine cheaply and then consumes them. The Rabbis reason that if the meat and wine were expensive, then the son would not be so prone to purchase them and would not be led to evil. There is an ethic behind this exception: Indeed, in our contemporary society, we are told the plethora of inexpensive, fast foods is a serious factor in the growth of obesity of our children. We might similarly reason: If school knowledge were valuable, then perhaps it would not be treated so lightly as to be copied on scraps of paper to be snuck into test rooms or stolen from the works of others. Or avoided all together for the pleasures of knowledge desired. If knowledge was expensive, perhaps it would be offered in more cautious quantities; if knowledge was expensive, perhaps it would be consumed with greater regard; if knowledge was valued, perhaps it would not be so easily thrown up.

Rabbi Hanan said that the child still does not become liable—even if he consumed inexpensive wines and meat—unless the meat was raw and the wine undiluted. These conditions suggest consumption in barbarous and debauched states and reflect on the son's character. Again, we note that there is an ethic that lies behind the law; unlike in our schools, where our measured evaluation defines the good student, for the Rabbis the definition of stubborn and rebellious derives from the living ethic and not from the law. Other Rabbis go even further by referring to at least two other respected Rabbis (Rabbah and Joseph) who argued that even if the son ate raw meat and undiluted wine, he is not liable as a stubborn and rebellious son, though Rabina qualifies this exemption arguing that by raw meat and undiluted wine it is really meant *partially cooked meat*, "as thieves on the run would eat," *and insufficiently undiluted wine*, which people concerned with becoming drunk would consume. And, Rabbah and

Joseph say that if the son eats *pickled* meat or drinks wine from the vat—before it has matured, then the child is not stubborn and rebellious, because this food cannot be appealing to the child and therefore, would not be eaten gluttonously.

What a wonderful opinion of humanity is offered here: The Rabbis seem to assume that by choice the individual would prefer the properly cooked and sufficiently diluted wine. It would appear that the Rabbis are attempting to establish an ethic of eating and drinking more than laying blame, and here a stubborn and rebellious child is defined not by act but by intention. However, the ethic defined assures that the motives of the son—again, within a very brief three-month window of culpability—are obviously and clearly malicious, and suggest that it is to protect the child from his ultimate end that the punishment is meted out. But the exemptions are such that guilt would be difficult to achieve.

And the Rabbis are still not done with their exemptions. If one eats and drinks to excess, and even if this meat is partially cooked and the wine insufficiently diluted, if that consumption takes place in celebration of a religious festival, even if the celebration is undertaken in the company of wastrels and ne'er-do-wells, the child is not liable for execution, for in this celebratory consumption the son is enacting a mitzvot. And, furthermore, the Rabbis reason, it might be that in that generally evil company there would be a single good person who might set the wayward son aright. In the exercise of a spiritual life, "eating the second tithe in Jerusalem," the son is not liable, for 'in Jerusalem' there are no restrictions to the quantities one may eat and drink, and besides, in the exercise of a mitzvot, he would not be drawn to wickedness. Nor is the son liable if he ate *nebeloth* or *terefoth*, abominable or creeping things, Again, this exemption applies to quantity eaten: The Rabbis decree that if the son ate less than a *tartemar* of meat and finished his/her meal with *nebeloth*, he is not punished. That is, unless the child ate a tartemar of meat *and* a tartemar of abominable or creeping things, he is not liable. And if the child eats even these forbidden things in the exercise of a religious act—even if the son overeats—then he is not punished because the excess is mitigated by the good act. Furthermore, even if overeating and excess drinking is committed in transgression of the law, then the son is not liable for punishment because the Torah says that in their complaint the parents must say, "He will not obey our voice," while in the transgressive act it is God's voice that is being denied. I think of Hamlet who warned Polonious, 'Treat every man after his own deserts and who should 'scape whipping," But the Rabbis have argued that no one should ever be liable for such whipping.

WHAT DO I HAVE TO DO TO FAIL? NOTHING!

Finally, if there be anyone yet still culpable, the Rabbis erect still another fence around the suspected son. If the accused child ate any food but meat and drank any drink but wine, then the child is not liable. That is, it is only the consumption of meat and wine that makes the child culpable because Deuteronomy states that the accusation against the child calls him a glutton and a drunkard, and there is evidence that these appellations concern only meat and wine. Proverbs 23:20 declares "Be not among the wine-bibbers, among gluttonous eaters of flesh." Similarly, in Proverbs 23:21, the Rabbis note the statement, "For the glutton and the drunkard shall come to poverty; and drowsiness shall clothe a man with rags." Thus, since waywardness and rebelliousness has been linked to the gluttonous eating of meat and drunkenness has been identified with the consumption of wine, then it is only those two substances only which render a child culpable for execution.

And still the Rabbis are not through with their exemptions. They argue that "If he stole of his Father's and ate it in his father's domain, or [stole] of strangers and ate it in the domain of the strangers, or [stole] of strangers and ate it in his father's domain, he does not become a 'stubborn and rebellious son'" (*Sanhedrin* 71a). This is so because, in each of these situations, the consumption of the meat and wine would entail danger and the child will not do this often and cannot be declared stubborn and rebellious. I like this: The Rabbis hold that unconscious guilt will operate and even if the act is accomplished once, the overwhelming guilt and difficulty will prevent further occurrences. The Rabbis not only tolerate error, but expect teshuvah—the turning from it. Thus, the Rabbis conclude that only when the son steals from his father and eats it in the domain of strangers is the child culpable.

Rabbi Jose is willing to go even further. He avers that it is only when the child steals from the father *and* the mother that the son becomes liable. Other Rabbis object saying that one cannot steal from the mother because she does not legally own anything: "whatever a woman acquires belongs to her husband . . ." (*Sanhedrin*, 71a). And Rabbi Jose responds: It means that if the son stole from a meal prepared by the mother for the father, only then is he liable. But, objects Rabbi Hanan, didn't the Rabbis just finish arguing that the child must buy the meat and wine cheaply and eat them? And the response again is exculpatory: Rabbi Jose means that the son has stolen money that is set aside for a meal for the father and the mother. And there is also an alternative explanation: The reference is to a gift to the mother from a stranger who has expressly stipulated that her husband has no rights to the gift. Thus, a woman could acquire of her own. Thus, the son must steal from both the mother and the father to be liable to execution.

AND WHO MAY SPEAK AGAINST THIS CHILD?

And more. Since the law (*Deuteronomy* 21: 19) reads, "Then shall his father and his mother lay hold of him," therefore, a child whose parents have lost a hand or fingers is not liable; and since the law reads that the parents must bring the child out, then the child of parents who are lame is not liable; since the law reads that the parents must announce that the accused is "this, our son," then the child of parents who are dumb is not liable. And since the law reads that the parents must point to the child and say "this, our son," then the child of parents who are blind is exempt, since in the absence of sight, certainty is impossible. And since the law reads, "he will not obey our voice," then the child of parents who are deaf is exempt, since they cannot be certain that when they have ordered their child to do something that he has, indeed, refused. And since the Rabbis decree that unless the three judges who originally whipped the boy are part of the court of twenty-three judges who condemn him, the son is not liable, because the law reads "this, our son," and the Rabbis interpret the relative pronoun, *this*, to mean "*this* our son who was whipped in your presence" ((*Sanhedrin,* 71a).

The daily accusation of our leaders concerning our educational failures is shamed by the Rabbis' desire to exempt all from summative judgement. Our willingness to stone the stubborn and rebellious child reflects not on our children but on ourselves. The enormous growth in the children classified as ADD (attention deficit disorder) and ADHD (attention deficit hyperactivity disorder) may be attributed to the demands of the social and pedagogical order rather than to any pathological condition of the child. René Helmerichs (2002, 76) writes that "stubborn, rebellious, and self-serving behavior became a trade mark in the first cases of 'moral defect' children studies by [G. F.] Still in 1902. Still is considered a pioneer in the development of attention-deficit behavior disorders." The Rabbis desire to exempt from culpability is set in serious relief by our willingness to include.

The law next reads, "If his father desires [his execution], but not his mother, or the reverse, he is not treated as stubborn and rebellious child, unless they both desire it" (*Sanhedrin,* 71a). Consider how such required agreement amongst the teachers might exempt not a few children from failure. Rabbi Judah says that "If his mother is not fit for his father, he does not become a stubborn and rebellious child" (*Sanhedrin,* 71a). What, the Rabbis wonder, does this phrase, "not fit" mean? And they decide that it must mean that the father and the mother are not physically alike. Others wonder on what justification could this exemption be made. Rabbi Judah says that since the holy law says "he will not obey our voice," and the Rabbis have declared that this must surely mean that the parents voices must be identical when they accuse the boy, that "since they must be alike in voice, they must be also [alike] in stature and appearance" (*Sanhedrin,* 71a).

Well, we can see where this is leading. The conclusion is reached: "There never has been a 'stubborn and rebellious son', and never will be" (*Sanhedrin,* 71a). But the Rabbis wonder: If the law is not executable, then why should there even be such a law in the first place. Why would Torah create a law that cannot be carried out? And the response to this puzzlement is the most pedagogically wonderful response I might imagine: "Why then was this law written? That you may study it and receive reward" (*Sanhedrin,* 71a). The whole purpose of the law is not to actually carry it out, but to use it as a stimulus to study!

NOT TO EVALUATE, BUT TO STUDY VALUATION!

And in a remarkable way, we have returned to Joseph Schwab. He held that the purpose of tests and evaluation ought to be not as means for executing students, but as means of provoking study. Schwab declared that rather than create tests for evaluating students, "Far more desirable would be tests and usages of statistical data which kept the teacher alert to the incomplete and merely representational character of the moment-to-moment content of a curriculum, and which aided and stimulated his effort to put incomplete parts into relation with one another, to make symbols more vividly representative, and to search out and invent mans for replacing shadows by the things themselves"(1978, 279). That is, tests and evaluative procedures ought measure not the student who cannot be held accountable for the incompleteness and ephemerality of curriculum. Rather, these tests and evaluative procedures might be used to measure the curriculum itself and its makers. "As examiners, we are unclear as to the meaning of 'validity.' As curriculum makers, we are more often wrong or incomplete than right about the nature of our subject matter" (1978, 279). I think Joseph Schwab thought very much like the Talmudic masters.

And so, to prove their point that the development of exegetical brilliance—built on a foundational ethic that respects the life of every other human being—is the real purpose of the law, though acknowledging there never was a stubborn and rebellious son and never will be, the Rabbis actually continue their discussion regarding the identity of the culpable stubborn and rebellious son. They reason that since the Torah says the parents must lay their hands on the child to bring him before the judges, then neither of the parents can be missing fingers or limbs. And since the Torah says that the parents must accuse the rebellious child of not listening to our voice, neither can the parents be dumb. If the parents have no physical voice, the child may not be culpable. And since the Torah says that the parents must lay their hands on the child and declare "This our son," then parents who are blind cannot have a rebellious son because they cannot be certain that the child on whom they have laid their hands is indeed, their child. And since Torah says that the stubborn and rebellious child does obey the voice of the parents, if the parents are deaf then they cannot know what the child responds when they speak, and so the child of deaf parents is exempt.

NO BEGINNING AND NO END

This chapter has no end. Or rather, its end is obvious. Finally, the Rabbis argue that no stubborn or rebellious child should ever be executed. The *Pirke Avot* (4:17) says, "One hour of return in this world is better than the entire world to come." The Rabbis mean to establish an ethic that makes such return possible. The ethic upon which we build our educational system should be the same. We ought to execute no one in the schools by grades and evaluation. I think Joseph Schwab would agree with this judgment.

Chapter Six

"WHO HOLDS THIS BOOK" Ethics, Reading, and Responsibility

Walt Whitman contained in each edition of *Leaves of Grass* the hopeful appeal, "Who holds this book holds a man." Perhaps I have always presumptuously assumed some insight into the meaning of this phrase. I considered: *Leaves of Grass* was the physical presence of the spiritual expression of Walt Whitman, a human being. Held in those leaves were the emanations of the soul and the evocation of the body of an actual man! These leaves were the embodiment and essence of a man. Who holds this book, *Leaves of Grass,* holds the man, Walt Whitman. Whitman's words wonderfully encumber my reading. But I ponder now, how exactly am I made responsible to the man through the book or obligated to the book through the man? Whitman's imperative demands from me an acknowledgment that his volume is no mere physical object; rather, it is the physical presence of a spiritual man for whom I must care. In Hasidic reading, the reader "transcends being a reader of the tradition, and, in a sense, become his text" (Magid, 2002, 39). In reading, the reader enacts the text in praxis: One becomes the text. In Hasidic ideology, what is crucial is not *what* is known, but *how* what is known is transformed into praxis. The reader becomes the text. The writer becomes her own first reader. The reader becomes the writer. Rabbi Nachman of Bratslav, said, speaking of his own text, "This entire book is mine/me. If I did not exist, this book would never exist in the world" (Magid, 2002, 40). The tzaddik, the righteous wise man, translates the tradition—the story—into praxis, and "shows how nonhalakhic[1] aspects of Torah are only external constructs for devotional living" (Magid, 2002, 40). And one seeks in the tales that are told aspects of the divine.

Hasidic practice and the caution of Walt Whitman encumber me to read with concern and care and responsibility. Whitman's *Leaves of Grass* is the physical evocation of a man's life in the process of being lived; to read *Leaves of Grass* is to participate with its author in life. To

[1]These would be aspects that are extra-legal. Halakhic aspects must be adhered to, though the Rabbis will debate what that adherence entails.

read *Leaves of Grass* is to engage in the active process of making a new life for the active reader. His life and mine, and the life of all of his readers. All texts read may be thus, read strongly, to use Harold Bloom's phrase (1975), an act of misprision in which the reader *misreads* in order to achieve self. In such a process, I am made responsible in my reading to both the author and my Self. And so, I wonder now, what is a responsible reading? What are the obligations attendant on this responsibility? How might I read to discover and care for the man in the book and the book in the man? How in my reading am I obliged? How in my reading am I made responsible? For it is also true that to read *Leaves of Grass* is to hold yet another man—myself—as well. In the reading, I might create and care for myself! I must be more attentive.

I think that in his essay, "Enquiry and the Reading Process," Joseph Schwab (1978) turned his attention to the pedagogy of reading and addressed some of these same issues. Consistent with the direction of his entire corpus, this essay decries the inability of present curriculum theory and practices to develop an intelligent populace. Though capable of great learning, students were traditionally not offered an education appropriate either to their potential or to education's ultimate purpose. "*Sub specie aeternitatis,*" Schwab argued, "the young are potentially capable of a vast and omnivorous appetite for learning, for deliberate as opposed to capricious action, and for aesthetic and creative experience" (1978, 108). But, Schwab asserted, present pedagogies, "though capable of leading a reader to water, [were] *not* capable of making him think" (1978, 150). Thought ought to be not a measurable quantity but an immeasurable quality of intellectual activity that would be then practiced in the activity of living. If education should produce smart people, then by smart Schwab included a capacity for understanding how knowledge was constructed and a capacity (and ability) to construct such informed knowledge. Schwab knew that all knowledge—even that in the sciences—was a human construction and that intellect ought to be developed to recognize and deal with such constructions. "For it is the structure of the discipline which lets us know what restricted chunk of the world was studied by the investigation which gave rise to the principle" (1978, 238). In this formulation, Schwab preceded and transcended the limited "structure of the discipline" ideology of the early 1960s promulgated most prominently by Jerome Bruner (1960/1977) and Philip Phenix (1964), and served as forerunner to the contemporary complaint that in the establishment of curriculum and in the hegemony of methods, schools falsely portrayed knowledge as absolute and seamless requiring of students mere absorption and passive learning. Frank Smith (1990, 129), for example, would years later state that in schools, "Students learn from the way that they are taught the illusion that 'knowledge' exists, that it can be trusted (unless specifically labeled *myth* or *propaganda*), and that the transmitters of knowledge can be trusted." Smith echoes Schwab's indictment of curriculum: Meaning in schools was presented to be passively received, and students never did learn to independently think.

If meaning were to have validity, thought Schwab, it required contextualization through enquiry and discourse. Schwab agreed that the ability to think had to develop from the ability to doubt and question and that unless schools offered this pedagogical practice they were miseducating students. "Most of these competence deficiencies point unmistakably and in the most conventional sense to deficiencies of curriculum" (1969b, 29). In this sense, present reading pedagogy does not open the world to the student, nor establish a possibility of praxis—or responsibility but, rather, presents a total world to the student that she/he must blindly accept. Schwab argued that a "[P]articipative interpretation moves from mere reading of a given discourse to anticipation of a larger whole of which the given discourse is a part" (1978, 163). In this sense, reading becomes the world and we become selves in reading. Certainly, here Schwab anticipated Harold Bloom who declared in 1975 that "the relationship between texts . . . depend upon a critical act, a misreading or misprision, that one poet performs upon another, and that does not differ in kind from the necessary critical acts performed by every strong reader upon every text he encounters" (3). Schwab's pedagogy meant to create strong readers.

Schwab hoped to change reading pedagogy to include elements that were not presently included in traditional reading instruction but which, so included, would promote enquiry. These elements, Schwab believed, would add a fourth level of interpretation in which "a whole discourse is 'placed' as providing such-and-such a treatment, in *these* terms but not *those*, of a certain part of a large subject disjoined from other parts, and providing a solution to this but not that problem involved in the subject" (1978, 153). Effective reading must seek the contexts of "subject, principles and conclusions in relation to subjects, principles and conclusions of other, related inquiries" (1978, 153). Schwab sought to add to reading pedagogy—as he did for all curriculum—what he referred to as the problem of dialectic—that every enquiry should point to the incompleteness of knowledge and the responsibility of further study. Schwab held that reading was more than an instrumental practice. Reading, reflecting, and remembering "were to eventuate in something more than efficient coping with the bread-and-butter problems of existence. [They] were to yield the capacity for rewarding experience, a doing and undergoing not merely for the sake of the material outcome; often, not for the outcome at all, but for the satisfaction of the work itself" (1978, 182). Reading, more than an instrumental, but always a practical event, must be based first in the metaphysical and ethical. "Who holds this book holds a man." "This entire book is mine/me. If I did not exist, this book would never exist in the world." In Schwab's essay, as in his entire educational program, he was concerned with the process by which meaning is made from text—*in* reading and *by* thought—and the contributive role that the "humanist" teacher might make to general education in the pedagogy of this practice. Schwab declared in the opening paragraph of the essay: "This document invites the humanist to make a contribution to general education which no one else—least of all the scientist—is as competent to make" (1978, 149). It is in the reading process and its pedagogy that Schwab saw a key to the renaissance of curriculum he would soon demand, and it was the reading process which would enable such learning.

The participative reader—the constructor of meaning and of the self's meaning—engaged in language. Language was not transparent, however, but opaque, and it was the construction of meaning rather than its reception that was the focus of Schwab's pedagogy. "[I]t is of the *construction* of valid meanings that I speak" (1978, 150). Language is not a lens through which one can look and discover meaning; rather, language creates realities, "full not of information but of the possibilities of experience" (Smith, 1990, 110). Unless the teacher aimed to enable all students to achieve a competence in what Schwab would call the reflective dynamic of intellectual space, then the teacher must "fail to test the possibility of a democratic society, to capitulate to the notion of Mass and Class—the latter managerial and manipulative; the former, managed servants, unaware" (Schwab, 1978, 183). The pedagogy of reading should sit, then, at the center of curriculum. Schwab's pedagogical interest was to develop and enable a keen and practical intelligence, one operational and essential for living daily life. In the dramatically changing world of the latter part of the twentieth century, Schwab declared that "the need is not for discard of the generalized liberal arts but for additional means which will supplement them and enable us to specify them to meet the new requirements involved in judgment and decisions about specialized problems" (1978, 139). Schwab thought that intelligence should serve our common lives. Enquiry and the reading process was a means to this pedagogy; reading was an essential tool, not only for learning but for thinking as well.

Schwab was not sanguine about the possibilities of educational reform. It was exactly for the failure of this pedagogical imperative that Schwab criticized the schools during the better part of his long intellectual career. In 1969, Schwab had written that student ineptitudes and ignorances were ascribable to the evils, neglects, distortions, and mistreatments of the curriculum (1969b). What the student learned—if indeed, the student learned anything at all—was not effective as education. Schwab argued that "The practical competences of deliberation are not, of course, traditional obligations of the academic curriculum [though] there is every reason why they should become so" (1969b, 29). By deliberation, Schwab meant the active participation in meaningful conversation, choice, and mutual criticism, "of a pooling of diversities of experience and insights" sufficient enough to cause the experience of education to be satisfying. "The heart of the matter," Schwab declared (1969b, 214-15), "is scope for recovery of meaning and relation, for education of perception and sensibility, in materials traditional to the traditional fields of learning." Settled solidly in a classical perspective, Schwab nevertheless believed that students must be taught to develop "competences which enable us to look at pictures instead of through them, to listen to music instead of being soothed by it, to find in works of literary art not only instruction but a high order of durable satisfaction, and to construct, with some clarity and niceness of distinction, communications of our own thought and experience" (1969b, 216). It was not that the students did not learn; rather, Schwab claimed, most of what they learned was inconsequential, meaningless, and boring. "Students are irresponsible about facts and what they mean, about words and their reference, about ideas and their relationship to facts, because we have left them ignorant of the complex structure of knowledge, innocent of the exacting work involved in a responsible concern for truth, and undisciplined in the discrimination of meaning and the estimation of probability" (1969b, 21). It was no wonder that students seemed to Schwab so irresponsible and ignorant.

They had been failed by the curriculum. "They do not know because, on the one hand, we have not taught them and because, on the other hand, we have mistaught them by making them on occasion both witness and victim of bad decisions badly made" (Schwab, 1969b, 7). What Schwab advocated for was an education that would "return to the curriculum an intellectual challenge to students and the fullest possible opportunity to develop the arts of recovery, enquiry, and criticism appropriate to each discipline" (1969b, 183). Schwab wanted students to learn a) that meaning is constructed, b) how meaning is constructed, and c) how students might themselves construct meaning. It is engagement in this curriculum that Schwab believed would enable the development of a more active and keen intellectual growth, an awareness of and sensitivity to diversity, and an understanding of the complexity of knowledge construction and decision making.

In his essay, "Enquiry and the Reading Process" (1958/1978), Schwab argued against what he described as the traditional paradigm of working with the textual structures from which meaning may be derived. Schwab believed such pedagogies inadequate and incomplete, and in this essay advocated for instruction of a crucial fourth level by which meaning would be actively constructed by a participative reader. This Deweyan constructivism—and Bloom's misprision—predates the present emphasis on constructivism in contemporary pedagogical theory, though, as I will suggest, this pedagogy postdates the earlier constructivism and strong misreadings of the Talmudic doctors. This fourth level of reading that Schwab advocated also is not unlike what will be referred to during the next decades as deconstructive philosophy and intertextual strategies. As I have already suggested, and will continue to demonstrate, this pedagogy is already integral to scholarly activity and exegesis of the Torah by the Talmudic Rabbis. It is, in summary, a method for enabling intelligence. Schwab argued that "The process of initiating the student into participative rhetorical and dialectical interpretation must also be a process of initiating him into the existence of enquiry, of exhibiting to him the extent to which organized knowledge depends on terms chosen and subjects defined, and of showing him how he can identify these terms and definitions and trace their effects upon the knowledge which embodies them" (1978, 158). Consistent with Schwab's entire ideological position, reading was taken to be an active process of enquiry, itself the purpose and end of a general education.

In life, as in reading, understanding of the part in light of the whole offers knowledge not only of the whole but fuller knowledge of any one part of that whole. Similarly, knowledge of the context in which discourses are placed and out of which they arise offers a fuller knowledge of the scope and meaning not only of that particular discourse, but of the larger perspective of which that discourse is a part, and of the context from which it draws and to which it adds. "To the question how big a context constitutes the proper context for a reported enquiry, there is no answer. But the principle which should govern a practical context is clear enough: any apparently definitive or highly persuasive solution to a clearly defined problem ought to appear in a context which will indicate that there is yet more to know or more to know about"(Schwab, 1978, 153). There is never enough background knowledge—what is already known—nor is there an end to what can be learned. Participative rhetorical and dialectical interpretation is the process of inquiry that seeks the contexts of meanings grasped, of whether "those meanings are grasped which accrue to an inquiry by seeing its subject, principles, and conclusion in relation to subjects, principles, and conclusions of other, related inquiries" (1978, 153). To read is to participate in community; reading as participative interpretation—as the activity of living, occurs as a result of community, [2] even as the reading process has the potential to create community. To teach one to read is to teach one how one might live intelligently in the world. "Not only the means, however, but also the ends of liberal education involve the Eros. For the end includes not only knowledge gained but knowledge desired and knowledge sought" (1978, 109). Reading pedagogy, central to a liberal education, must engage Eros.

Traditionally, Schwab argued, reading pedagogy operated on three levels: the semantic, syntactic, and rhetorical. These three levels operate as meaning systems, and knowledge of these levels enables the derivation of meaning. Pedagogies of reading (and writing) address competences on these levels. "When a writer wonders whether she is communicating, or a reader wonders if she is understanding, the question is usually addressed to three levels of his system of symbols (Schwab, 1978, 150). On the semantic level, the writer/reader is concerned with whether the words are "within the reach of the audience and sufficiently unambiguous in

---

[2] I think here of Fish's (1980) interpretive community.

their reference." The second level, the syntactic, wonders whether the sentences are constructed so as to serve their purpose? Are the words properly and appropriately ordered? Finally, on the rhetorical level of interpretation, the writer/reader concerns herself with the order of sentences and paragraphs and, in longer works, even chapters, and wonders how the discourse makes meaning. "To understand the meaning of each word, to understand the structure of the sentences in which they appear, and to understand the significance of the order of sentences and paragraphs would seem to constitute understanding of the discourse" (1978, 150). Reading traditionally is theorized as a logical process requiring formal instruction at each level. This ideology appears as the traditional subskill approach to reading prevalent in our schools today, a pedagogy increasingly mandated by the imposition of standards and the insistence on phonics instruction as the primary methods for the teaching of reading. "[I]f a reader has a proper store of language knowledge and skill in certain language arts," then it is assumed that meaning can be found wholly within the discourse. Vocabulary, prescriptive grammars, and literary forms and genres organize such a curriculum, and "so equipped, the reader *receives* the meaning of a sentence, of a paragraph, or of an entire discourse." There is always in this pedagogy a separation between reader and text: Meaning is in the text and must be discovered by the reader. Reader and text are opposed. Teachers practice a pedagogy for development at each level; there are proper and improper methods for discovery and reception of proper meaning. Language is assumed to be complex but transparent. One must become skillful in language use, but meaning is inherent in the language. "Language is treated as if it were a battery of flawless and focused lenses through which one can simply look and thereby apprehend everything thought and experienced which anyone sufficiently master of language has seen fit to report" (1978, 149). Here Schwab succinctly describes the ideology of the classical, formal approach to interpretation, or New Criticism, a form still widely taught and practiced in the schools in the contemporary United States. It is a pedagogy of the correct methods and the correct answers. It is a hierarchically structured system through which students may be raised to levels of academic competencies in thinking and reading.

Schwab's designation of the levels of meaning systems correspond to the three levels of comprehension discussed in traditional pedagogical texts concerned with reading instruction. For example, in *Teaching Reading in Today's Elementary Schools* (Burns et al., 1992, 258-264), the authors distinguish between literal and higher order comprehension. The former is defined as the acquisition of information that is directly stated in the text, whereas, higher-order comprehension, based on the higher-order thinking processes of interpretation, analysis and synthesis of information (these processes correspond to the higher levels of Bloom's taxonomy of educational objectives in the cognitive domain), is based on literal comprehension but goes beyond it. Last, critical reading—a further component of higher order comprehension—corresponds to the final level of Bloom's taxonomy, evaluation. The critical reader "must be an active reader, questioning, searching for facts, and suspending judgment until he or she has considered all the material. Critical reading depends on both literal and interpretive comprehension, and grasping implied ideas is especially important" (Burns et al., 1992, 278). This reification of critical thinking is decried by Frank Smith, for one, who argues, with Schwab, that "Children learn to think critically when they have opportunities and reason to think in critical ways; when they see (or hear) others engaged in critical thinking; and when they are admitted into arguments, challenges, and debates based on respect rather than power or exploitation" (1990, 107). Schwab had earlier complained that students "usually have been taught to conceive the structure of a whole work as a mere 'outline,' a convenience by which a large subject is broken into parts for presentation in theme or essay." For such a pedagogy, Schwab said, to be engaged in reading is to derive meaning *from* a text rather than to construct meaning *with* it. This belief speaks as if the meaning of a discourse could be found entire in the given statement, and the separation of text and reader is maintained. Traditional reading pedagogy assumes that the text can be—or ought to be—relatively transparent. Thus, students are asked "why" a particular piece was written—as if that question is explicit in texts—rather than asked to consider what effect the piece of writing has had on the reader. Students are asked about the author's approach to the material rather than the author's use of the material. Students are asked *what* the text means and not *how* the text means. Students are asked to measure a text based in external standards—and they are evaluated on those standards—purpose, point of view, style and tone, accuracy and timeliness, and appropriateness of presented material, as well as indications of bias and factual insistence.

Schwab argues, however, that though each level may have some real existence and might be understood as a pedagogy, each is mistakenly premised on the belief that language is transparent and that the meaning of words (semantic level), and sentences (syntactical levels) and entire discourses (rhetorical level) can be accomplished by a logical and universally applicable reading "apparatus." Moreover, Schwab (1978, 151) argues that such pedagogy is only partially valid and therefore, always incomplete and misleading: "The alleged potency of the apparatus rests on the assumption that there are only a few ways of treating a subject and only a few kinds of subjects, each with its own fixed kinds of parts." That is, the reader can discover the subject by the application of clear and universal rules. Students never learn of the greater discourse out of which the present has been drawn. Students do not learn how to discern.

Furthermore, Schwab asserts, this "reading apparatus" assumes that language is transparent, itself a result of firmly held beliefs concerning "the fixed nature of the world and corresponding fixed capacities of the human mind' (1978, 152). These beliefs reflect the persistence in educational philosophies of nineteenth century faculty psychology (despite the growing interest in the world following World War II of cognitive psychology), which held that mental powers of logic and reason and rhetoric also made up the components of discourse, and that the development (or training) of these powers would make comprehension possible. The limitation of this method, Schwab avers, rests strongly in the assumption that "the meaning of a discourse could be found entire in the given statement." Thus, pedagogies of reading consists largely of "uncovering, a learning, of what the speech or essay has to tell us. And the search for meaning is treated as largely an uncovering, a learning, of what the speech or essay has to tell us" (1978, 152). Schwab argued, to the contrary, that students must be taught to "construct" meaning rather than to discover it. That construction must discover not only what is said, but also what has been not said. Students must learn not only what a discourse says, but how that discourse speaks at all because of what it has not said. Such a reading would be responsible to the complexities of knowledge and of the world. In any case, "we will have been led to construct an inquiry with outcomes of worthwhile meaning which were never in the author's intention" (1978, 157). In the reading process, we would have created ourselves in our meaning-making.

Where is meaning and how is it constructed? I think the Rabbis antedated Schwab by a considerable number of years, themselves wondering about the issue of meaning and responsibility. They were very concerned with textuality—with reading and interpretation. After all, they had a text—Torah—and it demanded interpretation. The enactment of Torah was to live the daily life in manner of holiness. What I would like to suggest is that Schwab's advocacy for a reading pedagogy has its precedent in Rabbinic practice. David Kraemer writes (1996, 20): "The Talmudic sugya communicates by means of detailed argumentation, in which details provide the bricks and give-and-take the mortar of the final Talmudic structure. The meaning of the communication depends upon both the nature of the bricks and how they are assembled. . . . Moreover, the Talmud demands that the reader provide some of the 'mortar' himself. Always, we, as readers, insist—there will be meaning in this construction. What it is will depend upon the unique formulation of a given sugya and the response this formulation evokes in the reader/student." Schwab argues that reading pedagogy which "initiates the student into participative rhetorical and dialectical interpretation, must also be a process of initiating him into the existence of enquiry, of exhibiting to him the extent to which organized knowledge depends on terms chosen and subjects defined, and of showing him how he can identify these terms and definitions and trace their effects upon the knowledge which embodies them" (1978, 158). Schwab calls here for a reading pedagogy that suggests plurality of meaning and offers method for meaning-making that depends on plurality. Schwab's methods are rabbinic in origin.

IT IS NOT IN HEAVEN

The Torah (as are all texts) is meant for study. But the text of Torah, though given to Moshe on Sinai, was passed on by him in the oral tradition. The *Pirke Avot* (1:1) says, "Moshe received the Torah from Sinai and transmitted it to Joshua; Joshua to the Elders, the Elders to the Prophets; and the Prophets transmitted it to the Men of the Great Assembly." The tradition may be oral, but that tradition derives from writing. In Derridean terms, the Rabbis describe writing as precedent to speech, and gives authority to the oral tradition. Unlike in Socratic ideology, where writing is denied authority because it lacks its own voice, the Rabbis insist that the oral tradition does not exist without the prior written text; the Rabbis did not set priorities of authority, deeming oral and written Torah absolutely equal. Harold Bloom writes that "The *Soferim,* or Men of the Book, the true Scribes, centered authority upon the Book, insisting that everything was already in it, necessarily including all of their readings. Torah was true text, and their interpretations did not falsify it, but gave it context, and always through contemporary authority, 'the judge that shall be in those days'" (Bloom, 1975, 42). The dialectic between the written text and its necessitous oral interpretation gives no priority to either tradition but insists that all meaning is already within the text awaiting interpretation. The Torah, according to the Talmudic doctors, must be [orally] interpreted—and this, Talmud suggests, must be undertaken in accordance with local custom ("the judge that shall be in those days") and be wholly dependent on context. "If the same verse can be the subject of diverse interpretations," Max Kadushin writes (1952/1972, 72), "each interpretation must be considered independent and none as more authoritative than the others." That context, as Schwab declared more than thirteen hundred years following the redaction of the Talmud, must be understood in order for meaning to be made. "A given discourse has a context of other discourses in the same way that one of its paragraphs has a context of other paragraphs. And a reader brings meanings to symbols, just as symbols bring meaning to him" (1978, 152).

Enquiry—thought—occurs through the understanding of the several contexts of which a discourse is comprised. This acceptance ensures that meaning is always situational and always tentative. In the individual's construction of meaning, account must be made of the semantic, the individual meaning of words; the syntactic, the organization of words; and the rhetorical, the larger organization of sentences, paragraphs and chapters. Further, Schwab understood, one must understand the context of discourses in which the particular discourse is a part. "The Men of the Great Assembly said three things: 'Be deliberate in judgement; develop many disciples, and make a fence for the Torah'" (*Pirke Avot* 1:1). One interesting interpretation of the fence to be built about Torah argues that that the fence refers to the maintenance of a certain teaching tradition, a reading pedagogy, one practiced by Jewish sages that resulted in the discursive practice known as Talmud. It is a fence that Schwab must have appreciated. "[T]he process of initiating the student into participative rhetorical and dialectical interpretation must also be a process of initiating him into the existence of inquiry, of exhibiting to him the extent to which organized knowledge depends on terms chosen and subjects defined, and of showing him how he can identify these terms and definitions and trace their effects upon the knowledge which embodies them" (Schwab, 1978, 158). Though there are hermeneutical principles that valorize technique, interpretation must not disregard local custom; indeed, the whole purpose of interpretation is to discover how a discourse is constructed. That is, though I may maintain my own opinion, I must recognize it as only my opinion and not law.

There is a story: Rabbi Elazer disagreed with the rulings of his fellow Rabbis. Despite Elazer's insightful arguments, the rabbis did not follow his opinion.

> [Elazer] said to them: "If the halakhah is in accordance with me, let this carob tree prove it." The carob tree was uprooted from its place one hundred cubits—and some say four hundred cubits. They said to him: "One does not bring proof from a carob tree." He then said to them: "If the halakhah is in accordance with me, let the channel of water prove it." The channel of water turned backward. They said to him: "One does not bring proof from a channel of water." He then said to them: "If the halakhah is in accordance with me, let the walls of the House of Study prove it." The walls of the House of Study leaned to fall. Rabbi Yehoshua rebuked them, [and] said to them [the walls]: "If Talmudic Sages argue with one another about the Halakhah, what affair is it of yours?" They did not fall, out of respect for Rabbi Yehoushua; but they did not straighten, out of respect for Rabbi Elazer. He [Elazer] then said to them: "If the Halakhah is in accordance with me, let it be proved from Heaven." A [heavenly] voice went forth and said: "Why are you [disputing] with Rabbi Elazer, for the Halakhah is in accordance with him everywhere?" Rabbi Yehoshua rose to his feel and said: "It is not in heaven."
>
> What does "it is not in heaven" [mean]?
>
> Rabbi Yirmeyah said: That the Torah was already given on Mount Sinai, [and] we do not pay attention to a [heavenly] voice, for You already wrote in the Torah at Mount Sinai: "After the majority to incline."

Despite the brilliance of Elazer's reasoning, despite even the support of his opinion from the heavenly voice, the Rabbis reject Elazer's arguments. Neither nature nor the heavenly voice could dissuade the Rabbis from their own opinions. "It is not in heaven" means that though the words were given on Sinai, their meaning is an earthly matter. It is not that the words are unimportant; rather, the words are crucial; it is just that they are opaque. It is the meaning to be fashioned of those words to which attendance is paid and that meaning is dependent on context and is always dependent on the local. Elazar's failure is a failure to acknowledge that his interpretation remains only his own understanding and interpretation of the text, and it does not have universal application.

Nor need Elazar's interpretation it be universally accepted, regardless of his scholarly reputation.

That is a comfort to me as I sit with my own and my daughters' meanings. However, when I go to where the reference is made to Torah (the words)—when I read in Deuteronomy 30:12 I am surprised by what I discover:

> For this commandment that I command you today—it is not hidden from you and it is not distant. *It is not in heaven*. . . . Rather, the matter is very near to you—in your mouth and your heart—to perform it (italics added).

The reference in Deuteronomy suggests that the mitzvot (the commandments) are not strange to human behavior but are, rather, intrinsic to an understanding of what it means to be human. The meanings and matter of the commandments are not strange nor distant. "The matter" of the mitzvot is very near to me. Torah states, the commandments are not in heaven; they are here, on earth to be acted upon in daily life in my daily communings with the world, which includes other beings. The meanings of the mitzvot are not obscure but apparent. According to Torah, it would seem that interpretation must be relatively unnecessary. There is nothing local about it at all; indeed, meaning is universal.

I am surprised then by the Rabbis' mild misreading of "it is not in heaven." In their view, the phrase valorizes interpretation as a human and local prerogative. The meaning of mitzvot must be decided here and not in heaven. For the Rabbis "it is not in heaven" makes interpretation the central activity of study, though the end of study is clearly performance. Torah has said that the mitzvot are not about heavenly authority nor even scholarly activity but about earthly responsibility. A relationship to God is a relationship to human beings. Torah states that these mitzvot are not obscured as is the top of Sinai by clouds of smoke; they are clear and readily understood down here on the earth. The mitzvot, however, are to be performed; they are based in ethics and they must be enacted—I am Holy and you should be Holy—but the ***meaning*** of the mitzvot issues not from heavenly edict but from earthly exegesis. The meaning of the mitzvot derive from human action—interpretation—and must be negotiated in personal encounters, such as Talmudic-like discourse. "It is not in Heaven" means we are ultimately free. The Rabbis mild misreading offers me the opportunity to link interpretation and action and to make interpretation an ethical presence. I wonder at how our classrooms might alter if the teacher would assume such a stance. "What does this mean, teacher?" "It is not in heaven . . . but in your mouth and your heart to perform it."

But when I seek the second reference, "After the majority to incline," the Rabbis urging to subscribe to majority opinion, I discover a strong misreading. Exodus 23:2 actually says:

> Do not be a follower of the majority for evil; and do not respond to a grievance by yielding to the majority to pervert [the law].

Indeed, in their response to Elazar, the Rabbis have turned the Biblical negative into a rabbinic positive: Exodus says DON'T follow the majority into evil and the Rabbis contend that, in fact, one *must* follow the majority in interpretation. This strong misreading is effected to reinforce the notion that all is according to custom—meaning, is not in Heaven. Interpretation defines the mitzvot; human beings perform interpretation and meaning is made possible through the awareness of local custom. Of course, the Rabbis have valorized the scholar's interpretation; they are scholars and they have invested themselves with ultimate authority! But they inadvertently valorized also the interpretation of the many scholars who would succeed them—some of whom reside in our classrooms. Even the Heavenly voice might not cancel these interpretations. I welcome the dissent. But in our schools the question is still asked our daughters: "Which of the following most matches the author's purpose in writing this passage?" I urge Emma and Anna Rose not to fill in any bubble, but instead to pencil in the reply: "It is not in heaven! After the majority to incline." And what machine will read their response?

I think the Rabbis meant to ensure that interpretation must have human application and that interpretation must address local custom. Authorized meanings must be livable, which is to say, ethical. And the entire ethics is based on the world's foundation: Torah, service, and kindness. In the oral interpretation derived from reading Torah, one learns the practice of service and the manner of committing acts of kindness. But these acts are dependent on local custom.

In sum, the Rabbis and Joseph Schwab have antedated Stanley Fish's interpretive community, but encumber that community to transform its reading into praxis. Schwab held that such a pedagogy of reading enquiry institutes "collaborative community and the beginning of discovery of the existence and value of diverse habits of mind" (1969b, 61). Such a discussion will reveal "imperfect opinions, raw materials for *conjoint* scrutiny aimed at discovery and repair of . . . errors and omissions, and formulations of a better or best opinion by the group as a whole and not as contestants in a sparring match" (1969b, 61). That is, this reading pedagogy facilitates learning and community and action. Reading pedagogy ought to become praxis. Who holds this book holds a man. This entire book is mine/me. If I did not exist, this book would never exist in the world.

INTO THE MYSTIC

Schwab avers that there is a fourth and crucial level that must be attached to reading instruction—the dialectical. At this level the reader is concerned with "whether those meanings grasped which accrue to an inquiry by seeing its subject, principles and conclusions in relations to subjects, principles, and conclusions of other, related inquiries" (Schwab, 1978, 153). For Schwab, education should result in intellectual, ethical and practical ends; these were the Rabbis' concerns as well. I think Schwab's pedagogy and method can be observed in Kabbalistic notion of reading and then in a talmudic discussion concerning the care of texts.

For Joseph Schwab, to read would be to move in and through worlds towards responsibility and obligation. It is a pedagogy that makes reading an ethical act. There is precedent for this approach. The *Zohar*, a central text of Kabbalah (Matt, 1983, 136), establishes a geography and pedagogy of reading.

> Come and see: There is a garment visible to all.
> When those fools see someone in a good-looking garment they look no further.
> But the essence of the garment is the body;
> the essence of the body is the soul.
>
> So it is with Torah.
> She has a body: the commandments of Torah,
> called 'the embodiment of Torah.'
> This body is clothed in garments: the stories of this world.
> Fools of the world look only at that garment, the story of Torah;
> they know nothing more.
> They do not look at what is under that garment.

> Those who know more do not look at the garment,
> but rather at the body under the garment.
> The wise ones, servants of the King on high,
> those who stood at Mount Sinai,
> look only at the soul, root of all, real Torah.
> In the time to come, they are destined to look at the soul of the soul of Torah.

There are, the *Zohar* cautions, levels of reading, and there are obligations for the reader immanent at each level. The *Zohar* suggests a method that respects what Whitman might mean when he advises me that to hold the book is to hold the man. The *Zohar* anticipates Schwab's call for a responsible reading pedagogy. And Walt Whitman and Rabbi Nachman, before Joseph Schwab, counsel me to be a compassionate, mindful reader, and to be a mindful and compassionate man. Schwab cautions that "any apparently definitive or highly persuasive solution to a clearly defined problem ought to appear in a context which will indicate that there is yet more to know or more to know about" (1978, 153). To read thus is to recognize the body under the garment and the soul under the body. In this acknowledgment my reading and my living becomes an ethics—a stance in the world. What is the ethics? How and to what am I obliged? For example, I know it is to Whitman, the man, for whom I must care, but how might I engage with him in my reading of the book to care for the man? How might I engage with him in my life? If every book exists as a result of my existence, then what am I? What am I to do?

WORLDS OF BEING AND READING

We learn in Kabbalah that there are four levels of world that correspond to four levels of being and four levels of reading. The lowest level is the world of action, *asi-ah*, the empirical world of physical things, the arena where daily life occurs. In reading, this level of being and world corresponds to the world of narrative and is referred to as *p'shat*, the world of plot. It might be thought of as, perhaps, the poem's narrative. To move in this world of *asi-ah* is to inhabit and acknowledge the world's order and to accept the dominion of cause and effect. In the world of *p'shat*, the reader recognizes the tale, or story. The obligation is to follow and respect, even perhaps to comprehend its path. For example, we might look at the story of Jacob and his wrestle with the angel. On the level of *p'shat*, there is the story as it is narrated in *Bereshit*. There we read that Jacob "was left alone" at night, and a man wrestled with him until the break of dawn. This man could not defeat Jacob, but struck the socket of Jacob's hip and dislocated it. And when the man offered to end the struggle, Jacob insisted that he first be blessed. And the man changed Jacob's name to Israel.

The next level is the world of formation, *Yetzirah*, the place of feelings where everything is in flux, constantly moving and changing. Reading at this level is called *remez* and is identified as the level of one's emotional response to the poetic text. Here one reads the text and feels its emotions. This is the level of metaphor—what is there in the text inspires in us a remembrance of something else. Here, the feelings inspired by the text suggest another story. I think, perhaps, that this is the reverse of Eliot's (very Catholic) objective correlative. Eliot defines the objective correlative (1962, 793) as "the only way of expressing emotion in the form of art . . . a set of objects, a situation, a chain of events which shall be the formula of that *particular* emotion, such that when the external facts, which must terminate in sensory experience, are given, the emotion is immediately evoked." Eliot's objective correlative determines the emotional response, but at the level of *remez*, metaphor, the emotions lead us rather to discover and to care for an entirely other body. The action of the story, *p'shat*, remains clear, but there is more in my understanding than the action to the story, there are worlds *in formation* and I am obliged to recognize and even know about their existence. In this world, I accept that every story opens to another. One story inspires the next. At the level of *remez*, the level of metaphor, the story arouses in me (today) feelings associated with struggle: with colleagues, wives, friends, but not with enemies. The angel in the story is not Jacob's enemy, only his adversary. The angel who fights with Jacob does not mean to kill him or even to defeat him. Though this angel injures Jacob in the end, this event only suggests that he could have hurt him earlier but did not do so. When Jacob arises from the fight, however, he is given a new name, Israel, but this new name is not for use always, but only for use at times. This suggests to me that we often rise to new occasions and that this new name/new person cannot be ignored even when not visible present.

The third level of world is that of creation, *Bri-ah*, where the very principles of creation are operative and where the narrative may be read as a portrayal of creation even as the narrative is read in terms of the principles of creation: This is *drash*, the world of allegory. At this level of reading, the story itself contains the secrets of creation and of its own creation. At this level I am obliged to recognize that nothing is only itself, and that reality is known, even created, through our ability to imaginatively see it in its symbols. The world is created in symbol making. Perhaps one *drash* on the story of Jacob suggests that without struggle we cannot be born—without struggle, there can be no new creation. The story of Jacob is the story of a birth—but when the struggle is over, there is not a single but, rather, two persons, the old *and* the new, Jacob *and* Israel.

Finally, there is the world of emanation, *atzilut*. This is the world of secret spiritual meaning and is the ultimate source of wisdom. It is a world finally ineffable, inexpressible, invisible—in religious terms, it is, of course, God. But to read at this level directs us toward the creator's will. It is always unreachable, but for which we must yet reach. At this level of reading, *sod*, we become the story—we tell it and teach it to others. And it is in this telling that the work of *tikkun*, of healing, occurs. At the level of *sod*, we raise the story by using the story. This use of the story effects healing; we repair in recovering our meaning and give it to others. Healing is human purpose.

It is taught that if God is everywhere, then in what space could the creation of the world have occurred. Thus, the Kabbalists say, God must first have willingly withdrawn God's self to make room for creation. This withdrawal is referred to as *tzimtzum*. In the process of creation, however, the light that emanated from God ("And God said, 'Let there be light'") shattered the vessels through which the light was channeled, and the light fell as sparks into the material world, even as the pieces of the vessels scattered on the ground. "When the shards descended to the bottom of the world of actualization, they were transformed into the four elements—fire, air, water, and earth—from which evolved the stages of mineral, vegetable, animal and human." It is the human task to raise these sparks (and shards) "by the power of the soul," and return them to divinity—their divine status. When we tell the story rather than merely hear it, we effect change: "We raise these scattered sparks and arrange them into worlds, constructed within us, in our private and social lives. In proportion to the sparks we raise, our lives are enriched. Everything accords with how we act. The higher the aspiration, the greater the action, the deeper the insight, the higher the aspiration" (Matt, 1983, 152). We participate in creation by restoring the holy sparks to their source by our work. In the process of reading, in making meaning of holy text, we are engaged in creation and the work of *tikkun.*

To consider the process of reading in this fashion—as movement in worlds—is to understand reading as a social act. I think this is something Schwab understood. Reading becomes ethical. When we read and reread-Whitman's *Leaves of Grass* requires rereading because Whitman spent his entire life writing and rewriting it—we have the opportunity to move through levels of world and being in our deepening levels of reading. To hold *Leaves of Grass,* I think, is to have available the whole world in the man and the man in the world. It is an awesome obligation, I think. In *Zohar* (Matt, 1983, 137), we read:

> Woe to the wicked who say that Torah is merely a story!
> They look at the garment and no further.
> Happy are the righteous who look at Torah properly.
> As wine must sit in a jar, so Torah must sit in this garment.
> So look only at what is under the garment.
> All those words and all those stories are garments.

When we read, we become lovers of the books we read. We become, too, lovers of the book's writer. It must be love and not violence that permits us to see under the garments. I must read with care and with love.

I am a teacher. I teach from books. I teach the love of books. I am a learner. I learn with books. I am curious now to consider what it is I have been doing when I learn and what it is I do when I teach with texts. It is no small piece of learning I here interrogate since I spend so much of my life amongst books. It is no small piece of teaching about which I wonder, since I spend my life in the classroom with students reading books. And besides, I am a parent who has surrounded his children with books. Who holds this book holds a man, Walt Whitman alerts me. What have I taught about this holding? Perhaps Whitman's appeal (or is it, perhaps, his statement?) reminds me that there is an intimate connection between the book and its author in which I participate and about which I must be sensitive. Learning to hold the book might teach me how to hold the man; learning to hold the man might even teach me how to hold myself, my children and my students who hold books. My classrooms are occupied by living beings and they hold books. I hold books and perhaps, I also hold students.

In our dealings with books, there is, of course, a holding that is the physical expression of love, the world of *p'shat.* There is the sensuous nature of gazing at the books—consider Nick Caraway's wonderment while gazing at Gatsby's library. There is the sensible touching of the pages of the book, the caressful turning of the book's pages, the physical resting of them on our own bodies as we read. I myself love to touch the smooth pages imprinted almost imperceptibly with words which I am free to manipulate as I will. I breathe sensuously the book's odors. I gaze at the book lovingly. The *Zohar* tells me that this expression of physical love might be a response to the books' garments, and the *Zohar* demands that I look beyond the garment to the body and beyond that to the soul. The *Zohar* insists that in my reading I participate in the "raising of sparks." I think that in this manner of "holding" we might give simple response to a demand for love and/or respect and/or human sympathy. In our classrooms and with our books, we might respond to the urgings of the other: Who holds this book holds a man.

But I am still unclear: To my mind now, those words—love, respect, sympathy—are the big words that Hemingway's Frederic Henry did not understand. And in this era of deconstruction and cultural critique, of conservative compassion and benign neglect, the book's author may be subject to a skeptical holding. I am leery of the caution and respect with which the book is ofttimes held at the expense of that author. D. H. Lawrence's dictum (1964, 2), "Never trust the artist. Trust the tale," may be suitable to the age of the death of the author, but Whitman demands I hold the living author. I have spent my entire life holding books and holding authors. There is a pedagogical world of which I have been complicit in Whitman's dictum; there is an ethical world explicit in it as well. I must teach not only technique but obligation. It is also Schwab's urging.

I know the Torah teaches us to "love thy neighbor as thyself." It is an ideal love expressed here, I think, but one to which Whitman obliges me in my reading, nevertheless. The Biblical statement does not say what I must do, only what I must feel. Freud (1961, 30) suggests that there is no "golden rule which applies to everyone: every man must find out for himself in what particular fashion he can be saved." I like that. There is the anticipation of salvation in my love, but what do I tell my children when they ask practically, "What should we do?" For Freud, love is not so much indefinable as it is delusional. He asks, "Why should we do it?

What good will it do us? But above all, how can we achieve it? How can it be possible? My love is something valuable to me which I ought not to throw away without reflection. It imposes duties on me for whose fulfillment I must be ready to make sacrifices" (1961, 56). Freud is legitimately skeptical of human willingness to self-sacrifice. Yet Whitman and the *Zohar* commit me to the achievement of an absolute love for another, to the obligation to hold the book and the man as I would myself. I wonder how I might operationalize loving myself without causing harm to another? How to love the other without causing harm to myself? If to hold this book—any book—is to hold the man, then how can I hold this book recognizing I hold a man—even myself—as well.

Perhaps to love another as our self is to set the minimum standard. As well as we can love ourselves, so must we love another. We would treat the book as we treat ourselves. But my twelve-year-old daughter asks, "What if the person doesn't love herself? What if she smokes or does drugs or engages in promiscuous sex or hurts herself? Should she treat others like that?" It is a good question. I say to Emma that perhaps those behaviors are knowingly self-destructive but beyond control. They may not be so much expressions of love as of hate. But how, Emma asks, can she know the difference? Indeed, she has asked a wonderful question: I am aware that love manifests itself often in difficult ways. For example, does my daughter know—and how does she come to know it—that I love her when out of love I insist she do her homework, or practice her violin, or adhere to curfew, even if her friends beckon? How does my daughter recognize love from within reprimand and even punishment? Rabbi Akiva interpreted the Biblical injunction to "love they neighbor as thyself" as "Do not do to any neighbor what you wouldn't want him to do to you." Love is in this sense a negative command: It is what I should not do rather than what I must do. And that does not answer the question about those who willingly hurt themselves.

Or perhaps the command to love another as oneself is an impossible dictum, as Freud avers and, therefore, one easily avoided. There is a dangerous ethic there, and an equally perilous pedagogy that facilitates avoidance and detachment and disinterest. If to hold *Leaves of Grass*—to hold any book—is to hold the man, Whitman and myself, then I would learn what this love entails that I might begin to practice and to teach. And Schwab too, knew that reading was a social act and entailed responsibility and an ethical stance.

LOST PROPERTY: IF ONE FINDS LOST SCROLLS

I would like to understand how to hold a man by holding the book—how and to whom am I responsible when I hold a book. What obligations are incurred when I love another as I love myself. How can I read so responsibly? I think the Rabbis of the Talmud wondered about this question and these connections as well: They engaged in long, involved discussion concerning the obligations to return lost property. The Rabbis must have considered that the responsibility incurred upon finding lost objects represented the responsibility to the owner of such property. That is, we are obliged to the other even when the other is not only not present but when she/he is unknown. It is a wonderful ideal actualized: I am obliged to the other as the unknown Other. There is no mediation between our humanness. Books were one category of lost property with which the Rabbis dealt. "If one finds scrolls . . .," our Mishnah (*Bava Metzia*, 29b) begins. I consider whether Whitman's statement "Who holds this book holds a man" alludes to the obligation of the reader to address the author in her/his lostness. As a reader and as an author, I know that to let a writing go is to lose control over its meaning. The author loses her work to the reader and must depend on that reader to raise the sparks, as it were, and by such action return the author from her lostness. Perhaps Whitman appeals to the reader to safeguard the author from becoming lost. Meaning is, after all, always lost until I return it; when the author lets go of the creation, it is I who must return meaning to it. Without such return, there is neither book nor author. I must remember that this book is a man even as it is a book. I think that it is also true that without meaning neither does the reader exist. Thus, to make meaning is to return me to myself.

The extent to which I must go to return lost property is my concern: What indeed are the limits of my obligation. This concern regarding such limits addresses, I think, the practices of reading discussed earlier. To read is to accept obligation, and for such reading the *Zohar* suggests a pedagogy. I have much to learn. And in this section of Talmud, the Rabbis offer a method to operationalize that pedagogy. Here they state that "Where one would lead back his own [lost property], he must lead back his neighbor's too. And where one would unload and load his own [lost property], he must do so for his neighbor's." Ah, here indeed, is the enactment of loving my neighbor as myself. What I would do for myself in recovering lost property, that must I do for neighbor. Whatever I would do to regain and recover my own property, I must do for that of my neighbor. Whatever has meaning for me, so, too, must I acknowledge for my neighbor. I would also in turn be acknowledged by my neighbor as having meaning. My self-consciousness—my reflectiveness—both gives testament to and enacts the leading back of my property and its loading and unloading. I am, in my thought, forever concerned with the retrieval of myself; thus, according to the Rabbis, as I would lead back my own lost property, so must I lead back that of my neighbor. I am obliged to constantly acknowledge the meaning of the other. The book I hold has meaning; I have an obligation to load and unload that meaning; I must, as it were, lead it back. In this endeavor, the *Zohar* compels me to look beyond the garment to the body and beyond the body to the soul. I am obliged to lead back the lost property, meaning; I am obliged to discover the author.

Actually, however, though the Rabbis declare that returning lost property is imperative, in actuality they qualify this obligation. They say that I am obliged *only so long as* the return, and/or the loading and unloading of the lost property, does not lead to a loss of dignity to myself, the finder (*Bava Metzia* 30a-b). I am reminded of Hillel who acknowledged that the establishment of my meaning—"If I am not for myself, who will be?"—*prepares* for the meaning of the other—"if I am only for myself, what am I?" I can care for no one unless I first care for myself, but if I care only for my own meaning, then I am not part of the human community. Applying Hillel to the *Zohar*'s levels of reading, I suggest that if I make no meaning for myself, then I can certainly find no meaning outside of me and I can be of little service to others. However, it is also the case that if I cannot discover meaning outside of me, then neither am I part of the human community. In the present case, the Rabbis state that "If one finds a sack or a basket, or any object which it is undignified for him to take, he need not take it" (*Bava Metzia* 29b). If I find lost property and it would harm my dignity to retrieve it, then I need not do so. That is, the Rabbis insist that in my engagement with the book—lost property—I not compromise my own integrity. I like that: There are books, I know, which I would not read for they would dishonor me. I say with Bartleby, "I prefer not to." Rather, there are in this world so many books' meanings I would prefer to return and load and unload!!

However, I remember my absolute opposition to the banning and censoring of books, and I wonder what the Rabbis might mean by being dishonored in the act of taking a sack or a basket or a book, or of aiding my neighbor in the loading and unloading of objects, such as meaning. Parents claim that reading *Catcher in the Rye* would soil the children; parents argue that Judy Blume's books are inappropriate—I think "inappropriate" is a fancy word for "undignified." So many books are denied children because they are considered inglorious in some form or another. There are books I would not have my child read, but I would not censor or ban a book. If I need not hold a book or the man that would dishonor me, then how can I recognize that object before even having read it?

And I am glad that the Rabbis anticipate my concern. Or so it seems. They tell this story: Rabbi Ishmael was walking along the road when he saw a man carrying a load of sticks. The man put down the sticks and after a short rest and, perhaps, even pleasant conversation with the Rabbi, the man requested that Rabbi Ishmael help him lift them. But the bundle was heavy and Rabbi Ishmael was old and not strong. Rabbi Ishmael asked the man what the chore was worth—what was the worth of the bunch of sticks to the man—and the man answered, *"half a zuz,"* whereupon Rabbi Ishmael gave him the half a zuz, declared the property ownerless, and believed his obligation was met. It would have been undignified for Rabbi Ishmael to lift the sticks, but it would have been unethical not to help his neighbor. But the man regained possession of the now ownerless sticks and once again asked Ishmael to help him lift them, and once again Ishmael gave the man *half a zuz*. The man bent down yet again to pick up the sticks and, therefore, reacquire them; Ishmael declared the property ownerless to everyone *but* the man, and in this way prevented the man from reacquiring them and thus, obliging Ishmael to engage in activity beyond his dignity. Ishmael did not hide this lost property—rather, he declared it *ownerless to all but the man,* and thereby he was released from all obligation to recover it from its lostness, for to that man it was not lost. You see, the man might still lift the bundle, but Ishmael was merely relieved of the obligation to assist.

What would an undignified reading be such that I need not do it? Or even assist in it? Perhaps it is one that denigrates my humanity, as would Ishmael's effort to pick up the sticks hurt his humanity. Indeed, such activity might have killed him. But how might a book be so harmful? To paraphrase the National Rifle Association, "Books do not kill, people do." And I am also reminded of the child's taunt: "Sticks and stones may break my bones, but names can never harm me." Of course, neither the National Rifle Association nor the children's taunt is accurate. I think a harmful book—or any speech—could harm me if it refused to acknowledge respect for me, its reader, by espousing ideas that reduce me, the reader, to a cipher. Levinas teaches us that you can only kill what you cannot look at face to face. Books can kill as can guns. The present passage of hate speech laws notwithstanding, the Rabbis had many centuries earlier unequivocally condemned calumny, slander, and hate-filled speech as the most heinous and unforgivable act. The Rabbis justify this teaching by referring, of course, to the text of Torah. They argue that the dictum, "Ye shall not therefore wrong one another" *(Leviticus* 25:17), must refer specifically to verbal wrongs, because an earlier reference in *Leviticus* 25:14, "When you make a sale to your fellow or make a purchase from the hand of your fellow, do not wrong one another," spoke specifically of not wronging one another *in monetary matters*. Since, the Rabbis assume, Torah contains no needless repetition, then the second reference to "'wrong" in verse 17 must refer to verbal wrongs. Indeed, the Rabbis say, for the commission of verbal wrongs there is no restoration possible. "All who descend into *Gehenna* [subsequently] reascend, excepting three, who descend but do not reascend, viz., He who commits adultery with a married woman, publicly shames his neighbor, or fastens an evil epithet [nickname] upon his neighbor" (*Bava Metzia*, 58b). Books that would harm my dignity are books that publicly shame me or attach evil epithets to me. These I need not pick up. These I need not read. These I declare ownerless to everyone—but their author.

But actually, to my delighted dismay and wonder, in the present case the Rabbis address another issue altogether than the nature of an act that is beneath one's dignity. I am glad of that, for I would not be responsible for censorship. Rather, the Rabbis wondered instead if Ishmael's statement declaring the item ownerless to all but the man had any validity at all. Could one selectively declare property lost to all but one? It is a difficult question. By what authority can one single out an individual for exclusionary purposes. By what authority do we prepare appropriate reading matters? Perhaps it is not an unrelated issue to that pertaining to loss of dignity in the engagement of activity. By what authority can I declare this item ownerless for everyone but this person; by what authority can I declare this book readable by all but these individuals? The Rabbis wisely avoid confronting this issue directly. Rather, they look to the broader issue—what does Rabbi Ishmael's behavior suggest to us about our obligations to the other. Ishmael was a good man; what does his behavior teach us about our behavior?

One rabbi wonders if Ishmael's effort was unnecessary because as an elder he must have already known that he was exempt from effort below his dignity. That is, Ishmael must have known that he need not have assisted the man *at all* in raising the sticks. Nevertheless, the Rabbis acknowledge, Ishmael acted, and for the Rabbis, Ishmael's action is originally fraught with meaning. The Rabbis respond that to lift the sticks—or, in Rabbi Ishmael's case, to maintain his dignity by paying *half a zuz* in order to acquire them and then to declare them ownerless to fulfill his obligation to recover his neighbor's property—Ishmael went beyond the limits of the law. Indeed, the Rabbis suggest, according to law, Ishmael need not have been obliged to lift the sticks ***at all*** because to do so would have been an undignified act for a man of his age. That Ishmael did do so, however, becomes itself interpretable as Torah law. The Rabbis declare that though Ishmael was by law absolved of responsibility, he acted *as if* his responsibility were not contained by the law but extended beyond it. In their interpretation of *Exodus* 18:20, ". . . *and you shall make known to them the path in which they should go and* ***the deeds that they should do,***" the Rabbis declare that the meaning of "***the deeds that they should do***" refers, in fact, to going *beyond* the requirements of the law. Though the law is indeed, the law, it sets only the minimum standard. The law is *the path in which they should go*, but then there are *the deeds that they should do.* To act in an ethical manner is to be obliged to go beyond the law. Though it may be true that Ishmael might not have had the authority to declare the stick lost to all but the man, nevertheless, we might learn from his actions that simply obeying the law is not sufficient ethics. We are obliged always to go beyond the requirements of law. Indeed, Rabbi Johanan (*Bava Metzia,* 30b) declares that Jerusalem was destroyed because its citizens "gave judgements therein in accordance with Biblical law." Johanan avers that, ironically, by merely obeying only the law the people brought about the destruction of the city. By adhering exactly to the letter of the law they ignored the law's spirit "and did not go beyond the requirements of the law." In adhering to the law, the people committed injustice. Thus, loving another as oneself begins to be operationalized—it is to go beyond the law and to do more both for oneself and, therefore, for another than even the law requires.

"THAT THEY SHALL DO"

How does one go beyond the requirements of the law? How can one behave in a way that is immanent yet unexpressed. How does one love beyond what is love explicitly defined? What is the minimum expressed in law which is already insufficient to save Jerusalem? If Whitman suggests that to hold a man is equivalent to holding the book, then what are our minimum obligations in holding the book and the man? More, how in our care may we go beyond the requirements of law? At the minimum we must consider that in schools books are loaned to students and they are required to cover them and not to write in them; they are encumbered to treat them "with respect." At the University of Wisconsin-Stout, students may rent textbooks, though they are not required to cover the books nor need they refrain from writing in them. They must, however, return the books at semester's end. Students get homework assignments from these books—to read within them, and to answer questions posed by them, and to study for exams suggested from them. People take books from libraries and read them; though bookstores do not proliferate, there are yet no dearth of bookstores. We read books. These are the requirements of law. But I wonder how we might teach our students and ourselves to save Jerusalem by going beyond the requirements of law? How must they deal with books both as exemplars of lost property and as men and women? Isn't there a pedagogy here? There is certainly an ethics. Let us look first at the law.

IF ONE FINDS SCROLLS . . .

The Mishnah (*Bava Metzia, 29b*) states: "If one finds scrolls, he must read them every thirty days; if he cannot read, he must roll them. But he must not study [a subject] therein for the first time. Nor may another person read with him." I do not think scrolls are these days found—the days of scroll-finding are long since past. But it is frequent that one finds books—in offices, on buses and trains, in hotel rooms, and even on shelves on the walls of restaurants. And the Rabbis are concerned with my responsibility to the book—to lost property. The discovery of lost property obligates me to the unknown owner. Indeed, I am so obligated to the owner that the Rabbis say that if the property I discover may perish in the time before I discover the owner, I must sell the property and lay the money received aside in the event the owner is finally discovered. I am absolutely and materially obligated to the unknown owner. "Samuel said, 'If one finds phylacteries in a sack, he must immediately turn them into money [i.e., sell them] and lay the money by'" (*Bava Metzia*, 29b). That is, I am ultimately obligated to the owner and not to the property. Whitman reminds me, of course, that who holds a book holds a man. It is, then, no small matter to find a book at all. To discover a book is to immediately and irrevocably oblige me to its author. The Rabbis say that if I find a scroll—a book—and if I pick up a lost book, then I must read it at least once every thirty days. I think again of Jay Gatsby, whose bookshelves are filled with volumes whose pages remain uncut. All those authors rendered silent—imprisoned, lost, as it were. But then, though Gatsby might have been a dreamer, he was not a very nice man. The Rabbis' insistence that the scrolls be read indicates at the first degree a concern that without opening and therefore, airing the scrolls, the moisture contained within them would cause them to rot. This would destroy the scrolls. Who holds a book holds a man!

But the Rabbis insist not that the scrolls be merely unrolled, but that they be read as well.

I like that. It is one thing to perform the beneficial act of unrolling, to engage in the mere act. The deed is not empty; indeed, without the unrolling, the scrolls might rot. And remaining rolled, the scrolls certainly could not be read. Our students do not always find lost books—often they are directed to the books they pick up. But the Rabbis say not merely that the scrolls be unrolled—physically cared for—they insist that if one *can* read them, then one *must* read the scrolls *at least* once every thirty days. You see, the book is already an obligation: It is not simply an object. And once we begin to read, our acknowledgment of the levels of worlds and reading and raising the sparks embedded in the text obligates us to our reading. Once every thirty days is the law—but to go beyond the law is to commit ourselves to the text and to the worlds of being and reading. To read is to commit ourselves to *tikkun*. We obligate ourselves to the raising of sparks. There is a pedagogy here. There is an ethic here with which we could live.

Perhaps we must first teach our children that the scrolls must be unrolled for the care of the book *and* for the good of the author and the world. The scrolls must be unrolled at least once every thirty days if they are new. And *if we can read*, then we must read the scrolls. We are obliged to do so. But that, I recall, is merely the law. Jerusalem may be saved only if the people go beyond the requirements of the law. It would seem that there would be no limit in aspiring to fulfill the directive "that they shall do." What a redemptive obligation that would be!

However, the Rabbis qualify their dictum. They decree that one may not study a subject for the first time in these found scrolls. Perhaps the Rabbis are concerned that we may begin to study in the scrolls, and the owner may come and reclaim the scroll and our study would remain incomplete—surface level—at the level of *p'shat.* Or more seriously, our original reading and study would provoke us to decline to return the lost object. But, perhaps the Rabbis reason, that if we had read the material before, then it may be that we have once owned the scroll, or at least know where, if we had not found the book at this fortuitous moment, a copy of the scroll may be presently found. In such a case, perhaps, we would not be led to covet the book, knowing where we might otherwise find it. The Rabbis ensure here that our lives may never be aggrandized even at the unknown expense of another. Our lives may not be enriched by taking advantage of another's property, even when that person has lost that property, and we do not know even know the identity of that person.

The Rabbis have also above insisted that while fulfilling the obligation to read the scrolls at least once every thirty days, the finder may not study a subject for the first time, "nor may another person read it together with him." This latter interdiction seems so antisocial and even anti-intellectual. But I think there is no contradiction in the Rabbis mandate for study: This prohibition represents an ethical stance toward the yet unknown property owner. Here, the Rabbis are concerned that we must not share what is not ours to share—our obligation is to the book's owner whom we do not know and who is absent, even before it is to the friend who would study with us and is present. Furthermore, if two—even friends—were studying together a scroll, then it is possible that they might disagree on what to study or might differ during study. The friends might pull and push and bend and turn the text: They might mistreat the book! Who holds a book holds a man! Or study might provoke an altercation, and they would abuse not only the book but their friendship. Who holds a book holds a man! Study might be valorized in Rabbinic Judaism, but not at the expense of the book's owner or of the book itself or of amity. Scrolls and books are sacred, in part at least, because they are lost property. Finding them and holding them incur responsibility.

Earlier the Rabbis were concerned with the responsibilities incurred upon finding a scroll—lost property. Now, the issue turns to our obligation to a scroll that has been intentionally borrowed or purposely deposited with us for our care. The Gemara says: "If one borrows a scroll of Torah from his neighbor, he may not lend it to another. He may open and read it, providing, however, that he does not study a subject therein for the first time, nor may another person read it together with him. Likewise, if one deposits a Scroll of the Torah with this neighbor, he [the depositee] must roll it once every twelve months, and may open and read it; but if he opens it in his own interest, it is forbidden" (*Bava Metzia*, 29b). It is a curious proscription. Why would anyone borrow a scroll from his neighbor unless he intended to read it? How do we borrow books from our neighbors? Often we begin conversation with 'What are you reading?" It is an attempt, perhaps, to locate our colleague and ourselves. It might be also be an invitation to change direction. We ask: Is there something you are reading from which you think I might benefit? Isn't sharing books not unlike sharing selves? Perhaps to borrow a book in the fashion dictated by the Rabbis is founded on the idea that to borrow a book is to hold close the one from whom it is borrowed: Who holds this book holds a man! The Rabbis are ensuring, perhaps, that since I know for what purpose I have borrowed the book, I will be more apt not only to study the text but to care for it as well.

Of course, in schools, often, this depositing of books is a regular practice: Students are given texts whose purpose they do not know. Since they have not studied in them for the first time, according to the Rabbis, they ought to be forbidden to open them. Many times they do not!!

But on this issue of borrowing the Rabbis express a similar puzzlement. They declare, "He may open and read it: This is obvious" (*Bava Metzia*, 29b). It is obvious, they say, that if one borrows a book it is the borrower's intention to read it. Then why is it necessary to state these regulations regarding borrowing books? Clearly, something is not obvious at all.

If I borrow an important book from my neighbor—what more important book to borrow than Torah—then it is entrusted to me and I may not lend it out again. This is obvious. And that is, I think, the point of the law. One would think that one would be pleased to have our book disseminated to others so that they might enjoy the wisdom within contained. One would think that I would not be offended if my friend lent my book to another. Indeed, we are always anxious to share our books and our stories with others. We are forever recommending books to friends and colleagues and students: To accept our book is to accept ourselves. Who holds this book holds a man! And so what the Rabbis suggest here is that what is even more valuable than wisdom is care and obligation to the other. Therefore, the statement that we may not lend the book out again is necessary because it reminds us that even that which may enlighten comes not free from encumbrances and constraints and obligations. Even the absolute wisdom of Torah might not be freely disseminated if in its dissemination another human might be mistreated.

Too, I might think that if I borrowed the scroll, then it is because I have precise interests with it—the Rabbis suggest that it is a specific book I have asked for and not just any book; in the latter case my discovery would be like lost property. The specific purpose for which I have borrowed the book ensures that I will care for the book. And that is exactly why the Rabbis find it necessary to say that I may read it so long as I am not studying the material for the first time. In the latter case, I am not certain what it is I have borrowed. Either I have , borrowed the book with no serious intention or specific purpose and hence, I might not remain watchful as I flip through the text; I might be careless. Or it might be that without some prior learning the book would escape me. It might be that this book could prove invaluable; it may be that this book may be central to my life, but unless I am immediately purposeful in my intent, then it might be through mindless carelessness that I would even unintentionally harm the book. To prevent this failure of communication, the Rabbis forbid our studying in a borrowed book material we have not yet studied once.

Similarly, the Rabbis argue that if a scroll or book is left for safekeeping, then the one entrusted with it must care for the book but may not study in it. The text was left for care but not for use. But, the Rabbis note, there appears to be a contradiction—it would seem that it has already been stated that "if one deposits a scroll of the Torah with his neighbor, [the latter] must roll it once every twelve months, and may open and read it; but if he opens it in his own interests, it is forbidden." If he may read it, then how can he not open it in his own interests? And the Rabbis respond, that the neighbor is obliged to roll the scroll regardless of his ability to read, but if while he is rolling the scroll he reads the words in it, it is permitted. While scrolling it would have to be something with which we were already familiar to which our consciousness responds. Then, it is suggested, we may read. We would not be studying for the first time, as it were; if through the fulfillment of our duty to the one who has deposited the scroll with us we might also benefit in further study, then certainly it is acceptable to the Rabbis. However, just because a scroll is deposited, it is not assumed that it may be used for one's own purposes. Again, study might be deemed important, though not at the (unknown) owner's (unknown) expense.

The Rabbis continue: They say that one may not study a subject for the first time, nor may one study with another within the scroll a subject previously begun. It is possible, perhaps, that the second scholar may not have studied the same material as has the first and, hence, he has no right to study in the text since one may not study a subject in the text that has not previously been studied. No advantage may be taken of lost or borrowed property. Human relationships and trust take precedence over even the study of Torah. And that is merely the law; what if we were obligated—as indeed, we are—to go beyond the law. What care might we take toward others. Also, the Rabbis are ensuring that concern be taken with the text—two anxious scholars studying together might pull or rip the text searching through different sections. Or they might scroll rapidly and somewhat incautiously between diverse places in the scroll. Recall, scrolls needed to be rolled. Thus the Rabbis mandate that not more than three columns be opened at a time.

Finally, the Rabbis argue that three may never study together from the same text—nor may two read together. Isn't this yet another contradiction? No, says Abaye, the reference to reading together refers to a single subject, whereas the interdiction of two to read together is to two different subjects. That event might subject the book to ill use.

And these are only the requirements of law. But how do we go beyond the law in such matters? It interests me to consider that I still don't know. Perhaps I must acknowledge that to go beyond the law is to be forever obligated. And how might that alter our lives in schools as students and teachers?

Who holds this book, holds a man. I think I begin to understand now how I might show concern for the man in the holding of the book and how the holding of the man shows concern for the book. It would seem that the Rabbis have made me infinitely obligated to both. I think this is an ethic with which I can live.

Schwab believed that the work of curriculum must be a practical endeavor. Seymour Fox says that "By practical, we mean that no conception of Jewish history or thought, or for that matter of any discipline, as attractive as it may be in the form presented, is viable or useful unless actual students and teachers in real classrooms can and will apply these ideas" (1977, 106). Schwab believed that the curriculum in the schools ought to prepare students not by offering specific skills to practice in a life; rather, curriculum should enable engagement with life by enlarging the capacities to engage effectively in it. I think the Rabbis have offered a curriculum, a pedagogy, and an ethic with which and by which, we can live and thrive. "[I]t is still the case," Schwab writes, "that the heart of the matter is scope for recovery of meaning and relation, for education of perception and sensibility, in materials traditional to the traditional fields of learning" (1969b, 215). Schwab strove to improve the quality of our daily living; it was not an economic but an ethical solution he sought.

Chapter Seven

"They Sound the Alarm Immediately"

Anti-intellectualism in Teacher Education

In *Ta'anit*, the ninth tractate of the second order of the Babylonian Talmud,[1] the Rabbis concern themselves with the laws instituting and regulating public fast days and especially those fasts that have no appointed date and time, unlike those to be held on Yom Kippur (which falls always on the tenth of Tishri)[2] or Tisha b'Av (observed always on the ninth of Av).[3] Rather, in *Ta'anit*, the Rabbis address those fasts that are called as a response to unnatural conditions—late and absent rains, the sudden stoppage of rains, unnatural plant growths, plague, military presence (even if that presence represents merely a passing-through of the territory by the military), and building collapse, all of which threaten the well-being of the community and the nation. In the first chapter of *Ta'anit*, the Rabbis discuss the institution and practice of the fasts that are to be undertaken in response to the absence of expected rain ("The rains in due season") and the impending threat of serious and life-threatening conditions that will result immediately from this drought. In subsequent chapters, the Rabbis address other unnatural portents of national calamity for which the fast might provide medicament.

In the absence of the expected rains in the appointed seasons, the Rabbis prescribe a series of three sets of communal fasts. During the course of the specified time when the rains ought to come, the Rabbis institute a total of thirteen fasts that are to be observed. The stringency of the fasts increase with each succeeding series as does, it is expected, the penitence of the community. Adin Steinsaltz writes that the practice

---

[1]The Talmud (200 C.E.-600 C.E.) is a remarkably complex text that represents centuries of conversations by Jewish leaders and scholars concerning the edited system of laws and custom.

[2]Yom Kippur is the holiest day of the Jewish year, when the community is commanded to "afflict their souls" and pray for repentance.

[3]Tisha b'Av commemorates the destruction of the First and Second Temples and is a period of national mourning.

of fasting is based on the principle that "nothing occurs in this world by accident. The causes that determine events are not only physical but spiritual. Good deeds are rewarded and evil is punished. Divine providence responds to men's actions, both those of individuals as well as those of the community or the nation as a whole" (Steinsaltz, 1995, 2). It is hoped that the communal penance explicit in the fast will avert the severe decree and prevent the tragedies that the natural (and unnatural) disasters portend.

The form of the penance—abstinence from food and drink and other worldly pleasures (such as bathing, and wearing shoes, and marital relations) though necessary, is not, however, an end in itself; fasting must be accompanied by earnest prayer. Fasting, says Adin Steinsaltz, is the "means by which the community is to arrive at a spiritual awakening and true repentance" (Steinsaltz, 1995, 1). In the absence of the public sacrifice which could not take place outside the Temple which was destroyed in 70 C.E., the Rabbis had instituted prayer as the agency by which holiness might be attained and maintained. Fasting was a physical affliction of the body, but that abstinence should be accompanied by and facilitate the purity of the prayer. Concerning the ceremony instituting the fast, it is scripted: An elder of the community, probably the eldest of the leaders, would stand before the assembled people, and citing from the book of *Jonah* (3:10), announce to them: "It is not said about the people of Nineveh: 'And God saw their sackcloth and their fast,' but rather: 'And God saw their deeds, that they had returned from their evil way'" (Steinsaltz, 1995, 15A). With these words the leader cautioned the people that it was not their fast alone that would redeem their city; rather, it would be their engagement in prayer that would ultimately save the Ninevites from tragedy. Then, the leader would call to the people from the prophecy of Joel, who himself had warned of an impending plague of locust. The leader cautioned, "Rend your hearts and not your garments. . . ." (*Joel*, 2:13), again indicating that the fast was meant as a spiritual questing toward holiness and not merely a physical deprivation. Having determined in Chapter I the immediacy, order and rigor of the fasts, the Rabbis concern themselves in Chapter II of *Ta'anit* with the constitution of appropriate prayer services for the days of public fast and inserting special supplicatory prayers into the discipline of the regularly established service to recognize and to accompany the fast day.

In the observance of the fast, humans acknowledge their failings and aspire to improvement. The fast becomes a moment of *teshuvah,* a

Hebrew word the meaning of which remains yet open to me. All of my life I have understood the word *teshuvah* to mean "repentance." Repentance, as commonly accepted, is sorrow for our misdeeds, our misthoughts, our mistakes. The institution of the fast may be thought of as the Rabbinic establishment of a public act of *teshuvah*. Martin Buber (1967, 67-8), however, suggests that *teshuvah* might be understood as something more than mere "repentance." *Teshuvah*, he says, can be understood as the name given to the act of turning to the world to work towards the world's redemption. *Teshuvah,* according to Buber, is more than an act of personal (or even public) contrition; it is, rather, an act of personal (or even public) commitment. In *teshuvah*, we turn toward the world to begin the healing that our ethical absence from it has made necessary. That is, *teshuvah* is an affirmation of our commitment to the process of *tikkun olam*—a raising of the sparks and the repair of the world. In that engagement, we achieve our own healing as well. *Teshuvah* is not simply repentance for the past, but a responsibility to the future. "Teshuvah," Buber says (1967, 67), "is the name given to the act of decision in its ultimate intensification; it denotes the decisive turning point in a man's life, the renewing, total reversal in the midst of the normal course of his existence." *Teshuvah* is the decision to change one's life. The *Pirke Avot* (4:17) says, "One hour of return in this world is better than the entire world to come." The fast acknowledges our having turned away; the fast acknowledges as well our turning toward. The fast is the public manifestation of our hour of return, *as long as the fast is accompanied by appropriate spiritual awakening and elevation.* The public abstinence must lead to public action.

> Rabbi Bunam once asked his students, "Now that we no longer have prophets, how can we tell if our sins have been pardoned?" Several of his students enthusiastically offered learned responses to the teacher's questions, citing chapters and verses from throughout the Tanakh. But he refused all of them. When the room fell to silence, Bunam responded, 'We can tell our sins have been forgiven by the fact that we no longer commit that sin." (Buber, 1991, 253).

The fast acknowledges our guilt, but it is our action that effects redemption.

It would seem from the media and from the words and actions of public officials and the public government that the educational system is in a crisis that would require the institution of a fast. Our leaders stand before the assembled multitude and decry the miserable state of education in the United States today. The critics bemoan the inability of our students to read and to do simple arithmetical operations. Our leaders threaten dire national consequences if the schools do not improve. The status of our world power, we are adjured, depends on the quality of our schools. Failing schools are unacceptable, it would seem, failing societies notwithstanding. And by a standard definition, a school that fails is a school whose test scores remain below the nationally established standard on tests that have been quantitatively standardized. The recent government institution of tests in English and Mathematics for every child in grades 3-8 is a response to the supposed calamity of language and mathematical ignorance. The earlier 1983 polemic entitled "A Nation at Risk" warned of dire national calamities if the educational system was not seriously repaired. Diane Ravitch's repeated jeremiads (1995, 2000) concerning the dangers of progressivism in the twentieth century (the century of curriculum) speak to the perceived crises plaguing our educational system and hence, our nation's future. William Bennett (2001) declares that "In America, the longer you stay in school, the dumber you get in relation to your peers in other industrialized nations." It would seem from these prophecies that a fast would be in order. And what, I ask, ought be our prayer? I would, indeed, speak to the identity of this prayer in the academy, but I think, perhaps, that the identity of the supplications I would offer would address a different crisis.

I here speak of a serious and unnatural scarcity that threatens the well-being of the community for which the Rabbis instituted the practice of the fast. I speak to those in the academy who refer to our students as clients or customers, to those who aspire not to teach but to please, and to those who argue that their role is to prepare students for the educational marketplace rather than to be critics of that marketplace and its products. I speak to those who quake in fear of the accrediting agencies whose very existence assumes our incompetence. I address those who have become too busy to engage in reflective and critical thought. I would speak of plague, and unnatural plant growths, and military presence in the academy. I would speak of educational programs in which students are practiced in technique and regimen, but not in thought and critical reflection. I would speak to the crisis of intellectual drought pervading our classrooms. In *Ta'anit*, the Rabbis decree, "For these [events], "they sound the alarm in all places." I am here sounding an alarm.

In the academy today, and I speak here of the educational institution at primary, secondary and post-secondary levels, teachers have ceased learning for the ease of mere teaching. We have eschewed intellectual questioning for the safety of the answer. We wait for the word from governmental agencies for our deliverance. In 1969b, Joseph Schwab decried the scarcity of models in the intellectual communities then available to students to nurture intellectual activity. His accusation thirty years ago still has relevance today. Schwab (1969b, 18) complained that "the faculty have no professional lives apart from their teaching. They make no music. They write no books. They uncover no new knowledge. They forge no new policies. They are not conspicuously engaged in honorable public service. They administer little apart from their homes and classrooms. They teach, to be sure, but their teaching is a full-time service they perform, not a flowering or a sharing of expertise of scholarship. . . ." At larger universities, Schwab (1969b, 18) accused, "The visible bulk of the faculty of being very busy indeed but not at their own business. They are not doing what flows from their talents but what is marketable. . . ." Students lacked a model of intellectual passion and honesty.

Finally, Schwab bemoaned, in many places "there is an intellectual community, but the students don't belong to it, not even as second-class citizens" (1969b, 18-19). Schools neither require nor invite students to participate in intellectual pursuit; rather, students are assigned minimum standards and evaluated on their achievement of that minimum standard. Schwab complained (1969b, 19) that the undergraduate curriculum "is a mere inculcation of . . . a rhetoric of conclusions and of a body of rote methods for solving rote problems." Schwab worried, indeed, that the young were not being properly educated; he accused the educational community of a virulent form of anti-intellectualism. In his book, *College Curriculum and Student Protest*, Schwab called for a curative. "This book, is, in a sense, medical. It is, first, an examination of the style, the expression, and some of the content of student protest as presenting symptoms of evils of their education; student ineptitude and ignorance indicating neglects by the curriculum; perversities indicating distortions and mistreatments"(1969b, 3). Schwab called for an intellectual exemplification of the public fast.

Today, we have yet evidences of serious malaise and ineptitudes in our educational institutions, indicated not by low test scores but by low intellectual expectations; epitomized not by intellectual inadequacies, but by avoidance of intellectual challenge. Our schools are characterized not by intellectual rigor nor active pursuit of meaning and meaning making, but by intellectual retreat and cravenness. Recently, at the institution at which I teach, the faculty has undertaken to revise all of their courses to satisfy the newest regulations from the state Department of Public Instruction. Not a word was uttered in defense of the work we had been doing. Not a word was uttered questioning the efficacy of the program changes. Not a word was uttered in protest. Recently, at the institution in which I teach, the introductory course on Curriculum has been replaced by a course entitled Classroom Management. Students will be engaged not with the struggle of understanding curriculum but the technique of managing it; they will never be required to interrogate what *it*—the curriculum—might be and if it might be different. Nor will our students be asked to wonder about those whom they teach or why they have chosen to do such work in the first place. Rather, our students will memorize the algorithms of how to manage *them* for reasons and outcomes that will never be addressed.

Our students have been taught to desire only to be told what to do. Our faculty desire only to be told what to do. In so many classrooms, teaching is only about methods: the pedagogy of the how-to. Students demand of me: "Please, just tell me how to do this and I will do it. I will do it well. Just please, please don't trouble me with ideas." Methods proliferate. Methods classes proliferate. Teaching has been transformed into a set of directions not unlike those I cannot follow when putting together my children's toys, or my furniture, or anything else that comes in a carton with directions written by someone skilled in writing directions. Peruse any methods book and discover the myriad numbered lists of how-tos, or read the plethora of acronyms referring to methods and techniques. Teaching is almost never a conversation about studying, but a set of instructions and objectives about the mandated content of study; teaching is not about learning but about achieving, not about healing but about administering and assessing.

Indeed, our students are taught how not to study. My students would prefer not to read. They say, "This reading was hard." And what do they expect? They frighten me: I always know who they are from day to day. They rarely ask questions; they rarely seek answers to the questions they do ask; rather, they look to me in the front of the class and live in terror of the question. The past has truly passed for them. They say, "Just tell me what to do now and I will do it. I will even do it well. But I don't understand why I have to know what the nineteenth century thought of curriculum or even how they practiced it. We've advanced since then, haven't we? Don't we know now how to do it correctly?" My students are interested in the answer and not the conversation. Forty years ago Bob Dylan taught what yet remains true: "Teachers teach that knowledge waits, can lead to hundred dollar plates." From their teachers students have learned that if there is no immediate product, then the activity is immediately useless.

I would have teachers for our children with greater curiosity. I would have teachers for our children with greater respect for contingency and less faith in certainty. I would have teachers for our children who have authority rather than those who merely cast about for it. "For these [events]", the Rabbis (Steinsaltz, 1995, 19a) say, "they sound the alarm in all places: For blight, and for mildew, and for locusts, and for *hasil*, and for wild beasts, and for the sword. They sound the alarm for it, because it is a calamity that spreads." I am sounding the alarm. It is a calamity that spreads. You see, we have children in the schools who will be taught by the students presently in our classrooms.

And so Chapter III of *Ta'anit* concerns the obligations of the community for fast and prayer in the event of a calamity other than late rains. The chapter begins (Steinsaltz, 18b), "The order of the fasts that was said . . . applies with respect to [the period of] the first rainfall. But if plants have changed, they sound the alarm for them immediately." They sound the alarm for them immediately. There is no time to delay. In the earlier chapters, the Rabbis may have recognized that late rains might indicate Divine correction at work, and they, therefore, had mandated a series of fasts of increasing severity to enact communal penitence. The Rabbis hoped that during the observances of the early fasts, the penitence of the community would suffice and the rains would fall. But here in Chapter III, the Rabbis address a different situation: What if the rains come on time, but then they cease; or if the plants grow bizarrely, or if plague besets the town or wild animals begin to dangerously prowl the city? What if armed soldiers are seen within the borders of the city even in times of peace? The Rabbis reason that these situations clearly indicate a heavenly decree against the community, and they order that the alarm be immediately sounded and the more severe fasts summarily instituted. Interestingly, however, despite the calamitous results from these conditions, and despite the seeming danger to the community, much of this chapter concerns not so much explication of the law concerning the fast or the appropriate prayers but the miraculous responses of the righteous to these actual or impending calamities. This chapter is filled not so much with law as with legend. This chapter is filled with stories of those whose prayers helped avert catastrophe. And to speak to my purposes here, many of those people are teachers. It is the "prayers" of the teachers that averted the severe decree.

> When the rains were late, the Rabbis would send schoolchildren to find Hanan HaNehba. They would grab him by the hem of his cloak and cry, "Father, Father, give us rain!." And Hanan HaNehba would pray and the rains would come. (*Ta'anit*, 23b)

It is the content of the teachers' characters rather than that of their prayers—since others would say the same prayers—that produce miraculous outcomes.

I think we might look to the portrayal of these teachers by the Rabbis as an insight into our work in schools today. It is to this crisis of anti-intellectualism in the academy that I would now speak, for the conditions Schwab decried in 1969 have recurred. I believe that though the rains might have fallen in the appointed seasons, the plants have since changed and the rains have since ceased. I believe that wild animals have invaded the cities and that plague has overcome us. There are armed soldiers moving about in our community. I am sounding the alarm immediately. I say that the intellectuals in our community have abandoned their practice; we have succumbed to the will of the politicians whose motives must be always suspect, and we have forsworn our professions. We have ceased our unending quest for wisdom for the safety of standards and measurable products. We have ceased being curious for the ease of complacency. We cater to those whose power seems greater than ours because we have disregarded and/or abandoned our own powers. A story:

> Once, Rabbi Bunam went on a long journey. He took with him some of his finest students. They stopped at an inn for lunch and the innkeeper was so honored that Bunam and his students had stopped at his inn that he asked them to have dinner with him. Rabbi Bunam sat down at the table, but his students went into the kitchen to inquire of the purity of the meal. "Was the animal that they were to eat unblemished; was the butcher sufficiently skilled and did he execute his task according to strict law. How carefully had the meat been salted?" A man dressed in rags stood up and spoke. "O, you hasidim, you make a big to-do about what you put into your mouths being clean, but you

> don't worry half as much about the purity of what comes out of your mouths." (Buber, 1991, 229)

So today in the academy: we are so concerned with our ease and purity, that we have ceased to care what it is that comes out of our mouths.

We no longer institute public fast days, though we do occasionally still call for a day of prayer. I would here offer exemplars of teachers whose prayers in time of public distress saved the community. I would set these teachers as our models and learn their practices. It is to them we must look to save us from intellectual drought, and academic plague, and legislative wild beasts. We must not abandon the academy and our offices and our library seats for the safety of the legislative halls or even the quiet of our homes. As Bob Dylan writes, "It's bad out there," but "out there" is where we belong.

> Once, Rabbi Bunam stopped at an inn to pray, but the people there jostled and pushed him and he could not enter the room nor stop there to pray. He left. Later, he said to his students, "Sometimes it is impossible to pray in a certain place and one seeks out another place. But that is not the right thing to do. For the place we have quitted cries out mournfully: 'Why did you refuse to make your devotions here with me? If you met with obstacles, it was a sign that it was up to you to redeem me.'" (Buber, 1991, 256)

We must take our stance where we live despite the difficulties we confront there.

What should that stance be at this present moment? Indeed, at any moment? Certainly we live in time of physical and emotional plague. Dylan writes, "Things are breaking up out there." Plague besets the city, and our buildings collapse. We live, I think, in unstable and dilapidated houses. We worry for our lives and livelihood, and we have ceased to serve our students. The Rabbis tell the tale of a teacher.

> Nahum Gam Zu, was blind in both eyes, both his hands were cut off, both his legs were amputated, and his entire body was full of boils. And he was lying in a dilapidated house, and the legs of his bed were placed in bowls of water so that the ants would not climb on him. His students wished to move Gam Zuinto another residence and they set out to pack up all of his belongings. But Gam Zu stopped them. He said, "Remove the utensils and then remove me for I have been assured that as long as I am in the house it will not fall." And so the students removed all of the belongings and then they removed Gam Zu, and sure enough, as soon as he had been taken from the residence, it fell

> to the ground. His students asked Gam Zu how he could suffer such a horrible fate when he was so rightous that as long as he remained in it the building would not fall. And Gam Zu answered, "Once I was traveling on the road to the house of my father-in-law and I had with me a load [that was being carried] on three asses, one of food, and one of drink, and one with various kinds of delicacies. A poor man came and stood in front of me on the road, and said to me: 'My teacher, sustain me!' I said to him: 'Wait until I unload my ass.'" And Gam Zu began to unload his animal. He continued the story: "I did not have time to unload the ass before his soul departed. I went and fell on his face, and I said, 'Let my eyes, which had no compassion for your eyes, become blind. Let my hands, which had no compassion for your hands, be cut off. Let my legs which had no compassion for your legs be amputated. And my mind did not become calm until I said, 'Let my entire body be full of boils.'" His students looked at him and cried, "Oh teacher, alas for us that we had seen you like this," and Gam Zu responded, "My students, alas for me if you had not seen me like this." (*Ta'anit*, 21A)

Gam Zu's suffering resulted from his failure to sustain his students; was Gam Zu, perhaps, not too concerned with delivering his father-in-law's goods? Or with his own comfort? But Gam Zu's righteousness derives from his willingness to accept his responsibility and his failure. It is the righteousness of this wonderful teacher that keeps the building from collapsing.

And what does it mean to say that a teacher sustains? "Teacher, sustain me," cried the student to Gam Zu. I think first and foremost a teacher sustains by caring. And what could be meant by "caring." To care, says Nel Noddings (1999, 52), "is not to act by rule but by affection and regard.We act not to achieve for ourselves a commendation but to protect and enhance the welfare of the cared-for." Needless to say, our institutions as they are presently constituted are not established to admit caring as a factor in teaching behavior. Caring, rather, is equated to the concern that all be held to a universal standard for which no exemplar might in fact, ever be found. It is at present always incumbent upon us to unload our asses before we ever attend to our students' sustenance. We do not sustain in this manner. Martha Nussbaum argues from Aristotle that this adherence to a scientific rationality is at best incomplete, but at worst, actually false. Nussbaum writes: "But Aristotle's point in all these cases is that the rule or algorithm represents a falling off from full practical rationality, not its flourishing or completion" (1990, 73). Rather, Nussbaum says, it is in the particular that discernment lies. "What degree and type of divergence [from the normative] is blameworthy, it is not easy to express in any general principle: for the discernment lies in the particulars and in perception" (1990, 69). That is, rational choice must derive from the knowledge of the particular. The single standards that we establish and to which teachers blindly adhere inevitably falsify the situation. Nussbaum continues: "Principles are authoritative only insofar as they are correct: But they are correct only insofar as they do not err with regard to the particulars. And it is not possible for a formulation intended to cover many different particulars to achieve a high degree of correctness" (1990, 69).

This is not dissimilar to what Schwab argued about the particularities of curriculum. The Rabbis phrase it somewhat differently. They say that "All is according to local custom." Today, our silence in the face of the imposition of standards and our adherence to those standards bespeaks the dilapidation of our buildings and the presence of armed soldiers in our midst, even if we do not feel threatened by them. Perhaps it is our concern for our ease that speaks of the presence of plague. We are like Tennyson's Lotus-Eaters, "In the hollow Lotos-land to live and lie reclined/On the hills like Gods together, careless of mankind"(ll. 154-55). Though Hanan HaNehba's prayers for the children might bring rain, it is also said that he was called HaNehba because though his prayers might be effective, he once hid himself in the bathroom to avoid being called to responsibility (*Ta'anit*, 23b). Caring is immediate and personal and free from authoritative principles.

But perhaps, we are never capable of such absolute care, despite the present propagandistic drivel about selfless patriotism and the absurd romantic notions of selfless love. Does that impossibility obviate our commitments? Mary Anne Raywid (1999, 62) argues against the selflessness of caring by pointing out that were such selfless care to be true, there could only be one caring relationship in a person's life and no work would ever get done. In the present case, Gam Zu had not attempted to avoid responsibility; he had asked merely that the student wait until Gam Zu had unloaded his ass. Here is the case of an individual who desires to aid the student, but only after he has put down his own burden. Perhaps, in this situation, it is not intellectual sustenance that the student seeks at all but mere physical relief. Perhaps Gam Zu's failure is not intellectual at all!

But then again, perhaps it is . . .

The Rabbis tell another story in this chapter:

> Rav happened to come to a place which was experiencing a great drought. Rav declared as fast, but still the rains did not come. Another prayer leader came down and led the communal prayers. During the course of the service the prayer leader recited, "Who causes the wind to blow," and suddenly, the wind began to blow. When during the prayer service he said, ""Who causes the rain to fall," the rains began to fall. Rav asked the man what he did, and the man said, "I am a teacher of young children, and I teach the children of the poor just like the children of the rich. And whoever is unable [to pay] I do not take anything from him. And I have a fishpond, and whoever is lazy, I bribe him with them, and I prepare for him, and I mollify him, until he comes and studies." (*Ta'anit*, 24a)

Would I were such a teacher, with seemingly infinite resources and infinite patience. Perhaps we might understand this teacher as someone whose first priority is that the student learn. In this story the teacher *sustains* because he is prepared to go to any lengths for every student to facilitate learning. The caring here is an intellectual concern and is not exclusive. Indeed, it occurs in the discernment of the particular. Perhaps Gam Zu could have sustained by earlier accepting his responsibility.

There is evidence that in *Ta'anit*, the Rabbis identify sustenance and care with the intellectual work of which learning is comprised. I begin this exegesis with a related story from another tractate of the Babylonian Talmud, *Bava Metzia*, about another great teacher, Rabbi Hiyya.

> When Rabbi Hanina and Rabbi Hiyya would quarrel, Rabbi Hanina said to Rabbi Hiyya: "Do you quarrel with me? If, God forbid, the Torah were to be forgotten in Israel, I would bring it back with my argumentation." Rabbi Hiyya said to Rabbi Hanina: "Do you quarrel with me, who has labored for the Torah that it not be forgotten in Israel? What do I do? I go and sow flax, and I weave nets [from it], and I catch deer, and I give their meat to orphans. And I prepare scrolls and write the Five Books [of Torah]. And I go to a town and teach five children the Five Books [of the Torah], and I teach six children the six orders [of the Mishnah]. And I say to them: 'Until I come back, teach each other Torah and teach each other Mishnah.' And [thus] I labor for the Torah that it is not forgotten in Israel." This is what Rabbi said: "How great are the deeds of Hiyya!" (*Bava Metzia*, 85b)

Here, two sages argue about their respective superiority. Each claims to be the better scholar/teacher. Hanina argues that he must be the better teacher because his sagacity and rhetorical brilliance would be able to recreate Torah even if it were completely forgotten in Israel. Hanina claims that through his own genius, he could recreate Torah.

But Hiyya argues passionately. His merits as a teacher derive, he exclaims, not merely from his knowledge of Torah which is at least equal to that of Hanina, but from his ability to construct an environment suffused not only with teaching but with learning as well. Hiyya's counter acknowledges that his work as a scholar requires students. Hiyya claims that his power and reputation as a teacher derive not only from his ability to reason engaged with a text, but from his capacities to support the environment in which the teaching of text will occur. This activity includes the care and preparation of those who will continue the tradition, the education, that is, of future teachers. Whereas Hanina is concerned with preserving the past in the present, Hiyya seems engaged in transmitting the past into the future by attending to the present. Furthermore, whereas Hanina's merits maintain the tradition within himself, Hiyya opens the tradition democratically. Hiyya supports and teaches the children of the poor who will then teach others. I think we have here at least in part the Jewish roots of the Lancastrian or monitorial method of education. Sustenance here is for the sake of learning and is not delimited to mere physical support. Hiyya offers total care to his students; he is a single stop social agency catering predominantly to the poor. Hiyya's care includes the intellect but is not confined to it.

In our present discussion, however, our nameless teacher (!) argues that he teaches *both* rich and poor alike, and that his fish pond is not for feeding the resistant students but for "bribing them," as it were, to study. That is, what this story suggests is that what is primary is that students learn and not that they are taught. Our nameless teacher needs no class in management; he knows perfectly well how to engage students as they learn. The sustenance he offers is for the sake of their learning; it is all the construction of an intellectual environment. It is his remarkable abilities to do so which account for his righteousness. And it is this teacher's prayers that bring the rains.

There is another story that further suggests the intellectual nature of teaching.

> Rabbi Yohanan grew angry at his student, Resh Lakish., for disagreeing with him in the classroom. The student, Lakish, was overwrought and became ill at the idea of offending his teacher. But despite the pleas of Lakish's wife (who

> happened also to be Yohanan's sister), Yohanan would not forgive. Lakish died. And Yohanan mourned and too, in deep depression, began to wither.
>
> The Rabbis said, "Who will go [and] relieve his mind? Let Rabbi Elazar ben Pedat go, for his statements are sharp." He went [and] sat before him. [After] everything that Rabbi Yohanan said, ben Pedat said to him: "There is a baraita that supports you." Yohanan said, "Are you like the son of Lakish? When I would say something, Lakish would raise twenty-four objections against me, and I would give him twenty-four answers, and the statement would thereby be clarified. And you say: 'There is a Baraita that supports you.' Do I not know that what I have said is right?" He went on rending his clothes and weeping, and said, "Where are you, Lakish? Where are you, Lakish?" And he cried out until his mind slipped from him. The Rabbis pleaded for mercy on his behalf and Yohanan died. (*Bava Metzia*, 84a)

No sooner does Yohanan lose his student, then he mourns Lakish's loss and falls into what we would today refer to as a deep depression. In the absence of Prozac, the scholarly Rabbis advocate that relief ought to come in the form of intellectual disquisition. How better to revive Yohanan's failed spirits than engagement in scholarly conversation! The rabbis send their best scholar, Elazar ben Pedat, who listens in awe to Yohanan's brilliant discourses. But Yohanan is not assuaged; the conversation bores him. He accuses Elazar: What good are you? Don't I know that I am right. I need you, he says, to tell me I am wrong. You must argue with me, Yohanan scolds Elazar, you must contradict me that I might continue to learn. How can I be a student, the teacher asks the student, if you, the student, will not be the teacher? Yohanan has learned that the student's value is not in agreeing with the teacher but in disagreement. Lakish's brilliance rests not only in what he learned, but in what he could help Yohanan learn. Yohanan has lost his best teacher and his best student when Lakish dies. Yohanan cannot go on. It is questioning in teaching that is essential, but that questioning must be one in which revealing answers is not the aim. Our academies have forgone the question for the answer.

This idea of teaching as intellectual challenge is strengthened in a further story in *Ta'anit* concerning a righteous teacher.

> Two students who were before Rabbi Yithak ben Elyahisv said to him, "Ask for mercy, Sir, on our behalf that we may become wise." He said to them, "It was with me, but I sent it away" (*Ta'anit*, 23b)

That is, Rabbi Yitzhak ben Elyashiv had the power to make his students wise, but he refrained from doing so. One might say that he did so because he did not mean to trouble God with petty human details.

But I would prefer to think that this teacher knew that wisdom comes from engagement in the work itself, and cannot be simply passed on as today's standards are transmitted. Indeed, even Moses had to write down the law on the second set of tablets, and he spent forty days and nights in disquisition with God concerning them.

Another story to suggest of what this intellectual work of the academy might consist. Again, this story derives from Rabbi Bunam, who was asked by his students about a phrase from Torah.

> They said to him: "We read in Exodus 19:6, 'And ye shall be unto me a kingdom of priests, and a holy nation. These are the words which thou shalt speak unto the children of Israel.' But," says the students, "Rashi, our teacher, argues that this phrase means, 'These are the words, no more and no less.' What does Rashi mean by that—no more and no less?" And Bunam answered: "Moses, our teacher, was good. He wanted to reveal more to the people, but he was not allowed. For it was God's will that the people make an effort of their own. Moses was to say just these words to them, no more and no less, so that they might feel: something is hidden here, and we must strive to discover it for ourselves. That is why, further on, in Exodus 19:7, we read: 'And he set before them all these words. No more and no less'" (Buber, 1991, 261).

The teacher must help the student learn. Learning is interpretation and not declamation. There is nothing but interpretation, except indoctrination.

We must teach interpretation, but first must we must enact it ourselves. We must abandon not the teaching of Ralph Tyler, but our use of him. We must teach our students how to engage in discourse with Tyler and with Dewey and with ourselves. Meaning issues not from heavenly edict but from earthly exegesis. Meaning derives from human action—interpretation—and must be negotiated in personal encounters—Talmudic-like discourse. "It is not in Heaven" means we are ultimately free. The Rabbis' mild misreading offers me the opportunity to link interpretation and action and to make interpretation an ethical presence. I wonder at how our classrooms might alter if the teacher would assume such a stance. "What does this mean, teacher?" "It is not in heaven . . . but in your mouth and your heart to perform it." We must offer texts that require interpretation; we must read books that require interpretation. As of the present, however, we read only the imposed regulations and sometimes the newspapers and our academic journals.

I tell a final story.

> Our Rabbis taught that once there was a great period of drought, and the Rabbis called for a series of thirteen fasts. At the conclusion of the fast the rains had still not fallen and the people rose from their prayers, and they turned for home. Rabbi Eliezer called to them from the pulpit: "And have you prepared graves for yourselves?" For Eliezer knew that in the absence of rain the people would surely die. The people burst out crying, and suddenly the rain fell. (25b)

I would inquire now of the academics: And have you prepared graves for yourselves?

Chapter Eight

OBLIGATION'S TIME

It might have been one of the last formal publications in a long career of publishing. In the third issue of the thirteenth volume of *Curriculum Inquiry* (1983), Joseph Schwab placed his final formal article of the series of articles he referred to as "The Practical." This last article was entitled "The Practical 4: Something for Curriculum Professors to Do." *Something for curriculum professors to do*: I like that. I am a professor *of* curriculum, and before that I was a professor *with* curriculum. And I have often wondered what there might be to do. For years—for as long as I can recall—I have been drawn to Lenin's title, "What is to be Done?" For years I have stood in classrooms and wondered what I was to do there. Oh, not that there was any lack of objectives, but I regularly wondered about the efficacy of them and about the final value of what was done with them—or even to them. As advocates of strict standards assert, I should know "what students should know and be able to do" (Ravitch, 1995, 133) and, therefore, I should know what I was supposed to do. Standards notwithstanding, I remained not confident that what I did would "ensure that all students learn to use their minds well, so that they may be prepared for responsible citizenship, further learning, and productive employment in our Nation's modern economy" (Ravitch, 1995, 188). I mean, some of my dear friends are unemployed. Some of my dear friends protest vigorously against the policies of the government, and our present president says that their opposition is akin to treachery.

I do not know what it means to use a mind well, unless it means that everyone's mind should work like mine. And as for lifelong habits of learning, well, each of us learns everyday, and sometimes despite our presence in school. C. Wright Mills once said that successful criminals are merely the genius of the streets. I think you do not have to go to school to learn to use your mind. And furthermore, if content standards "define what is to be learned, not the kind of behavior, attitudes, or personal qualities that students should display when the course is concluded," (Ravitch, 1995, 133), then to focus on *measurable* content standards is to shoot my arrow in the air only to kill my sisters and my brothers. Knowledge, as Schwab noted, is not objective. "Organizing forms (atoms, electrons, wave-motion, reflex arcs, cultures, civilizations) are not the forms of things, an ultimate or 'true' picture of the state of our knowledge, but the forms which serve us well, in the present state of our knowledge, as means for pursuing more knowledge" (Schwab, 1978, 177). Schwab held that "reflection, in the light of knowledge of means and ends and [reflection] on the knowledge in the light of what science has to offer" could be the only real base of curriculum. To ignore this "pragmatic intellectual space" (1978, 178-9), was to ignore the greater part of education and to relegate the greater part of the student population to ignorance.

Lenin's question derives, I think, from Marx's charge that philosophers must not merely interpret the world in various ways, but must work to change it. Schwab meant education to be thus, progressive. Marx and Lenin, I recall, regardless of their practice, were immersed in a Judaism. So, too, was Joseph Schwab. Judaism is a religion of deeds; it wonders always not what is simply known, but how what is known must lead to action. Judaism is always about being holy by practicing holiness. Holiness is an activity in this world and not a state of being in preparation for the next one. Holiness is achieved in action and not derived by grace or divine conferral. And as Freud—another Jew—very practically argued, we must each find for him/herself the means to salvation. The Rabbis say that at Sinai, God's voice "went forth to all Israel, to each and every one in keeping with his particular capacity—to the elderly in keeping with their capacity, to young men in keeping with their capacity, to the little ones in keeping with their capacity, and to the women in keeping with their capacity"(Bialik & Ravnitzky, 1992, 80:40). What we hear and what we learn—what we might know from theory—is very much based in the individual. Schwab knew that educational problems could only be dealt with if autobiographical material were taken into account. "For example, the way I allocate my scarce resources is tied to my infantile experiences. My infantile experiences, in turn, were determined in part by my parents' economic resources, in part by their political allegiances, in part by their small-town milieu. It is just such a complex web which must somehow be taken into account if we are to effect durable solutions to educational problems" (Schwab, 1971, 501). We are always going to be only "partly right," Schwab averred. But, if content standards define "what is to be learned, not the kind of behavior, attitudes, or personal qualities that students should display when the course is concluded" (Ravitch, 1995, 133), then education must completely ignore the individual's role in learning and the personal quality of his/her knowledge. If we are always only "partly right," then advocates of standards are always going to be completely wrong. Perhaps, if students are apathetic, it is not because they are not intellectually challenged but because for them the work has neither personal meaning nor relevance.

Schwab argued that the curriculum must derive from the immediacy of the particular and local classroom. "It is not decided in Moscow and telegraphed to the provinces whether Moscow be conceived as the specialist in biology, or the specialist in curriculum, or the teacher claiming academic freedom, or the legislator or parents, or students" (1983, 240). Rather, curriculum is a local and personal process from which a plurality of outcomes may be derived. "The detail is this: I do not intend or expect one outcome or one cluster of outcomes but *any one* of several, a plurality. Recognizance of the several stems from consideration not of possible outcomes, but of the materials under treatment: pluralities of theory, their relations to the matter they try in their various ways to subsume, their relations to one another"(1978, 363). Indeed, curriculum is the discovery of these pluralities. Curriculum professors have the responsibility of enjoining the various constituencies in the conjoint study of all the theories and factors concerning schooling. "Again, we have an eye on more than one educational purpose: not only contribution to liberal knowledge of curriculum but practice in person-to-person rhetoric, as seminarians question practitioners and respond to their replies" (1983, 263). Furthermore, curriculum professors "would attend to what they perceive as evils and vicissitudes of our government and society. They would try to convince readers that these troubles exist, show the threats they pose, and suggest ways in which alternation of school practice might help ameliorate the conditions discussed" (1983, 263). Finally, as Schwab declared often enough, the end of a general education has "something to do with being a man and a citizen" (1978, 277). Of course, the definitions of each were open to dispute—nevertheless, the goal of education was a practical and not a theoretical one. The place of curriculum was in daily activity. And, by the practical, Schwab meant "a complex discipline . . . concerned with choice and action, in contrast with the theoretic, which is concerned with knowledge. Its methods lead to defensible decision . . ." (1969a, 1-2). Curriculum should enable each to make choices which would enable each indvidual to achieve success as a good person and a good citizen.

Thus, professors of curriculum must do more than transfer knowledge to, or inculcate knowledge in, students. Rather, they must "perform a similar task with respect to the tastes, mores, and attitudes of our fellow citizens in their daily lives . . . [they might] face the question of means by which schools could go beyond mere propinquity in lessening the xenophobias and racisms which afflict us" (Schwab, 1983, 263). There is, Schwab avers, much to be done. But this work insists that the theoretical be translated into the practical via the eclectic arts. It is the work of the professors of curriculum *to practice* and *to teach the practice* of these arts. Polyfocal conspectus, the term Schwab gave to the multiplicity of theoretical views, derives from a curriculum based in deliberation. Such a multifaceted approach acknowledges the incompleteness of all views and the possibilities of future learning. There is no cessation of possibility. "Hananiah son of R. Joshua's brother said: Just as in the sea there are ripples and wavelets between each major wave, so between each of the Ten Commandments there were Torah's unwritten minutiae, as well as all of Torah's letters" (Bialik & Ravnitsky, 1992, 80:39). Schwab's practical exists in all of those unwritten minutiae and letters for which theory, by its very nature, could not account. "The very fabric of the practical . . . consists of the richly endowed and variable particulars form which theory abstracts or idealizes its uniformities. [W]e will drive our car smoothly, convey *Billy Budd* effectively, and teach 'Tilda well only as we take account of conditions of each which are not included in the theories which describe them as roads, literature, and learning child" (Schwab, 1978, 324). Schwab's practical addressed each locality and each student *as a particularity*. There is no single answer to the question of what is to be done. Always there was available another interpretation and something else to do.

The Rabbis, too, desired to make the holy life possible, and to this end they interpreted the holy texts. For the Rabbis, whole passages of text were open to differing interpretation, and yet these different interpretations are placed in contiguity as independent and co-equal opinions. As a plurality of views, they do not contradict each other; rather, these various theories exist independently, but in contiguity. Contradiction might imply that one view is wrong; rather than offer to each proferred opinion a "but," the Rabbis tender an "and." Each interpretation has equal validity. Discourse is what the Rabbis sought and discourse, not dogma, is what they offer. "The absence of dogmatic formulation allowed the Rabbis . . . to dwell upon one doctrine, when there was need, rather than upon another; to enunciate religious ideas without spinning them out into creedal principles; to present aspects of a subject which may well be modified or qualified by other aspects of that subject" (Kadushin, 1957, 14). Always, however, the Rabbis' intent concerned what was to be done. The Rabbis' discourse interrogated the texts, searching for the text's meaning. They never discovered that meaning. Rather, they produced it. Individual Rabbis offered differing opinions of the meaning of verses, and these various meanings sit side by side in the text. "Another interpretation" can only mean that the preceding interpretation as well as that about to be given are each of them independent of the others and that all are of the same rank. And this prefatory term is employed profusely throughout all of midrashic literature" (Kadushin, 1957, 72).[1] The Rabbis did not produce meaning, but the means for making meaning. For the Rabbis, there could be no definitive interpretation; it is interpretation itself that is definitive, and the interpretation is always about doing.

It was a method Schwab not only understood, but to my mind, emulated during the course of his work and especially in his discussions of the Practical. When the Rabbis mandated a twice daily recitation of the *Sh'ma*—when you lie down and when you rise up—they did not specify exactly what was meant by these times. The obligation was without question, but within what time was one obliged to complete the recitation? Who exactly was obliged within that time? This is not a small issue—the daily recitation of the *Sh'ma* is the guiding principle of Jewish life—it was instituted to affirm the oneness of God and to insist that the words of that unitary God be spoken of "when you lie down and when you rise up." Education sits at the center of Jewish practice. The practicalities are obvious. But from what time may one recite the *Sh'ma* in the evening? From what time may one recite the *Sh'ma* in the morning? The advocates of standards would desire that a clear answer be given that it might be learned, but I—and I think Joseph Schwab—are relieved to

---

[1]Our Rabbis taught: "Adam was created [last of all beings] on the even of Sabbath. And why?–Lest the Sadducees say: The Holy One, blessed be God, had a partner [Adam] in his work. Another answer is: In order that, if a man's mind becomes too proud, he may be reminded that the gnats preceded him in the order of creation. Another answer is: That he might immediately enter upon the fulfillment of the precept [to observe the Sabbath]. Another answer is: That he might straightway go into the banquet,[that is, to partake of all of creation](*Sanhedrin*, 38a).

discover that such answers are not forthcoming. Rather, in what might appears to be a rambling and unfocused discussion, the Rabbis' discourse suggests not so much answers as ways of life, not so much content as ways of considering that content. Schwab argued, "Deliberation requires consideration of the widest possible variety of alternatives if it is to be most effective. Each alternative must be viewed in the widest variety of lights. Ramifying consequences must be traced to all parts of the curriculum. The desirability of each alternative must be felt out, 'rehearsed,' by a representative variety of all those who must live with the consequences of a chosen action. And a similar variety must deal with the identification of problems as well as with their solution" (1978, 319). Schwab was describing Talmudic discourse.

Education ought to be about doing and not about receiving. Schwab demanded that students be engaged in the only education appropriate to their lives: an education informed by the practical, the end of which is "improving the quality and quantity of self-determination" (1978, 145). Education should be not about the good life, but about having the intellectual resources to choose it. Curriculum ought to satisfy and increase desire. "Not only the means, however, but also the ends of liberal education involve the Eros. For the end includes not only knowledge gained but knowledge desire and knowledge sought. The outcome of a successful liberal curriculum is *actively* intelligent people" (1978, 109). As the Rabbis studied Torah to discover what should be done, so Schwab intended curriculum to be the study of texts to discover what should be done. And despite our beliefs concerning the nature of the good and happy life, regardless of our understanding of the characteristics of good humans and good citizens and good learners, Schwab averred that we could only ever be "partly right." "The generalities about science, about literature, about children in general, about children or teachers of some specified class or kind, may be true, but they attain this status in virtue of what they leave out" (1978, 310). These theories are always only abstractions, and therefore, in all of their complexities, always only oversimplifications. The understanding of our limitations becomes for Schwab our strength: We are constantly aware of our partial view; hence, we are always open to alternatives and new knowledge. Thus, in schools we recognize that whatever it is we offer as subject matter is always only partially correct and always incomplete; sometimes what we offer might in some ways be deemed incorrect.

The renaissance in curriculum Schwab sought would change the measure of education and curriculum from acquisition of matter, to the institution of methods by which matter may be considered and practically applied in and to the activities of life. Curriculum would satisfy desire rather than impart information. Education would be accomplished by the awareness that its success must be measured not by the material that is offered, but by that which is learned by action performed practically with the material offered. "It follows then, that practical problems intrinsically involve states of character and the possibility of character change" (Schwab, 1978, 289). Education—as is holiness—is for life. It is not that theory is irrelevant but, rather, that life is too complex to be satisfied by any one theory. The incompleteness of all theories must be first acknowledged, and then to every real problem a multiplicity of theories must be applied. "It is clear, I submit, that defensible curriculum or plan of curriculum must be one which somehow takes account of all these sub-subjects which pertain to man" (1969a, 9). Schwab sought a curriculum that would account for what theory by its very definition could not account, and he sought a curriculum based in a pedagogy that could define the known by the unknown and make the latter accessible through the former. Schwab sought an education that would create a community of learners. It was, I assert, a very Rabbinic ideal: "The very concepts that make for the special character of a group also make for the distinctiveness and uniqueness of the individual self, for the integrative process which *is* the self. There is no actual group mind. There are only individual minds, each of which employs the common heritage of value-concepts in an original and distinctive manner" (Kadushin, 1952/1972, 82). In this Rabbinic environment, we are also, of course, not far from Fish's interpretive community or Schwab's community of learners.

Schwab distinguished the Practical from the traditional curriculum. Whereas the traditional curriculum was based on imparting subject matter, the practical was to be founded on interrogation of that subject matter not for its substance but for its meaning. The Practical offered a curriculum that would deal with the practical life by recognizing the role of theory in our participation in that life. The Practical would also reveal theory's incompleteness and inadequacies. Because theory existed as an abstraction from life, the practical offered means to understand the necessary incompleteness of that abstraction. If theory imparted knowledge "which is supposed to be true, warranted, confidence-inspiring" (Schwab, 1978, 288), then the practical "ends in a decision, a selection and guide to trustworthy action." Decisions, Schwab asserts, are never certain. To the Rabbis' offer of "Another interpretation would be. . . ," Schwab offered, "Another theory. . . ." If another interpretation offered something different to be done, then another theory offered another solution in the practical life. Problems in the theoretic arise from states of mind—awarenesses of what we do not know mapped out by what it is that we do already know. But problems in the practical arise from states of affairs, from our own personal feelings of "fulfilled needs and satisfied desires" (Schwab,1978, 289). Outcomes from the theoretic are more knowledge, but outcomes from the practical are events.

Schwab argued that education ought to make possible a life more satisfying because "These [practical and eclectic] arts are addressed to the underlying structure of theories. They are arts which identify the devices which confer the appearances of completeness on the subject" (1978, 330). The eclectic arts suggest the incompleteness of our knowledge and open the way to reconceptualized action based in an awareness of what theory has by definition left out. The practical would help us know what is to be done. The Practical "cannot be inductive because the target of the method is not a generalization or explanation, but a decision about action in a concrete situation. It cannot be deductive because it deals with the concrete cases and not abstractions from cases, and the concrete case cannot be settled by mere application of a principle, for almost every concrete case falls under two or more principles, and is not, therefore, a complete instance of either principle" (1978, 318). The Practical was deliberative. Because all theories are incomplete, it requires a community to engage in discourse regarding curricular matters. "It will require the formation of a new public and new means of communication among its constituent members. Deliberation requires consideration of the widest possible variety of alternatives if it is to be most effective. Each alternative must be viewed in the widest variety of lights. Ramifying consequences must be traced to all parts of the curriculum. The desirability of each alternative must be felt out, 'rehearsed,' by a representative variety of all those who must live with the consequences of a chosen action. And a similar variety must deal with the identification of problems as well as with their solution" (1978, 319). The P*irke Avot* (1:2) begins, "On three things the world depends: study, doing God's work, and performing deeds of kindness." Of course, the three deeds are not unrelated: one studies to learn what it might be to do God's work, which must always be based in and leads to deeds of kindness. The Talmud begins in recognition that action and study are inextricably connected: its first words are a question: "From what time may the requirement of the recitation of the *Sh'ma* be said?" As it is incumbent upon the observant Jew to take the words to heart, and to teach them diligently to the children, and to recite them in the morning and in the evening, then learning and doing lead inevitably to ethical action.

Schwab's work in curriculum practiced the rationale and method of talmudic discourse. I think Schwab advocated that the renaissance in curriculum would occur when its discourses and methods would be modeled after the work of the Rabbis of early part of the past millennium. David Kraemer (1990, 189) says "the Bavli, makes the imperfect and imperfectible pursuit of divine truth the very center of its enterprise. It concerns itself and its students with multiple interpretations of scripture, with multiple opinions of law, that is, with multiple approaches (but only approaches) to the truth. Even when it renders decisions or favors particular interpretations, the Bavli makes it clear that the process, and not the conclusion, is its utmost concern." This is the model of Schwab's deliberation, and the exemplar of his polyfocal conspectus. The aim of the Rabbis was behavior, but the source of behavior was deliberative thought. Study and learning were the intended outcomes.

SOMETHING TO DO

From its title, this final article (1983) appeared to draw full circle the agenda Schwab had drawn up in 1969 with his original charge to these same professors. Then, his first point was that the work that the professors had been doing had either a) killed the field of curriculum altogether, and/or b) took place in the killing fields where the body lay slain and disgustingly decomposed. In either case, in 1969 Schwab bewailed the dreadful practices of education then (and alas, even now) being practiced in the schools. In a sweeping accusation Schwab attributed the burgeoning social unrest of the young in the 1960s to the inadequacies and errors of the education to which they had been subject in the schools. In 1969, in the first of the series of articles on the practical, Schwab had urged that there would be a renaissance in curriculum only if energies were diverted from the theoretical to the practical, to the quasi-practical, and to the eclectic arts. In each of the first three papers, Schwab examined the moribund body of curriculum that had been asphyxiated by an excess of theory and by an absence of attentiveness to the practical—the sustaining and necessary vibrancy of breath. Curriculum, Schwab cried, was incapable of doing its work and contributing to the education of the students. New principles and new methods were required. In these papers (1969-1973), Schwab performed the necessary autopsy, ascribed the causes of death, and then, like Elisha, worked to revive the body.

If the curriculum choked from a excess of theory, it also drowned in a flood of objectives. Neither the theoretical nor the behaviorally objective would suffice: Schwab argued that theory and practice must be inevitably linked if curriculum was to benefit. "First, the particularities of each practical problem can be sought in the practical situation itself, the search guided by resources much richer than any one theory can afford. Second, in each instance of application of a borrowed theory to a practical situation, incongruities can be adjusted by mutual accommodation. Third, restricted subject and limited treatment so characteristic of behavioral theories can be transcended by using more than one such theory" (Schwab, 1978, 323). The three seminal articles explored the process by which a polyfocal conspectus could be achieved: "It is concerned with imparting to students a measure of inclination toward and competence for examining education situations and problems in more than one set of terms" (1978, 356). Schwab explored (theoretically) the causes of curriculum's demise and then offered means for its resuscitation. Schwab understood that the focus of curriculum had to be not on the achievement of a body of knowledge, but the means to understand and work with knowledge. The three articles advocate for the necessity of curriculum reform; a rationale for and a method of teaching polyfocal conspectus; and a structure for curriculum planning, work and reform in the schools. But what role should curriculum professors play if the idea of theory is to be abandoned? What are curriculum professors to do?

Schwab defined curriculum as ". . . what is successfully conveyed to differing degrees to different students, by committed teachers using appropriate materials and actions, of legitimated bodies of knowledge, skill, taste, and propensity to act and react, which are chosen for instruction after serious reflection and communal decision by representatives of those involved in the teaching of a specified group of students who are known to the decision makers" (1983, 240). It is complex and even a remarkable definition. Schwab asserts that curriculum is not subject matter at all, but what is done with that subject matter. Curriculum is not the material given but the material received. Schwab's definition asserts that curriculum is subject matter ***chosen for*** instruction but is not necessarily the matter of instruction. That is, what Schwab refers to as "endless strings of objectives," the matter of texts and lessons plans, trivialize and sterilize knowledge. "A linear movement from ends to means is absurd" (1983, 241). Rather, Schwab asserted that the materials chosen are resources of curriculum, but that curriculum can be defined only in the student. "A curriculum ought to be known by the persons it produces, as well as by other signs and standards" (1983, 247). Schwab asserted that it was the student who defined the curriculum.

Hebrew is a consonantal language: Its script appears without vowels, and the Rabbis employed such silences to produce wonderfully ingenious readings. Thus, the sentence, "I fell off of the ***hrs***," could be variously interpreted literally, I fell off the ***horse***, or figuratively, I fell off the ***hours***. Of course, for the Rabbis, different interpretations—sometimes those that might be dramatically opposed—are linked to the foundational ethic, "I am holy therefore, you shall be Holy," but the specificity of particular behaviors is left open. And Schwab writes: "A curriculum ought to be known by the persons it produces, as well as by other signs and standards." In the language of the Rabbis, I would offer, "read not '***known***,' a situation in the past, but rather, read '***knowing***,' a process active in the present. A curriculum ought to be a process—a process of thought resulting in action. Curriculum is not a body of facts, but a method of thinking about those facts to effect a doing. Curriculum is activity and qualitative rather than ideal, objective and quantifiable.

And so for me the question remains: What is to be done? What should curriculum professors do? It would seem to me that Schwab's charge was that curriculum professors should enable conversation. And clearly, conversation should result in activity. The Rabbis, as I have said, were concerned with action: From what time may one recite the *Sh'ma* in the evening? That is, how might obligation be measured with regard to the constraints of time. This is not an uninteresting question to educators. We are constrained always by time; we ourselves constrain time. And I would like to suggest that not only does the Rabbis' conversation prefigure Schwab's calling for deliberation, but the conclusions that the Rabbis reach seem to me embedded in what Schwab will call "the practical." The Rabbis discussion of obligation reconfigures the relationship between time and obligation and, in a very pre-Schwabian manner, argue for a liberality and for a possibility of doing—the character of an education available to all. The Rabbis mean to enable all to fulfill obligation in a reconfigured relationship to time. All may find the road to holiness.

OF TIME

I think lately a great deal about time. As I myself grow older, I am increasingly concerned with temporality. Now in my sixth decade, I discover that like Prospero, every third thought is of the grave. Time has become central to my existence. I wonder how much time remains to me; I wonder how I might best use my time remaining? What commitments ought I to make in the remaining time? How can I fulfill best my commitments in the time which remains?

Of course, as a teacher, time has always been central to my existence. My classrooms have been governed by the clanging of bells, and by the carefully graphed and charted scopes and sequences of particular grade levels and subject matters; I have been obliged by deadlines and notions of finals and terminal degrees. The American mainstream curricula in which I have for a lifetime participated has been predicated on "best practices," time honored methods that seem most effective in achieving with greatest efficiency and effectiveness previously (and often, professionally) planned objectives. Education has been structured on the existence of carefully defined developmental stages—physiological, psychological and moral grades through which "normal" children naturally move and unfold, as it were.[2] Education has been traditionally organized by the notion of age-appropriate materials, materials defined by the externally and objectively marked physical/emotional/intellectual years of the audience to which they are addressed. I have been in the schools forever constrained by the exams—standardized or self-constructed—that served to precisely locate a student's present position (and status!) in the educational community. My year has been punctuated by precise moments of school openings and closings; my days have been

[2]My daughter now labors under the label "pre-adolescent." She studies in a middle-school where she is known more by her reputed hormonal level and her sociability than by her interests and desires.

organized into discretely constructed time-delineated class periods; my months fixed into symmetrically set and designed semesters. My evenings are occupied with homework. So, too, is my children's time ordered. And, so, perhaps, is that of yours. Yes, I have, as it were, been obsessed in schools with time. I function minutely, hourly, and daily under the authority of time.

More, what occurs in schools is founded on the notion of time's obligations: We teach for the future. What is important in education is what *will* occur—although that is, by definition, not yet existent and certainly unknown. Franklin Bobbitt (1918, 42), to whom is ascribed the first book on curriculum in America and whose work remains a primary influence on American education, tells us that the curriculum ought to be a means to a pre-determined end. The curriculum is, he says, "that series of experiences which children and youth must do and experience by way of developing abilities to do the things well that make up the affairs of adult life; and to be in all respects what adults should be." School is a training ground for adult life. The present, in this conception, is non-existent, and there are no children here. Objectives—behaviors that will be changed—define the present and determine the future. Learning is identified as a change in behavior; objectives define what the student will be able to do in the future. Learning theory is, for the most part, formulated as an explanation of how certain aspects of behavior are changed with the greatest effectiveness and efficiency.

In this system, the past exists only to be changed, the past must be simply erased, and the school is charged with the creation of a suitable environment that will permit attainment of those adult behaviors that are not already learned from general experience or that are, alas, learned imperfectly. It is our job as educational workers to find the disease and cure it. "*The curriculum of the directed training*," Bobbitt (1918, 45, italics added) writes, "*is to be discovered in the shortcomings of individuals after they have had all that can be given by the undirected training*." Ralph Tyler (1949/1971) says that behavioral objectives must define what behavior is to be changed, assuming, I suppose, that excision leaves no scars. And more recently, Diane Ravitch (1995, 103), a direct philosophical descendant of Bobbitt and Tyler, says that "Teachers who know what the students' preconceptions are can help them understand new ideas and replace misconceptions." This remarkable sentence follows her acknowledgment that knowledge is actually constructed and that all knowledge is based on previous knowledge, experience, and understanding. Yet here she cates the mere excision of old knowledge and the implanting of new by the teacher. Would teaching were so easy as removing an appendix and inserting, say, a new stomach. Nevertheless, this should be accomplished, such educational theorists argue, with the greatest effectiveness and efficiency. The Report of the Committee on Economy of Time in Education (in Schubert et al., 1993)—from whose dictates I do not think we have far drifted—states that, "The period of general education is too long. . . . In the elementary and secondary periods, economy through selection, elimination, vital methods, relation to modern life, would yield much better results, and little or nothing would be lost by the proposed change in time." Indeed, the invention of the middle school curriculum in the 1980s introduces job skills into the lives of *eleven years olds*. For the Committee, time is being wasted in the schools; our obligation is to the future. It is efficiency and not quality with which the committee is concerned; it is economy and not excellence that the committee seeks. Time has an objective status and can be handled and manipulated, but time is not itself a factor immanent within education. Time is not a human construct.

A semester begins, and I am again consumed with time's obligations. I must develop course syllabi under the constraint of the organizationally structured semester length of sixteen weeks. I must organize the course content and plan assignments. How much should students be obliged to read each week? How much should each student be obliged to complete by the end of the semester? During the sixteen weeks, how much of what I may know must I oblige students to actually learn? During the sixteen weeks, how much of what I may know might students be capable of learning? How much of what I know am I actually obliged to teach to students during the sixteen week semester? How much writing must students be obliged to produce during the sixteen weeks? How much time in reflection should I oblige them to engage? How much fulfilled obligation will earn a grade of "A?" Is obligation to be understood as only the completion of work directed by another? As the semester begins—indeed, as more than thirty beginnings of school years have begun—I am very much concerned with time's obligations, how I am bound and frustrated by time.

I am concerned, as well, with how I compel the time of others and by what authority I obligate that time. I want active engagement in learning, but what do I teach when I obligate the time of others? Do I define their reality by time or by the obligation? How does the reality of time impose and determine obligations? My life in schools has been defined by time's obligation. I realize that there is never enough time—all that I consider central to the learning could not be contained in even an eternal series of sixteen weeks. I inevitably must fail. Sometimes, I realize that there is just too much of time. Course work becomes defined by the time spent in expected attendance and passive hearing, which may not be listening at all! Requirements substitute for the idea of responsibility. Students look for only the minimum demanded so that they can complete them satisfactorily. Or not. I inevitably must fail. But recently, my readings and studies in Talmud and Joseph Schwab have begun to suggest another possibility. If the obligations imposed by time lead inevitably to failure, then how might I better succeed to consider the reverse: to understand that obligation defines time.

Of course, the Rabbis do not speak explicitly of curriculum, and I have always wondered in schools what is to be done. Nor does Schwab speak directly of the Rabbis, though his discourse seems solidly based in their teachings. But through the influence of one very dear friend, William Pinar, and discussions with three wonderful colleagues, Peter Appelbaum, Vicki Hillis and Molly Quinn, I had been rereading some of the work of Dwayne Huebner. On Bill's kind request, a recent reissue of his early book *Curriculum Studies: The Reconceptualization* (1975/2000) arrived at my office recently. That text has been declared one of the hundred greatest books concerning education in the twentieth century, and Huebner had contributed four essays to this wonderful collection. Vicki Hillis has been responsible for editing a wonderful collection of Huebner's essays, *The Lure of the Transcendent*, and Molly has long worked and studied under the influence of Huebner. For years, Peter and I have explored what is already Jewish about curriculum. As I read the Huebner essays, I felt as if I sat with my friend and colleagues. I was, as it were, obligated to them.

How all occasions do inform against me. Since I had already been thinking about time when this volume arrived, I was particularly drawn to Huebner's essay about time and education, "Curriculum as a Concern for Man's Temporality." Huebner asserts (1975/2000, 244) that as time "arises out of our human existence," then it is possible to consider that the human being might be cherished as time realized. Time, as Einstein has earlier suggested, is relative; it does not exist apart from our experience of it. Time is not an absolute entity existing everywhere alike and the same. Huebner (1975/2001) writes:

> Time is not a dimension in which we live—a series of "nows," some past and some in the future. Man does not have so many "nows" allotted. He does not simply await a future and look back upon a past. The very notion of time arises out of man's existence, which is emergent. The future is man facing himself in anticipation of his own potentiality for being. The past is finding himself already thrown into a world. . . .The present is the moment of vision when *Dasein*[3], finding himself thrown into a situation (the past) projects his own potentiality for being. (in Pinar, 2000, 244)

I near the end of my daily six-mile run. I am fatigued and I breathe heavily. One hundred yards before me my mailbox comes into view, and I anticipate the cessation of running and the end of my effort. Every stride—the present—draws me closer to my driveway—the future, and every step is filled with the twenty-five years of running steps that precede it—the past. Every step occurs in the moment. Every step contains all of the previous moments. And every step draws me closer not only to its cessation but toward tomorrow's run. The present is the accumulated past, only some of which is known (why, for example, did I choose to run in the first place?), and it projects and therefore contains a future that is also uncertain. Time is myself in the world. Time is my being-in-the world. In the creation and fulfillment of the obligation, I create time in the fulfilled obligation of running. When I run, I am a runner. I am time.

The dominant language of education eschews such realization. It clearly demarcates the past, a student's ability as measured by aptitude and/or achievement tests, from the future, the established (and standardized) educational objectives that define behavioral outcomes. Education ignores the present. But, Huebner suggests, to ignore the present is to negate the past and to deny the freedom the future offers. To ignore the present is to deny being-in-the-world. I may run every day, but what particular course I choose and what distance I run and speed I attain are always subject to variation depending on short and long term goals, as well as physical and mental conditions and environmental constraints. For example, where I live the wind chill can sometimes plummet to minus 30°F. There are days when I am all dressed up to run, but when I stick my head out, I pull it right back in and proceed to another activity. I think that to set objectives in terms of someone else's idea of a future without regard for the temporality of the human being is

---

[3]This is Heidegger's concept of "being-in-the-world."

to commit educational malpractice. To ignore the future is to ignore the potentiality of being and to disregard the hopes and dreams and desires of the student. To ignore the future is not to hear, or more seriously, to refuse to attend to the student's demand that ought to be the teacher's ultimate responsibility. The future is potential made available by freedom in the present. There are days when I take my thoughts out on the roads and discover the wonder of an additional several miles and a new route. Or an older route made anew. Huebner argues that the contemporary language and thought of education misrepresents the lived experience of time and, therefore, help organize a curriculum that refuses tragically to recognize the severe limits that present categories of educational objectives and experiences represent. To assume that learning occurs solely within the mind of the individual apart from that individual's being-in-the-world is to falsify the very notion of learning and to negate the humanity of the student.

Huebner argues (1975/2000, 244) that the challenge to the educator "is to find a way to talk about man's temporality which will increase his professional power in the world." I admire Huebner's subtlety here. I think his declaration suggests that the challenge to the educator is to find a way to talk about man's temporality so that the teacher can function at all. Without such concern, all effort would be fruitless. I am reminded of the disenchanted words of a student quoted in Herbert Kohl's essay, "I won't learn from you" (1994, 30). Paul says about his school experience: "People tell you if you don't go along with the program, you'll mess up your life . . . [but] It's their education. Not mine. It's their history, Not mine. It's their language. Not mine. You name it. It's theirs." What temporality is accounted for here? Who is paying attention to time at all? Without attention to temporality, there can be no attention to the student. Without attention to temporality, there is no obligation to the student. It is not to Paul's past, present or future with which the school is concerned. It is not to Paul that the school is obliged. Paul refuses to participate.

Huebner argues that unless curriculum accounts for human temporality, then it must ultimately fail exactly for those for whom it must be designed. Huebner writes: "The student, either by his own understanding or that of others, must be able to envision his own projected potentiality for being as it exists in the past-present-future. This is the uniquely human quality of the [educational] environment and requires the presence of human wisdom. This is the unique function of the teacher . . . who shares the rhythms of continuity and change, of necessity and freedom, with his students" (1975/2000, 249). That is, change in the present depends on the notion of continuity from the past; the necessity of the present should lead to freedom in the future. Schools must address the student as temporal beings. Marx had said that "Men make their own history, but they do not make it just as they please; they do not make it under circumstances chosen by themselves, but under circumstances directly encountered, given and transmitted from the past" (1984, 15). Curriculum must take account of the past, but it must also promote the student's capacity to envision and enact a future. Curriculum should provide the student with the power not only to dream, but with the willingness and command to strive for a fulfillment of those dreams. Curriculum is not something that happens to the student individually and in isolation, but something that connects the student to her/his world: stimulating an awareness of the world's effect on her/him, and authorizing her competence to change that world and her/himself in the world. Curriculum must, indeed, be concerned with human temporal concerns.

FROM WHAT TIME?

"From what time may one recite the *Sh'ma* in the evening?" (*Berakhot* 2a)

Over the past several years, I have been studying Talmud down here in my basement office. I think that the Rabbis of the Talmud have something to say about such curricular issues that now concern me. The first tractate of the Babylonian Talmud, *Berakhot*, is very much concerned with time. Indeed, the first subject in Talmud addresses this very issue concerning the relationship between time and obligation. The commandment to recite the *Sh'ma*, Judaism's central declaration of faith, is a Rabbinic creation; that is, unlike the overtly directive Ten Commandments and the approximately 613 positive and negative commandments in Scripture itself, there is nothing in Torah thatexactly mandates this central practice of the twice-daily recitation of the *Sh'ma*. Though the words of Torah state that *"You shall speak of them when you lie down and when you rise up,"* the Rabbis chose to interpret this phrase literally rather than figuratively. They had only to institutionalize the antecedent of "them." During the invention of the liturgy and the development of Jewish spiritual practice, the Rabbis established the regular recitation of this declaration of faith: "Hear O Israel, the Lord our God the Lord is One" (*Deuteronomy* 4:4). The complete prayer, called the *Sh'ma*, consists of this declaration and three appended paragraphs derived from three different parts of the *Torah*.[4] These three paragraphs (*Deuteronomy* 6:4-9; *Deuteronomy* 11:13-21; *Numbers* 15:37-41) were added to the original declarative statement on thematic grounds, noted below. Thus, the Rabbis declared that the original declaration (*Hear O Israel* . . .) and the three subsequent paragraphs constituted the entire *Sh'ma*, the prayer that required twice daily recitation. Contained within the first two paragraphs (*Deuteronomy* 6:7 and 11:19), which immediately follow the original declaration, is the Biblical command that you should *"speak of them when you lie down and when you rise up."* The antecedent to "them" in the first paragraph of the *Sh'ma* refers apparently to the declaration of love and loyalty to the One God; in the second paragraph "them" refers to Jewish beliefs and Jewish practices. The third paragraph institutes a pedagogical tool to ensure education—the wearing of tassels (*tzitzit*) to ensure that the obligation be remembered. The entire *Sh'ma* is the Jew's declaration of faith, of the need for ethical practice, and of the necessity for continued study and learning. These three paragraphs, asserts Elliot Dorff (1997, 88), "articulate the heart of Jewish faith." Their continued presence in the liturgy is integral to Jewish identity and practice, and the Rabbis regularized this praxis in their institution of the twice daily recitation.

However, since the Torah insists that these words (*them*) be recited "*when you lie down and when you rise up*," the Rabbis wonder from what time in the evening (*"when you lie down"*) and from what time in the morning (*"when you rise up"*) may the *Sh'ma* be said. When exactly does evening begin? When is evening ended? From what time may one say the morning *Sh'ma*? When begins the day? When is day over? When begins our obligation? When is our obligation ended? Time appears very much a factor in these questions. I think these questions about obligation and time are very relevant to the work of teachers.

The Rabbis trouble the notion of time in this section of Talmud. The mitzvot of the recitation of the *Sh'ma* must be accomplished in time, but when is time? What is time? We must remember that the fulfillment of mitzvot is the achievement of holiness—God's statement, "I am holy,

---

[4]The Torah is the first Five Books of Moses and comprises the Jewish Scriptures.

so you should be holy" (*Leviticus* 19:1) is the motive behind all of the hermeneutic scholarship concerning the meaning of Torah. The meaning of time is not abstract—it is practical and consequential. Hillel would say, "If I am not for myself, who will be; if I am only for myself, what am I; if not now, when?" Indeed, in the fulfillment of obligation, time can be understood as life-affirming.

Various individual, Rabbinic responses to the question "From what time . . ." are proffered. Some Rabbis say that evening begins from the time that the priests eat their offering; that is, evening begins when the sun has set. An alternative response is given by Rabbi Eliezer who declares that one may recite the evening *Sh'ma* from the end of the first watch—at least three or four hours into the night's passing. The sages—unnamed Rabbis—offer still another opinion. They say that the evening *Sh'ma* may be recited even after midnight. A last opinion is offered: Rabbi Gamaliel avers that one may recite the evening *Sh'ma* even to the moment right up until dawn! The movement here is toward the greater possibility of fulfilling the obligation rather than toward the insistence of its fulfillment in narrow time. The movement here is away from time's obligation to obligation's time. Here, fulfilling the obligation creates the time in which the obligation is fulfilled. The effect is the creation of a greater potential for the achievement of holiness. Time is created in the obligation, and the fulfillment of the obligation leads to holiness.

Indeed, so intent are the Rabbis to ensure observance, that Rabbi Shimon bar Yohai declares that one may even recite the *Sh'ma* twice during the night and, therefore, fulfill one's duty for the recitation of the *Sh'ma* for both night and day. One of Rabbi Shimon's colleagues raises a vigorous objection: This dissenting Rabbi points out that Rabbi Shimon bar Yohai's declaration represents a contradiction because to say that one may recite the *Sh'ma* twice at *night* implies that it *is* night and, therefore, the recitation would occur at night and obviously may not qualify for the fulfillment of the recitation of *Sh'ma* during the day. Not so, the Rabbis remarkably reason: There is no contradiction at all! The Rabbis maintain that Shimon bar Yohai's assertion is valid because though it may appear night to some here, it is, indeed, already day to someone somewhere else!! Thus, since day always exists somewhere, by this reasoning one fulfills the daytime obligation for the *Sh'ma* even if it is recited at night.

Actual time has become irrelevant and is replaced with by a time that comes into existence with the engagement in obligation.

A remarkable rationale I believe. The Rabbis have rationalized time into being—whenever one says the *Sh'ma*, then it is the right time of day. I am reminded of Thoreau, my ideal candidate for latter-day Talmudist. He contended that that day dawns *only to which we are awake*!! Thoreau felt measured time to be irrelevant; rather, time is defined by human action. For Thoreau, as for the Rabbis, time is defined by our actions rather than our actions being defined by the time in which they occur. If I thought Thoreau had read Talmud, I would ascribe Rabbinic influence to his thought. I believe that the Rabbis of the Talmud preceded Thoreau's philosophical position. It would seem that the fulfillment of the mitzvot is of greater consequence that the fulfillment of the mitzvot *in specific time*. We may say that for the Rabbis of the Talmud, the completion of the mitzvot defines time rather than time defining the performance of the mitzvot. Indeed, if the mitzvot are fulfilled *in time* but the performance and/or intention is suspect, then it is as if the mitzvot have not even been accomplished. For example, if one recites the paragraphs of the *Sh'ma* in an improper order, then the obligation remains unfulfilled even if it is recited at the proper time. Furthermore, the Rabbis say that, "the validity of the act [of reciting the *Sh'ma*] depends on the mental concentration." For the Rabbis, it would appear that time and being are equivalent and both exist materially in the world.

For the Rabbis of the Talmud, time comes into being in the fulfillment of our obligation. The fluid perspective taken on time by the Rabbis suggests that though we are obliged by time, in fact, our fulfillment of the obligation defines that time. Obligation's time. Our actions occur in time, but we are the time in which our actions are accomplished. We are time. And, since human beings are time, we are obligation. We stand, then, as ethics. To fulfill a mitzvot is to move toward holiness. As human beings we are our obligation. "If I am not for myself, who will be? If I am only for myself, what am I? If not now, when?"

TIME AND OBLIGATION

> Women, slaves and minors are exempt from reciting the *Sh'ma* and from putting on tefillin, but they are subject to the obligations of *tefillah* and *mezuzah* and grace after meals. (Berkhot, 17b)

As I have said, I have been thinking a great deal about time of late. And now, under the influence of the Rabbis, I begin to wonder not how our actions in school are obliged by time (of that I am already well aware), but how in schools we might *establish* time through our obligations. To conceptualize in this manner, my world in schools might be created in obligation. Time would come into existence through my obligation rather than time being the constraint on it. This differing notion of time would, I think, establish very different classrooms. Inevitably, time and obligations are intrinsic to the classroom; if curriculum must concern itself with human temporality, then it must as well be concerned with obligation. I know what an assignment might be, even must be, but how might the conceptualization of that school/classroom obligation change under Rabbinic influence. And so I am intrigued by how the Rabbis consider "obligation." I am aware of how obligation is often defined: the incumbency to effect a specific action. But how is responsibility for obligation ascribed? If obligation is eternal, then who is eternally obliged and what constitutes the obligation. In Chapter III of *Berakhot*, quoted above, the Rabbis address these issues in their intricate discussions concerning specific exemptions from obligation. Perhaps if the Rabbis can understand for whom and by what means exemption from obligation is fixed, then they might understand what obligation might be to those who are *halalchically*[5] bound.

A mishnah[6] in Chapter III in *Berakhot*, the first tractate of the voluminous Babylonian Talmud, states: "Women, slaves, and minors are exempt from reciting the *Sh'ma* and from putting on tefillin, but they are subject to the obligations of tefillah and mezuzah and grace after meals." Our Mishnah states that women, slaves, and minors are exempt from the recitation of the *Sh'ma* and from wearing tefillin, but they are nevertheless obliged to recite the thrice-daily silent prayer, place and acknowledge the mezuzah on the doorpost of the house, and recite grace

---

[5]This is an neologic hybrid. In Hebrew, *halacha* means "law," but the -ly suffix is an Americanism and transforms the word into an adverb meaning "by law."

[6]A statement of law.

after meals. Now, this mishnah seems to accord with another segment of law (*Kiddushin,* 29a) that frees women from all positive, time-bound *mitzvot. Mitzvot* are acts ordained (or forbidden) by Torah that must be fulfilled to live an exemplary practical and spiritual life. The fulfillment of *mitzvot* is compelled by Torah and are central to Judaism and Jewish practice. To participate in Judaism, to be a Jew, is to fulfill the mitzvot.

Now, as I have shown above, the Rabbis argued that time comes into existence by the fulfillment of obligation, rather than the obligation having to be fulfilled within an exactly specified time. It might be that women might be rabbinically freed from time-bound mitzvot, but, as the Rabbis themselves have argued, time only comes into existence with the fulfillment of obligation. Everything might be considered a time-bound mitzvot since fulfillment creates the time in which the obligation must be met. The Rabbis appear to have argued themselves into an uncomfortable and untenable position: They have obliged the recitation of the *Sh'ma* not to time but to being, but here they absolve women, slaves, and minors from being.

I suppose one could argue that, indeed, the misogyny of the Rabbis define women (and slaves and minors) as less than being, but the movement of their thinking reveals the Rabbis are struggling to overcome their own misogyny. I think they recognize their contradictions and work to explain them in a manner that seeks to enlarge their culturally-imposed bounds. This is the argument of Judith Hauptman in her book, *Rereading the Rabbis* (1998, 4). There she argues that though the Rabbis clearly upheld the patriarchy "as the preordained mode of social organization . . . they began to introduce numerous, significant, and occasionally bold corrective measures to ameliorate the lot of women . . . From their own perspective the rabbis were seeking to close the gap that had developed over time between more enlightened social thinking and women's more subordinate status as defined by the received texts, biblical and rabbinic, without openly opposing such texts." Daniel Boyarin argues in *Carnal Israel* (1993, 242) that Rabbinic texts may be read to recover "feminist" voices. "The texts when read in the way that I am proposing to read them do not only reflect a dissident proto-feminist voice within Classical Judaism; they constitute such a voice." I do not intend to deal here with the reasons why women, slaves, and minors are *halalchically* exempt from the fulfillment of time-bound mitzvot: This issue has been dealt with insightfully by Judith Hauptman (1998). Nor do I wish to excuse the misogyny expressed in too much of

Torah and liturgy. Hauptman argues (1998, 4) that the Rabbis struggled—sometimes even boldly—to "ameliorate the lot of women" who had been relegated to second-class social status. Clearly this present Mishnah strains to make sense of the apparent contradiction, and in so doing may offers not only a deconstruction of the Rabbis' own notion of class, but also offers insight into notions of time and obligation that might serve curriculum thought.

The Rabbis have shown how the mitzvot of the recitation of the *Sh'ma* is not, in fact, time-bound; indeed, it is the recitation of the *Sh'ma* that creates time. Thus, the Rabbis have apparently bound women, slaves, and children to that from which they have been already freed by another section of law; in the fulfillment of this mitzvot the Rabbis have made all equal. In defining time by obligation rather than defining the obligation by specific time, the Rabbis have included women, slaves, and minors to the obligations through which holiness is achieved. Indeed, by the Rabbi's standard, no one within the community could be exempt from obligation. If all obligation creates time, and we are all always obliged to holiness—you shall be to Me a community of priests—then we are forever obliged. Time is when we fulfill obligation. Time and obligation are synonymous.

It is at first interesting that the Rabbis have argued that the obligation in time to the fulfillment of the time-bound mitzvot may be liberally interpreted. That is, to ensure that the mitzvot are enacted, the Rabbis are prepared to define time by the action rather than to commit the valid action to a specific time. Thus, the recitation of the *Sh'ma* by men may occur—within clear limits[7]—in such a broad range of time as to render time's constraints veritably meaningless. Since by their reasoning the Rabbis have shown how the time-bound mitzvot of the recitation of the *Sh'ma* is not, in fact, time-bound, then the Rabbis are now bound to explain the specific exemption for women, minors, and slaves from a seeming, but not actual, -time-bound mitzvot. Here, the anonymous objector says that since women are exempt from time-bound mitzvot, then the statement in the present mishnah—that women are exempt from the saying of the *Sh'ma*—is obvious and therefore, unnecessary. It is redundant. Since redundancies must be explained, then an explanation

---

[7]For example, though one can say two *Sh'mas* at one time, this does not permit one to say seven *Sh'mas* to make up for a week of non-observance.

must be sought. Alternatively, it is reasoned, since the *Sh'ma* mentions the acceptance of the sovereignty of God, which is always true, then the *Sh'ma* is *not* a time-bound mitzvot and women, slaves, and minors ought to be bound to its recitation. We have already seen that though the *Sh'ma* is very much tied to time—*when you lie down and when you rise up*—that time has been liberally defined almost out of absolute existence. Whenever the mitzvot are fulfilled, then it is time. Thus, the Rabbis, apparently confronted with an untenable contradiction respond: This exemption must be stated explicitly in this Mishnah to indicate that though it would appear otherwise and that women, slaves, and minors ought to be bound, in fact women, slaves, and minors are not so obliged. But, by the Rabbi's reasoning, they apparently ought very much to be obligated.

One conclusion we might reach is that we are obligated until we are specifically exempted. Our obligation is forever confirmed; only an explicit exemption frees us. Since mitzvot lead to holiness, the Rabbis liberally make possible the fulfillment of them and, therefore, severely limit exemption. The Rabbis' reasoning suggests that these obligations are, as it were, ,*non*-time bound and, therefore, all human beings—regardless of gender, class or age—are bound to the mitzvot. Though the Rabbis will struggle with their cultural misogyny, finally they accede to the obligation for all. It is an interesting progression. Though the Rabbis specifically exempt women, slaves, and minors from fulfilling the *mitzvot*, by their own reasoning their exemption is invalid. The remainder of the Rabbis reasoning will, in fact, reinforce this obligation.

OBLIGATION'S TIME

Now, women are in this Mishnah bound by Rabbinic decree to the obligation of *mezuzah*—the placement of the words of the *Sh'ma* on the doorpost (*"and you shall write them upon the doorposts of your house and upon your gates," Deuteronomy* 6:9 and 11:20). Women are obliged, then, to the continual acknowledgment of God's sovereignty if not to the verbal recitation of it. Thus, it is reasoned, women, slaves and minors ought also to be obliged to putting on tefillin. This would be apparent because the *Sh'ma* mandates that you should *"Bind them as a sign upon your arm and let them be ornaments between your eyes"* (Deuteronomy 6:8 and 11:18). Thus, it is reasoned, if women, slaves, and minors are bound to the mitzvot of the mezuzah—writing the words on the doorposts—then they ought to be obliged to binding the words by putting on tefillin. The Rabbis once more aver that though it would *appear* that women, slaves, and minors must be so bound, this mishnah's specific exemption mandates that this is not so. Again, the Rabbis have to explicitly exempt women, slaves, and minors, because by their own logic, they should be obliged. But to my mind—and I think those of the Rabbis—the logic of the obligation carries far greater strength than the logic of the exemption from it. Though time appears to be a factor in the obligation to action, in fact, the Rabbis have reasoned that the action defines the time. Thus, there must be no exemption from obligation. Therefore, the Rabbis state that they must explicitly mention the exemption, but it is to my mind too obviously apparent that the exemption is a cultural artifact and not a religious one; that is, the exemption of women, slaves, and minors has nothing to do with God. Participation in these obligations is universal. Time has nothing to do with it.

Indeed, this appears to be the thrust of subsequent objections. How is it, it is asked, that women, slaves, and minors are subject to tefillah[8] since prayer, too, is time-bound? Indeed, the Rabbis quote *Psalm 55:18*: "evening, morning and noon I supplicate and moan; and God has heard my voice," to justify the notion of time bound prayer. If women are freed from time-bound mitzvot, then they ought not to be obliged to tefillah. The answer the Rabbis give is that just as the Rabbis specifically exempted women, slaves, and minors from the recitation of the *Sh'ma* to which they ought to be obliged, so do the Rabbis specifically oblige women to prayer, though by their own dictum they should be exempt. Again, the exemption is clearly of cultural origin and not religious.

Finally, women are said to be not exempt from the fulfillment of the commandment of *mezuzah*. The *mezuzah* is a scroll placed on the doorposts of the house (*"you shall place them on the doorposts of your house")*. This commandment, as well, is defined in the *Sh'ma* from which the Rabbis have legally exempted women, slaves, and minors, though they have, we have seen, by their logic, in fact, obliged them. Because the *mezuzah* are the words of Torah from which study women are exempt, then the Rabbis argue the explicit statement of obligation to the *mitzvot*

[8] *Tefillah* may refer to a period of prayer (morning, afternoon, and night) or it may refer to a specific prayer (the Silent Benediction–the Amidah), which Jews recite in each prayer service. Either way, women should be exempt from this time-bound commitment.

must be made. In each of these exceptions, the Rabbis suggest that, in fact, time is not at all the criteria for obligation. Rather, the responsibility for exemption is a cultural decision and must be owned as such. Obligation is complete. The Rabbis assume that responsibility of naming exemptions, but the logic of their explanations seems to oblige everyone all of the time.

It is apparent from the Rabbis' reasoning, that whatever leads to holiness ought not to be bound by time. Rather, the Rabbis' reasoning suggests that time actually comes into existence by the fulfillment of the *mitzvot.* Holiness is the attainment of a spirituality that governs our everyday stance in the world. I am holy, therefore you should be holy, are God's words in *Leviticus* (19:1). Try as they might, the Rabbis cannot exempt women, slaves, and minors from this imperative. And that is good, for we ought all be obliged to aspire to holy deeds. Heschel says: "It is not by the rare act of greatness that character is determined, but by everyday actions, by a constant effort to rend our callousness. It is constancy that sanctifies . . . Through the constant rhythm of prayers, disciplines, reminders, joys, [man] is taught not to forfeit his grandeur" (1955, 384). It is in our deeds that we achieve our humanity, and our deeds ought to be the fulfillment of mitzvot. No one—not men, women, slaves, or minors—must be exempt from these obligations, regardless of time: The Rabbis cannot find their way out of this mandate. Time cannot mitigate our obligation because our obligation creates the time in which it is fulfilled.

This is further shown in the next section of the discussion. The Rabbis have obliged women to recite grace after meals. Grace after meals is the only blessing explicitly required by Torah: It is a positive commandment. *Deuteronomy* 8:10 says, "You will eat and you will be satisfied, and bless Adonai, your God, for the good Land that God gave you." Moshe (*Exodus* 16:8, 12) defines the time of eating saying, "When, in the evening God gives you meat to eat and bread to satiety in the morning. . . . In the afternoon you shall eat meat and in the morning you shall be sated with bread, and you shall know that I am Adonai, your God." Therefore, it would appear that grace after meals ought also to be understood as a positive, time-bound Mitzvot from which women *ought to be* exempt. But, in fact, again the Rabbis argue that though it would *appear* that grace after meals is a positive time-bound mitzvot, this is not so. No further explanation is forthcoming at this time; though I will show there is one implicit. Women are, indeed, obliged to recite grace after meals, and from the acknowledgment of this obligation the Rabbis will negate the notion of time's obligation and impose the rule of obligation's time.

RABBINICAL OR SCRIPTURAL?

I am interested in the wonderful logic by which the Rabbis oblige women to time-bound mitzvot from which they ought to be exempt, and how they thus define time by obligation rather than defining obligation by time. The Rabbis are very much concerned with time in the present—wonderfully so, I think. How to set holiness as their goal and exempt some from the achievement of holiness is clearly an issue and a problem here. And so they move onto a related but separate topic: Women are obliged to sanctify the Sabbath—to make Kiddush over the fruit of the vine. Since the Sabbath is bound in time, sanctification is a time-bound mitzvot from which women ought to be exempt. And furthermore, says Abaye, the obligation to sanctify the Sabbath with wine is a rabbinical dictum; it is legally binding on all. The obligation here originates from human and not scriptural origin, but nevertheless it is recognized as completely valid and completely binding. Abaye returns to the issue of cultural mandates: The obligation to say Kiddush derives from Rabbinic authority; therefore, women may be bound since the Rabbis are established (and have been establishing themselves) as authoritative on halachic matters. But, says Raba, another discussant in the present issue, Torah commands that everyone must "Remember the Sabbath day." Either women ought to be included in "everyone" and obliged to sanctify the Sabbath by *scriptural* authority rather than by *rabbinic* authority, or else the sanctification of Sabbath according to scriptural authority is time bound from which women ought to be exempt. Besides, Raba acknowledges, if Rabbinic authority could subject them to sanctification of Sabbath, then why could not Rabbinic authority oblige them to all mitzvot.

Raba is cautious—he senses the slippery slope and so to validate the Rabbi's directives, he turns to the ultimate authority, Scripture, for justification. The *Kiddush*—the blessing over the wine—sanctifies the Sabbath day and, as the present case suggests, women are obliged to recite this blessing. However, since the sanctification of the Sabbath is subject to time, then women, slaves, and minors ought to be exempt.

The contradiction must be explained! Raba must be also cautious not to ascribe final authority to the Rabbis, lest they come to assert full authority for everything. Raba turns to two related passages: two versions of the ten commandments. *Exodus* 20:8 commands that the people must "*Remember* the Sabbath Day to sanctify it," and *Deuteronomy* 5:12 commands that the people must "*Observe* the Sabbath day to sanctify it." Thus, Raba explains, that whoever has to observe, to abstain from work, must also have to remember, to sanctify. Therefore, since women are obliged to observe the Sabbath day, they are also obliged to sanctify it. Sanctification is not a separate time-bound mitzvot nor one of Rabbinic authority—it is natural. Raba has effectively transformed time into human psychological terms—obligation is in this fashion, inevitable. And therefore, obligation is natural and not bound by time—rather, obligation creates time.

Once the can has been opened, the worms escape. The mishnah obligates women to say grace after meals, but the question is raised: Is the obligation of women to recite grace Scriptural or Rabbinic. The Rabbis wonder: Who cares? Isn't an obligation, regardless of its source, nevertheless binding? As long as the authority of the Rabbis is clear, then it is inconsequential whether the obligation derives from them or the scripture. Not so, a Rabbi objects. This Rabbi says that in fact, the source of the obligation is a factor, because if the obligation is only Rabbinically derived, then women, slaves, and minors may not perform the duty *on the behalf* of others. That is, only those bound by scripture may perform duties on behalf of another bound by scripture. But, if one is bound only by Rabbinic authority, then one may not fulfill the obligation for those who are bound by scripture. That is, how do we come to be obliged and, finally, for whom are we obliged? Some of the Rabbis may be attempting to redraw authority to ensure male dominance.

But there are some Rabbis who are yet uncomfortable in this area. The question is: Are women, slaves, and minors bound by Scripture or Rabbinic authority? That, the Rabbis argue, is not the question. They have already established (though, as I have shown above, they also contradict their own establishment) that only men are bound to time-bound mitzvot. Though it appears that grace is a time-bound mitzvah from which women, slaves, and minors ought to be exempt, the present discussion claims that they are obliged to say grace. The authority for this mandate is in question, however: If a person, in this case, women, slaves, and minors, is only Rabbinically bound, can they be responsible for one who is actually scripturally bound, that is, men? Can a son say grace for his father, or can a women say grace for her husband? Can a slave say grace for her master? The question here concerns under what circumstances may a person who is Rabbinically bound to the recitation of grace perform the obligation for another who is scripturally bound.

And the (ir)resolution of the contradiction astonishes me: "With what case are we dealing here? If, for instance, he ate a quantity for which he is only Rabbinically bound [to say grace], in which case one who is Rabbinically bound comes and performs the duty on behalf of one who is only Rabbinically bound." That is, if a person (a Jewish male) who might be (scripturally) obliged to say grace eats a quantity of food established by the Rabbis as requiring grace, but does not or cannot say grace, then one who is scripturally not bound to say grace but is Rabbinically so obliged (women, slaves and minors) may recite it for him.

WITH WHAT QUANTITY ARE WE DEALING HERE?

That is, the issue seems to concern what are the limits of our obligation to the other. Though the Torah mandates the saying of grace after eating, the Torah does not define what quantity constitutes a meal sufficient for grace. Oh, God states that "when you eat and are satisfied" you must bless God, but exactly what quantity constitutes satisfaction? And so the Rabbis establish a limit. They say (*Berakhot* 45a), "How much must one have eaten to count? As much as an olive; R. Judah says, as much as an egg." Rabbinically, one is bound to say grace after eating the volume equal to that of either an olive (Rabbi Meir) or an egg (Rabbi Judah). That is, a handful of M&Ms obliges us to give thanks for our blessings! Thus, the Rabbis reason, since the quantity requiring grace is Rabbinically defined, the obligation to say grace *for another* must be tied to the rabbinic quantity. If one eats so much as the quantity of an olive or an egg, then one is obliged to say grace. And since women are Rabbinically obliged to say grace, then they may say grace even for one who is scripturally bound and who has eaten a quantity prescribed by Rabbinic authority but for some reason is not capable of reciting grace. The Rabbis have obliged women (and, of course, men) to recite grace for another who has eaten even the smallest portion—our obligation is limitless and forever.

FROM WHAT TIME?

I think in the discussion concerning the times from which the *Sh'ma* must be recited, the Rabbis have effectively obviated the dominance of time in the achievement of holiness. Indeed, rather than time defining the observance of obligation, time comes into being with obligation. By effectively removing the structure of time's obligation, the Rabbis have effectively obliged everyone to the fulfillment of mitzvot. One of my favorite stories is Thoreau's narrative of the artist of Kouroo who was disposed to strive after perfection. That artist meant to make a staff, but considering that in an imperfect work time is an ingredient, but in a perfect work time does not enter as a factor, he set out to make a perfect work though he should do nothing else in his life.

> He proceeded instantly to the forest for wood, being resolved that it should not be made of unsuitable material, and as he searched for and rejected stick after stick, his friends gradually deserted him, for they grew old and died, but he grew not older by a moment. His singleness of purpose and resolution, and his elevated piety, endowed him, without his knowledge, with perennial youth. As he made no compromise with Time, Time kept out of his way, and only sighed at a distance because he could not overcome him. (Thoreau, 1970, 442)

It is not perfection the Rabbis seek, of course, it is holiness. Holiness is a relationship; that is, it is achieved in the exercise of daily lives lived in community. There are obligations inherent—ways of being that underlie all daily life: "You shall love your neighbor as yourself." Obligation is an achieving and not an achievement, and for the Rabbis as for the artist of Kouroo, time can be no limiting factor. Obligation is forever and for everyone. Our obligations are complete and in community. For Thoreau, the effort of the artist was an individual and singular one; while he endeavored to achieve perfection, all of his friends passed away and the world came to ruin. But for the Rabbis the purpose of mitzvot is the repair of the world—*tikkun olam*. For the Rabbis, it is not the ignorance of time that is paramount but rather, the sense of obligation that creates time. The *Sh'ma* is bound by time—its recitation must be daily recited. But the *Sh'ma*'s diurnal time is defined by its recitation—within the broadest of borders the *Sh'ma* must be said *when you lie down and when you rise up*. The Rabbis very liberally give humans the range of the entire day to fulfill the obligation. Indeed, when the obligation is fulfilled, then it is time. How might this emphasis change the nature of our classrooms?

The Rabbis have obviated the dictatorship of time to ensure that obligation may be fulfilled. We are always obliged because in the fulfillment of the obligation we create the time of its fulfillment. The Rabbis have bound women, slaves, and minors to a time-bound mitzvot from which they ought to be exempt. In the end what significance do the Rabbis ascribe to this move? It is, the Rabbis suggest, the basis of an ethical standard. The Rabbis have obliged women, slaves, and minors to say grace for a male who does not (or even will not) recite grace for himself. This act is bound by the consumption of as little as an olive or an egg. How significant is this particular obligation? The Rabbis respond that it is because of grace that God chooses the Jewish people as God's own. The Rabbis suggest that the practice of saying grace ties one to God; it is the Israelite practice of saying grace that endears the people to God.

> Rabbi 'Awira discoursed: sometimes in the name of R. Ammi, and sometimes in the name of R. Assi—as follows: The ministering angels said before the Holy One . . . Sovereign of the Universe, it is written in Thy law, *Who regardeth not persons nor taketh reward,* and dost Thou not regard the person of Israel, as it is written, *the Lord lift up God's countenance upon thee?* God replied to them: "And shall I not lift up My countenance for Israel, seeing that I wrote for them in the Torah, *And thou shalt eat and be satisfied and bless the Lord they God,* and they are particular [to say Grace] if the quantity is but an olive or an egg."

The angels wonder: if God does not show favorites (*Deuteronomy* 10:17), then why is it also written (*Numbers* 6:26) that God's countenance shines on the people of Israel. Isn't this latter phrase a sign of especial favor? God's remarkable response here is that since God mandates grace after meals, then the rabbinic decree that the quantity of an olive or an egg requires grace endears the people to God because it ensures a continual aspiring toward holiness. God recognizes the effort the people make to achieve holiness. That is, the Rabbis have imposed the obligation to the minimum quantity and not to time; therefore, all are bound by this non-time-bound mitzvot and, thus, all may attain holiness in equal fashion.

Thus, it seems to me that the Rabbis have completely negated the exemption of women from time-bound mitzvot. Indeed, not merely have the Rabbis suggested that the fulfillment of obligation creates the time in which that obligation may be fulfilled, but they have in the present case obliged women, slaves, and minors to a mitzvot from which they have been specifically exempted. A handful of M&Ms is sufficient to require saying of grace. Women, slaves, and minors are bound to this obligation if they have eaten a Rabbinically mandated quantity. Indeed, in my reading they may even say grace for one who has eaten a Rabbinically mandated amount: an olive or an egg. Despite the attempts to suggest that women are secondclass citizens, the Rabbis have here removed all exemption. Obligation is complete. The obligation binds us to practice and to the Other.

I do not argue that time is irrelevant in the schools. Nor do I believe that the reasoning of the Rabbis would suggest as much either. The Rabbis do not argue that the *Sh'ma* may be said whenever one desires. The commandment for the twice daily recitation of the *Sh'ma* mandates a *daily* recitation. Nor do the Rabbis suggest that one may recite the *Sh'ma* fourteen times at once and fulfill the mitzvot for a week. Rather, the effect of the Rabbi's reasoning is to ensure that the obligation of fulfilling is paramount. The Rabbis do not obviate the reality of time: The daily recitation of the *Sh'ma* must be accomplished twice daily; if one forgets to say the *Sh'ma* on one day, it is not permissible to say it four times the next. Nor is time unbounded; night becomes day and day becomes night. Human behavior cannot alter this order. However, within certain limits, it is the fulfillment of obligation that defines time rather than time governing the fulfillment of obligation. And obligation—to the eating of the quantity of an olive or an egg—is complete.

Abraham Joshua Heschel (1955, 291-2) writes: "The sense of obligation expresses a situation in which an idea, as it were, is waiting to be attained." I think that this is what the Rabbis meant in their discussions concerning from what time one might say the *Sh'ma*, and concerning the obligations for certain practices. I do not think Heschel speaks of an Platonic idealism; he seems eminently aware that all ideas must be expressed in action. Obligation is a daily behavior. Obligation is our stance in the world before the Other. Obligation for the other is almost illimitable—to the quantity of an egg or an olive. Education is a quest and not an achievement. It occurs in time, but the learning that is education creates the time of that obligation. When I learn, then it is time. As education is an obligation—it must be pursued and, therefore, requires human activity—education is also a commitment to the Other, a demand upon and not a conferral. Education must be measured not by what the educator prepares in the effort to achieve formal academic standards but by the degree to which we obliged by the student's demand. And we are obliged for Grace even to the quantity of an olive or an egg. The obligation to learn is comprehensive—the Rabbis have to my thinking and within their own acknowledged cultural bounds—made everyone responsible not only to the practice but to the fulfillment of the practice even for the Other. They have insisted on our responsibility. I think that this might be an education that practices and promotes a social justice with which we can live. The contemporary emphasis on education's products attenuates its purpose even as the quantification of its goals falsifies its design.

The Rabbis have not negated time; the twice daily recitation of the *Sh'ma* must be accomplished twice daily. But from what time may one recite the *Sh'ma* is answered not by the definition of time but by the insistence on fulfillment. Within clear limits, the act of obligation creates the time of that fulfillment. Time is defined more by the fulfillment of the obligation than is obligation constrained by time. And our obligation for ourselves and for another is veritably limitless. In another context (*Ta'anit* 11a), the Rabbis taught: "At a time when Israel is in distress, and one of them has separated himself, the two ministering angels who accompany a man come and place their hands on his head and say: 'This man, So-and So, who has separated himself from the community, let him not see the consolation of the community.'" This is not inconsistent with what the Rabbis have above discussed regarding obligation and time. Our obligation is always and complete. Our obligation is itself the reward. Time has little to do with it. For consumption of the quantity of an olive or an egg the obligation to say grace is as complete as for the satisfaction derived from a complete meal. In schools we might do well to remember this.

My seven-year-old daughter asks me if it is school tomorrow. I say it is school now. She asks if it is time to go, and I answer that we are already there. And what does she learn about time and her obligation here. And there?

Afterword

By Peter Appelbaum

STORY 1

Fresh out of graduate school I nervously drafted an email message to Alan Block, describing how I admired his work and politely asking if he might have the time to read some of my own writing. Professor Block's response was a quick message asking if I was going to the Bergamo Conference on curriculum theory and classroom practice and, if so, would I be interested in sharing a room. Thus began a professional and personal friendship that has grown over the last ten years. In that time, Professor Block, now Alan, has been a teacher and friend who has always challenged me and consistently prodded me to take theoretical and pedagogical risks. True to form, our first encounter was a template for many to follow: A question was met with a question, and Alan's questions are not transparently linked to the original question. I am not sure if he ever read that first paper I sent him, although he certainly has read numerous drafts of my work since; but surely his response was the one I would now prefer from a teacher/friend. My ideas and my teaching have changed and led to new questions through our regular contact.

STORY 2

In the last several years, the students in my curriculum theory course have consistently developed a favorite theorist. It is the same one each year. I assign one simple article by this person as part of a collection of responses to Ralph Tyler and the Tyler Rationale. Each time I teach this course, the same article resonates with my students' professional experience, and it is this article that helps them to figure out a semester project growing out of their current concerns in education that they believe will help them to move in a significant direction in their career. This one article is "The Practical: A Language for Curriculum," by Joseph Schwab, published in 1969. Why this article? Because it makes sense. Why does it make sense? Because it gives them practical ideas for what they can do. Why does it seem practical? Because instead of prescribing what to do, it gives them the freedom to say that groups meeting to deliberate is serious curriculum development work. Because instead of repeating what they know is not really met with satisfying results in their schools, again and again, it gives them a language that is new yet fits with what they do every day.

D'RASH 1

When Alan wrote me back that first time, did he have in mind the notion that he would be a better teacher/mentor by establishing ways for us to get to know each other over time rather than reading my writing in a vacuum? Did he think that he would be a better reader if we read each others' work over a period of years rather than reading what I had chosen to send him first? A cynic suggests he was worrying about the price of accommodations at the Bergamo Center and was possibly taking every opportunity to find someone to split expenses. A scholar counters that even if this were the case, the establishment of a relationship would still be the important act. It does not so much matter what his motives might have been but that he offered the opportunity for relation. A friend notes that in so doing, Professor Block cleverly transformed the system of exchange offered by the original email message, so that I would no longer be beholden to him for whatever kindness he might generously provide (in the form of reading my paper and in exchange giving me his response and advice); if that relation had been maintained, there would be little opportunity for us to begin a dialogue. The scholar asks if there were any potential reasons why Alan might not have acknowledged my email message. Other than uninteresting reasons, such as not checking his email that month or accidentally deleting it, he might have had reason to wonder whether or not it would be worth his time to read an unsolicited manuscript from an unknown person. What would he get in return for even opening the file should he agree to read it? By suggesting a professional relationship beyond the requested transaction (he gets the opportunity to read something he might find interesting; I get his feedback and guidance), the friend points out, he created a context in which there is a reason to read what I have written. After all, if we are going to be sharing a room at a conference, surely he might want to get to know more about what I write about. A student notes as well that he has shifted the direction of exchange: Can I do him the favor of sharing a room at a conference? The reciprocity of our initial encounter is now different. In responding to my request with a question he made it possible for a conversation to occur. Instead of evaluating my writing, we both now had the opportunity to learn, or, in Alan's words, we both might become "smart."

D'RASH 2

In the words of my students, Joseph Schwab seems to emphasize four themes: Practical knowledge and wisdom about curriculum development is found in the daily classroom decisions; thus the teacher is a major decision-maker in the curriculum development process; this rejects the view of the teacher as a technician; and henceforth it is possible to acknowledge that curriculum reflects the uniqueness of every group of teachers, students, administrators, families, community members, and others interested and involved in the daily life of the school and the school community. As Amie notes, Schwab says we should not understand our work as the production of lists of objectives and evaluation criteria; we must make it possible for our work as curriculum developers is primarily to effect the existence of ongoing meetings where as many different perspectives on the educational encounter participate. Roberta emphasizes that one important contribution to the deliberative experience of such meetings is to challenge those present to acknowledge that some viewpoints are absent, and thus, to work to create invitations to new members. Matt suggests that educational leadership is not necessarily a job of authority but rather one of facilitating democratic group processes. He offers that he could best be a leader by asking his colleagues to help him with his new course plans; thus leadership is to place the leadership in the hands of others. (A side discussion ensues about the leadership work of Ella Baker in the civil rights movement.) Geneva asks how much the parents and other family members can be expected to contribute, considering that they are not paid for their participation and have other family and work responsibilities outside of the school community. Alysa asks her students how they want to participate in the planning of their educational program. They plot together the ways that they might experiment with classroom organization, visit other classes in their school, make trips to local community associations, and design social action projects in science. Sam offers a study of a historical artifact from popular culture as a focal point for involving her students in the unfolding curriculum. Kate wonders what curriculum packages look like when the curriculum process is what is valued.

SCHWAB AS PROBLEM SOLVING?

Deliberation is at the center of Schwab's work and at the center of what my students tell me is missing from the curriculum work in their current educational contexts. Deliberation is how a group of educators responds to the implicit request made by their school community to formulate practical action within their practice. At the heart of this enterprise is the desire to find what is not readily apparent to those present, in order to either maintain something "good" that is not acknowledged, and thus to build on our strengths, or change practices that create "bad" things in our school environment, so that they are no longer causing unnecessary harm to the democratic pluralist community of which we are a part. As Nilton Bonder writes, a historically Jewish response is to move through four levels of deliberation, effectively traveling from discernment to commitment. In the area of discernment ("of what is apparent in essence") we can reach what is hidden from us through questions or ignorance. "The greater you understand your ignorance," writes Bonder, "The more efficiently you can make decisions within this sphere of reason. On this plane, what is hidden is revealed not by producing answers but by reframing the question(s)". Within the area of commitment, "of what is hidden, of what is ascertained empirically rather than relying on reason," we can reach what is hidden by recognizing that experience not only yields data on life but also provides us with knowledge on the extent of our ignorances. "The Hidden Realm of What is Hidden is the principle of acting first, which makes us rethink the questions." (1999, 96) A deliberative group must move from the apparent realm of what is apparent (using information to understand and elucidate) to the hidden realm of what is apparent (understanding by listening, learning, and teaching), and on to the apparent realm of what is hidden (the practice of wisdom made possible by safeguarding and performing) in order to make it to the hidden realm of what is hidden (a state of reverence reached through fulfilling one's commitments). Within this process, one is constantly reminded that the purpose of the problem solving process is to decide what to do now rather than to determine what is true or right. There is no way to know what is true or right, and we are condemned to act before we could ever find out, in retrospect, whether what we have done is indeed what we should have done.

RELATIONS COME FIRST, BEFORE PHILOSOPHY?

One of the interesting things about Alan's offer of sharing a room was that he made it clear that a relationship was primary and that scholarship was secondary. Schwab shares this view, stressing that communities must form sites of deliberation before they can undertake the serious tasks of curriculum development and design. Creating an infrastructure that promotes relationships among the diverse members of the school community is in this sense a new form of curriculum practice and a new discourse of curriculum design and development. Whereas people might have spent countless hours creating scope and sequence charts, or in formulating lessons that adhere to district or state guidelines, Schwab counsels us that any of that may be important and useful, but far more essential to serious curriculum reform is this infrastructure that makes it possible for relationships to flourish and grow. As a learning system, curriculum development work must speak in a new language, and therefore promote a new kind of practice. In this practice we must act before we can ever think about what is true or best. Nevertheless, we hold before us the primary ethical concern that what we do be the wisest ethical response.

This is what Alan Block has been doing throughout most of his career in education. His earlier works, including *Occupied Reading* and *I'm Only Bleeding*, pleaded with his readers to use new discourses in their professional work. With this latest of his efforts, we can see that he is in prestigious company. In Block's reading, this is really what Schwab was doing as well. In fact, he points out, it may be that there has been a long-standing tradition of such efforts that simply have not been understood as such just because we have not been reading Schwab in this light. Ira Stone (1998), in his interpretation of the philosopher Levinas, claims this turn of theory is really the introduction of Jewish approaches to a traditional Greek, Christian audience. In his reading of Levinas, the philosopher and Talmudic scholar is both describing Jewish Talmudic scholarship in traditional Western terms evolving out of ancient Greek philosophy and introducing Jews to Jewish tradition in the language of traditional Western philosophy. Block suggests this is what Schwab was doing in his work, too, whether he knew it or not. And whether there is any evidence that Schwab thought he was doing this or not is not to the point. Block is convincing. It makes sense. And it helps us to understand Schwab on his own terms.

WHY WAVES WHEN I WANT DIRECTIONS?

Readers of both Levinas and the Talmud both sometimes complain of the non-linearity, of the repeated returns to the same themes and subjects, only to drop them and turn to something else. The same has been said of Joseph Schwab, and perhaps this may also be said of Alan Block's writing about Schwab. Yet this seeming appearance of non-linearity translates into a new kind of ocean washing over the beach again and again, each time allowing us a chance to get wet in its new language, each time providing a new opportunity for a relationship with our subject. Every wave is a new wave, a different wave, yet each one shares with all of the others a family resemblance and a commonality that can help us to think about any particular wave that may come in the future. Life is like this, too: Every situation that we find ourselves in is new and different, yet we hope to think about all situations through the particularities of the one situation we are in at the moment. Curriculum work is characterized by the same characteristics. Each curriculum situation cries out for decisions and choices, for action, yet no two curricular moments are the same, and we can never be sure what the outcome of our choices and actions may be.

As Alan Block and Joseph Schwab teach us, curriculum is another Talmud, constantly interrupting itself in order to teach us that our search for a totality of understanding, a clear method, will always fail. The practical, everyday life experiences that form the body of the Talmud and the Talmudic curriculum are forever going to be self-interrupting in constantly repeating waves of unique but familiar constellations. We want prescribed methods, instructions for what to do; and instead we are confronted with neverending special cases that prove the inconsistency and unreliability of our methods and procedures. So how can we live with this? Schwab, Levinas, and Block each speak on their own terms to help us understand that relation comes first; once we create the infrastructure of deliberation—Talmudic study, communities of relation, we have already done the hard work of curriculum reform. We will no longer be disappointed in our methods and procedures. Instead, our methods and procedures, our policies, will help us to make decisions "in the moment," knowing full well that our memory of these choices and actions are likely to come back to haunt us as stories with their own interpretations in the future. They may be lessons of regret or case studies of hope, but each one will contribute to our quest for the structure we use to approach our decision-making process.

D'RASH 3

I take Schwab to be an insurgent multiculturalist. If we perpetually seek to disrupt our deliberations with the concern that we have not included all possible perspectives and constituent representatives in the deliberation process, then we are on our way to the enactment of a critical democratic process (Appelbaum, 2002). If we further make the processes of deliberation consistently challenge our acceptance of authority, then we can work to ensure that all voices will impact on policy. The quest is to make this happen. How can we do this? Alan Block suggests we can do this by modeling our deliberations after the structure of the Talmud. This is not meant to mean that we study Talmud, but that we create curriculum work as living Talmud. For example, if a group of people are meeting to discuss what should be done in their school, they each should make sure to present an important statement about what they bring to the table. These originating statements would be analogous to the center of the pages of a Curricular Talmud. Each person present at the meeting should re-introduce their own statements as interpretations of the others' originating comments. In this way, every person disrupts each others' isolated point of view and creates a series of relations. It is in the exchange of relation that concepts are nurtured and applied to new situations. Every conceivable application of any potential conclusion must be followed to its implications from every perspective in the deliberation process.

Oy—will we never get anything done? Won't we spend all of our lives creating one page of Curricular Talmud? The point of the meeting is not to make the decisions or to set policy but to learn the method of deliberation so that we can make the decisions readily outside of the meeting. Our lives make sense if we live the Talmud we make. We will be pretty darned good at listening to others, because we will learn that we only exist in time when we understand ourselves through others.

STORY 3

We're sitting in an elementary classroom where students are talking mathematics (Appelbaum, 1999). Last year, these students would often share their different strategies for solving mathematics problems. Occasionally, a student would understand another student's explanation better than the teacher's, and thus, would learn how to solve a particular type of problem. The experience of sharing their strategies had helped them to use oral as well as written language in mathematics. This current year, mathematics is experienced in another way. Students might still be seen sharing their strategies in the course of a typical day, but the purposes are different and the use of their presentations is different. Last year, there was little incentive to listen to another student, except perhaps the simple curiosity that one student might have for another's solution. Perhaps a student might have been motivated to be able to get correct answers, and therefore they may have listened to another student because they hoped to understand what they said. Most often, however, each student took their turn talking to please the teacher and to have his/her moment in the spotlight. It was common for students to repeat explanations very similar to ones that had been described moments earlier, typically because they were waiting their turn rather than listening to each other. But of course the conditions of exchange were different last year. Then, the students got praise and attention in return for participation. But as I said, this year is different.

This year, students use a particular mathematical question as an entry into deliberation. They discuss the meaning of the question and potential approaches of response. They take turns sharing strategies and solutions, but not in order to take turns doing so. This year, they are now used to the idea that they need to not only be able to get a correct answer, but also to be able to understand more than one alternative approach to the same question. Why must they understand each other? Because their class discussion does not stop at the point of shared strategies. The teacher this year agrees with John Dewey that in a democracy each member is heard, each member's statements matter. In this classroom, the participants make a point of learning to use each strategy offered; they then search for situations in which each possible approach would be the best. For example, in order to explain a solution to a younger child, one solution strategy might be best, but in a presentation to the city council, another approach might be more persuasive; another might be quickest, while yet another might be the one that students would use when they wanted to be most confident about the accuracy of their result. Students use the varying strategies in presentations to multiple audiences and discuss the alternative solution strategies in this context. On some days, however, no answers are found! Instead, students are led to surprising discoveries about mathematical ideas that they had not yet thought about. They may abandon the original question in favor of new ones. Most important in this classroom, however, is the emphasis on new questions. The teacher and students celebrate when a member of the class articulates a new question based on their work. This new question may become the focus for another mathematical investigation on the next day. Students often discuss what makes a mathematical question interesting or important. They sometimes find themselves arguing and unable to reach an agreement! Last year, students would often ask, when will we ever use this stuff in real life? This year, students come to class eager to share stories about how they have been using mathematics outside of school.

STORY 4

We are in a first-grade classroom that seems to be combining science and language arts. The class reads *Desert Giant* (Bash, 1989), a book about the life cycle of the saguaro cactus and how it interacts with the life cycles of people, other animals, and plants in its ecosystem. Whole-class discussion explores the multiple perspectives represented in the story (birds, people, insects, etc.); students write their own version of the story, extracting one of these perspectives. Later in the week, students take on a perspective of their own choice for field study in which they record in their notebooks observations of an ecosystem near the school. They write stories from the perspective they chose. Then, in groups, they weave multiple-perspective narratives about the eco-system they observed together.

STORY 5

A fourth-grade class is in the midst of a tree branch study (Appelbaum 2001). Over the course of a week they collect lists on large sheets of paper taped to the wall of the classroom: what they know and what they wonder. Groups form by interests growing out of the list of wonders and begin to collect data to help them guide an investigation about what they wonder about. Based on their initial data, and in consultation with other class members in whole-class meetings, the groups design research projects based on more refined data collection. All along, two students take on the job of anthropologists, and two others take on the job of the media. They study how the "scientists" are doing their work and give scholarly and media reports, representing the work of the scientists to the class. These fourth-graders are motivated to examine particulars of their own identification and rarely follow a linear process in developing their investigations. The representation of science in the usual textbook or hands-on activity rarely creates images of disorganization, illogic, intuition, and so on. In this classroom, the anthropologists and media reporters help students to reflect on the work of actual science. Rather than search for generality, students here might focus on particularities. They may create thought experiments, asking what-if-not questions about what they observe, moving into a realm of science fiction and fantasy. Problem posing might highlight the special method of "What-if-not?" taking illogic as the road to local, contextual validity that sheds light on the general. Such playful discussions happen once a week on Thursday afternoons, in a regular "Science Talk" (Gallas 1995).

STORY 6

Qishana reports to the class: "We needed to know, what do you have to add to 2/3 + 1/5 to get 1? We found, after a lot of work, 2/3 + 1/5 + 2/15 =1." And then Shareefa laughed and said, "We could've just multiplied the numerators and denominators instead of going through all that!" Then we laughed and said, "Course not, that makes no sense." But Shareefa and I went off and looked for other combinations of fractions that we could solve the "wrong way ." So we came up with. . . . Later, Roza asks, "So do we know now when multiplying works, and when it doesn't?" Shareefa: "We know it works when it works, and it doesn't work a lot; but your question—a good one—is still out there. We're thinking it's one of those questions that keeps us learning without ever finding the answer to the question" (Appelbaum, 2001, p.118).

STORY 7

We are on the education committee for a Jewish Sunday school, rewriting the goals and objectives for grades K-9 (Appelbaum 2003). One of us notes that all of our models for Jewish education originate in secular educational theory. We have taken on over the years the latest in educational theory in order to rid ourselves of the worst of American Jewish education, so often "bad pedagogy" promulgated by people whose sole qualifications were that they knew Hebrew. Now we are modern and use modern methods. But whatever happened to the idea of a "Jewish" education? What would be a genuinely Jewish educational encounter? The group begins to envision a school based on traditionally Jewish forms of education: study partners re-reading sections of Torah and Talmud; using holidays and preparation for important life-cycle events as the centerpieces for discussions of ethics and culture; social action projects as the focus of the curriculum, as an outgrowth of small group discussions of what is the best response; trying to determine the best course of action by reading excerpts of Yiddish literature; returning to old themes rather than moving on to new ones, in order to reconsider many more interpretations. Community deliberations about the new curriculum begin to be organized as study sessions about pedagogy. "We're making our own, new Talmud," declares someone taking minutes.

STORY 8

We are in a graduate course on the Cultural Foundations of Education. We are about to discuss several writings on diversity education. We start by "performing our reading." Students in attendance first write down their scripts: 1. a sentence (or two, if they must) from the readings that they feel is so important that, if this quote were left out of what they read, then the meaning of what they read would be changed; 2. a phrase—again from the reading and again so important that if it were left out then the meaning would be changed; 3. a word—the one word they would use to communicate what the readings are all about; and 4. their own word. We read with conviction our scripts around the room, maintaining our pace, the rhythm of our scripts, first the sentences, then the phrases, followed by the words, and ending in dramatic climax with our own words, one person following another counterclockwise. After a brief pause to reflect on the performance that we just created, the questions begin.

NEW QUESTIONS

If Alan's book is to make the impact it should on educational practice, then it must be read by many people. But these same people will have to believe it speaks to their questions and issues. But we begin entangled in a paradox. To introduce a new way of thinking is difficult precisely because the dominant discourse resists challenges to itself. Unlike Talmudic practice, curriculum does not disrupt itself nor does it seek disruption. Alan has pointed to the long history of educational thought ignoring Jewish philosophy and practice. How can we take this Schwabian deliberation, "the practical" into our work? How can we live our own Talmud in a secular world? Well, why could we not? There is nothing about Talmudic scholarship that presumes a particular religion or viewpoint; it is a method of interaction with text that highlights the ethics of response. Any text will do: Grab the first book you can reach and read it with others. Ask yourselves, what does this book say to us about how we should respond to the responsibilities we have? What does it not say? What might someone else say? Why would they say that? Suppose we imagined each of these possible ways of responding to our responsibilities. When would each option seem to be the best choice? Why? Would it matter who was considering the choice, or do we imagine any person would feel the same way? Are we sure? We is missing from our discussion? How did that happen? What are the implications? What might we *do*? What *should* we do?

What *will* we do?

What will *you* do?

What will you *do*?

Hosafah[1]

By Way of an Introduction

Another answer.

Rabbi Mendel's students asked him why he didn't write a book. He responded:

> Well, let's say I have written a book. Now who is going to buy it? Our own people will buy it. But when do our people get to read a book, since all through the week they are absorbed in earning their livelihood? They will get to read it on a Sabbath. And when will they get to read it on a Sabbath? First they have to take the ritual bath, then they must learn and pray, and then comes the Sabbath meal. But after the Sabbath meal is over, they have time to read. Well, suppose one of them stretches out on the sofa, takes the book, and opens it. But he is full and he feels drowsy, so he falls asleep and the book slips to the floor. Now tell me, why should I write a book?

THE BEGINNING

---

[1] A Hebrew word which means 'addition.'

REFERENCES

Appelbaum, P. (1999). Eight Critical Points for Mathematics. In S. Steinberg and J. Kincheloe (Eds.), *Perspectives in Critical Thinking: Essays by Teachers in Theory and Practice.* New York: Peter Lang.

Appelbaum, P. (2001). Pastiche Science: Bringing Cultural Studies of Science to Education and Education to the Cultural Studies of Science. In J. Weaver, P. Appelbaum, & M. Morris (Eds.), *(Post) Modern Science (Education).* New York: Peter Lang.

Appelbaum, P. (2002). *Multicultural and Diversity Education.* California: ABC-CLIO.

Appelbaum, P. (2003, May 28-31). What Is a Jewish Educational Experience? Philadelphia: Congress of Secular Jewish Organizations.

Babylonian Talmud, Bava Metzia. (1971). (I. Epstein, Ed.) (S. Daiches & H. Freedman, Trans.). Jerusalem: Soncino Press.

Babylonian Talmud, Berakhot. (1971). (I. Epstein, Ed.) (S. Daiches & H. Freedman, Trans.). Jerusalem: Soncino Press.

Babylonian Talmud, Sanhedrin. (1971). (I. Epstein, Ed.) (S. Daiches & H. Freedman, Trans.). Jerusalem: Soncino Press.

Babylonian Talmud, Ta'anit. (1971). (I. Epstein, Ed.) (S. Daiches & H. Freedman, Trans.). Jerusalem: Soncino Press.

Bash, B. (1989). *Desert Giant: The World of the Saguaro Cactus.* Boston: Little, Brown.

Benjamin, W. (1969). *Illuminations* (H. Arendt, Ed.) (H. Zohn, Trans.). New York: Schocken Press.

Bennett, William. (2001, March). "The State and Future of American Education." In a Speech to the Heritage Foundation.

Benson, J. (1998). *Wisconsin Model Academic Standards for Information and Technological Literacy*. Milwaukee: Wisconsin Department of Public Instruction.

Bialik H. N., & Ravnitzky, Y. H. (Eds.). (1992). *The Book of Legends*. (W. G. Braude, Trans.). New York: Schocken Books.

Bingham, E. (2003). *Mordecai: An Early American Family*. New York: Hill and Wang.

Bleich, D. (1999). The Living Text: Literary Pedagogy and Jewish Identity. In H. S. Shaprio (Ed.), *Strangers in the Land: Pedagogy, Modernity, and Jewish Identity*. New York: Peter Lang.

Block, A. A. (1997). *I'm Only Bleeding*. New York: Peter Lang.

Block, A. A. (1998). "'And he pretended to be a stranger to them:' Maxine Greene and Teacher as Stranger." In W. F. Pinar (Ed.), *The Passionate Mind of Maxine Greene: I am . . . Not Yet*. New York: Falmer Press.

Block, A. A. (1999-2000). Curriculum from the Back of the Bookstore. *Encounter: Education for Meaning and Social Justice, 12*(4).

Block, A. A. (2001). Ethics and Curriculum. *JCT: An Interdisciplinary Journal of Curriculum Studies, 17*(3), 23-38.

Bloom, A. (1987). *The Closing of the American Mind*. New York: Simon & Schuster.

Bloom, B. (Ed.). (1956). *Taxonomy of Educational Objectives*. New York: David McKay.

Bloom, H. (1975). *A Map of Misreading*. New York: Oxford University Press.

Bobbitt, F. (1918). *Curriculum*. Boston: Houghton Mifflin.

Bonder, N. (1999). *Yiddische Kop: Creative Problem Solving in Jewish Learning, Lore & Humor.* Boston: Shambala.

Boyarin, D. (1993). *Carnal Israel.* Berkeley: University of California Press.

Bracey, G. (2002, 16 January). What They Did on Vacation. *Washington Post,* A19.

Brody, R. (1998). *The Geonim of Babylonia and the Shaping of Medieval Jewish Culture.* New Haven: Yale University Press.

Bruner, J. (1960/1977). *The Process of Education.* Cambridge, MA: Harvard University Press.

Buber, M. (1967). *On Judaism* (N. N. Glatzer, Ed.). New York: Schocken Books.

Buber, M. (1991). *Tales of the Hasidim.* New York: Schocken Books.

Buber, M. (1999). *Gog and Magog* (L. Lewisohn, Trans.). Syracuse, New York: Syracuse University Press.

Burns, P. C., Roe, B. D., & Ross, E. P. (1992). *Teaching Reading in Today's Elementary Schools.* Boston: Houghton Mifflin.

Cracco, M., Weiler, K., & Munro, P. (1999). *Pedagogies of Resistance.* New York: Teachers College Press.

Cremin, L. (Ed.). (1957). *The Republic and the School: Horace Mann and the Education of Free Man.* New York: Teachers College Press.

Dewey, J. (1916/1966). *Democracy and Education.* New York.: The Free Press.

Dewey, J. (1934/1980). *Art as Experience.* New York.: Perigee Books.

Dewey, J. (1991). *How We Think.* Buffalo, New York: Prometheus Books.

Doll, W. E. J. (1993). *A Postmodern Perspective on Curriculum.* New York: Teachers College Press.

Dorff, E. (1997). *The Sh'ma and Its Blessings* (L. Hoffman, Ed.). Woodstock, VT.: Jewish Lights Publishing.

Douglas, M. (1999). *Leviticus as Literature.* New York: Oxford University Press.

Efros, I. (1964). *Ancient Jewish Philosophy.* New York: Bloch Publishing.

Eisner, E. (1984). No Easy Answers: Schwab's Contributions to Curriculum. *Curriculum Inquiry, 14*(2), 201-209.

Elias, J. (1995). *Philosophy of Education: Classical and Contemporary.* Malabar, Fl.: Kriefer Publishing.

Eliot, T.S. (1962) Hamlet and His Problems. In *Major Writers of America.* (Miller, Perry, ed.). New York: Harcourt, Brace & World.

Fiedler, L. (1991). *Fiedler on the Roof: Essays on Literature and Jewish Identity.* Boston: David Godine.

Fish, S. (1980). *Is There a Text in This Class?* Cambridge, MA.: Harvard University Press.

Fishbane, M. (1998). *The Exegetical Imagination.* Cambridge, Massachusetts: Harvard University Press.

Fox, S. (1985). The Vitality of Theory in Schwab's Conception of the Practical. *Curriculum Inquiry, 15*(1), 63-89.

Fox, S., & Rosenfield, G., (Eds.). (1977). *From the Scholar to the Classroom: Translating Jewish Tradition into Curriculum.* New York: Melton Research Center for Jewish Education.

Freud, S. (1960). *The Psychopathology of Everyday Life* (J. Strachey, Ed.) (A. Tyson, Trans.). New York: Norton.

Freud, S. (1961). *Civilization and Its Discontents* (J. Strachey, Trans.). New York: Norton.

Gallas, K. (1995). *Talking Their Way into Science: Hearing Children's Questions and Theories, Responding with Curricula.* New York: Teachers College Press.

Gehring, J. (2002, 21 July). NY Appeals Court Rebuffs Lower Court's Aid Ruling. *The New York Times,* 16.

Ginzburg, L. (1956). *Legends of the Bible.* Philadelphia: Jewish Publications Society.

Goldenberg, R. (1989). Talmud. In B. W. Holtz (Ed.), *Back to the Sources.* New York: Simon & Schuster.

Gould, S. J. (1983). *The Mismeasure of Man.* New York: Norton.

Greene, M. *Teacher as Stranger: Education Philosophy for the Modern Age.* (1973). Belmont, CA.: Wadsworth Publishing.

Gutek, G. (1972/1987). *A History of the Western Educational Experience.* Prospect, Illinois: Waveland Press.

Gutek, G. (1997). *Historical and Philosophical Foundations of Education: A Biographical Introduction.* New York: Prentice Hall.

Halbertal, M., & Halbertal, T. H. (1998). The Yeshiva. In A. O. Rorty (Ed.), *Philosophers on Education.* New York: Routledge.

Halivni, D. W. (1991). *Peshat & Derash.* New York: Oxford University Press.

Halivni, D. W. (1997). *Revelation Restored.* Boulder, Co.: Westview Press.

Handelman, S. (1982) *The Slayers of Moses.* New York: State University of New York Press.

Harvard University. (1946). *General Education in a Free Society.* Cambridge, MA.: Harvard University Press.

Hauptman, J. (1998). *Rereading the Rabbis: A Woman's Voice.* Boulder, Co.: Westview Press.

Helmerichs, R. (2002). *Historical Definitions and Nomneclatures of the label 'ADHD:' An Investigation into Attention-Deficit and Hyperactive Behavior through Time.* [Diss.] University of Wisconsin-Stout.

Heschel, A. J. (1955). *God in Search of Man.* New York: Noonday Press.

Heschel, A. J. (1996). *Moral Grandeur and Spiritual Audacity* (S. Heschel, Ed.). New York: Noonday Press.

Heschel, A. J (1959). *Between God and Man: An Interpretation of Judaism.* New York: The Free Press.

Huebner, D. (1975/2000). Curriculum as Concern for Man's Temporality. In W. F. Pinar (Ed.), *Curriculum Studies: The Reconceptualiization.* Berkeley, Ca.: McCutchan Publishing Company.

Jacobsen, D. A. (1999). *Philosophy in Classroom Teaching.* Upper Saddle River, NJ.: Merrill.

James, W. (1907/1970). *Pragmatism and Four Essays from The Meaning of Truth.* New York: Meridian Books.

Jardine, D. (2003). *Back to the Basics.* Hillsdale, NJ: Lawrence Erlbaum Associates.

Kaplan M. (1994/1934). *Judaism as a Civilization.* Philadelphia: Jewish Publication Society.

Katz, S. T. (1975). *Jewish Philosophers.* New York: Bloch Publishing.

Kadushin, M. (1952/1972). *The Rabbinic Mind.* New York: Bloch Publishing.

Kliebard, H. (1987). *The Struggle for the American Curriculum.* New York: Routledge & Kegan Paul.

Kohl, H. (1994). *"I Won't Learn from You," and Other Thoughts on Creative Maladjustment.* New York: New Press.

Kraemer, D. (1990). *The Mind of the Talmud.* New York: Oxford University Press.

Kraemer, D. (1996). *Reading the Rabbis.* New York: Oxford University Press.

Lawrence, D. H. (1964). *Studies in Classic American Literature.* New York: Viking Press.

Lemann, N. (1999). *The Big Test.* New York: Farrar Straus and Giroux.

Levinas, E. (1990a). *Difficult Freedom: Essays in Judaism* (S. Hand, Trans.). Baltimore: Johns Hopkins University Press.

Levinas, E. (1990b). *Nine Talmudic Readings* (A. Aronowicz, Trans.). Bloomington, In: Indiana University Press.

Magid, S. (2002). Associative Midrash. In S. Magid (Ed.), *God's Voice from the Void: Old and New Studies in Bratslav Hasidism.* Albany: State University of New York.

Marx, K. (1967). *Capital.* New York: International Publishers.

Marx. K. (1984). The 18th Brumaire of Louis Bonaparte. New York: International Publishers.

Matt, D.C. (1983). *The Essential Kabbalah.* San Francisco: HarperSanFrancisco.

McNeill, W. H. (1991). *Hutchin's University.* Chicago: University of Chicago Press.

Miller, P. (1955). *The Puritan Mind.* Cambridge, Ma: Harvard University Press.

Noddings, N. (1999). *Contemporary Curriculum Discourses* (Pinar, W F., Ed.). New York: Peter Lang.

Nussbaum, M. C. (1990). *Love's Knowledge.* New York: Oxford University Press.

Ouaknin, M.-A. (1995). *The Burnt Book: Reading the Talmud* (L. Brown, Trans.). Princeton, NJ: Princeton University Press.

Ozmon, H. A., & Craver, S. M. (1999) *Philosophical Foundations of Education.* New York: Prentice-Hall.

Phenix, P. (1964). *Realms of Meaning.* New York: McGraw Hill Book Company.

Pirke Avot: Ethics of the Fathers. (2002) (R. M. Davis, Ed.). Brooklyn, NY: Mesorah Publications.

Purpel, D. (1989). *Moral and Spiritual Crisis in Education.* Boston: Bergin and Garvey.

Purpel, D. (1999). On Being a Jew and a Boston Braves Fan: Alone and Afraid in a Land I Never Made. In S. H. Shapiro (Ed.), *Strangers in the Land: Pedagogy, Modernity, and Jewish Identity.* New York: Peter Lang.

Ravitch, D. (1995). *National Standards in American Education.* Washington, D.C.: Brookings Institution Press.

Ravitch, D. (2000). *Left Back: A Century of Failed School Reforms.* New York: Simon & Schuster.

Raywid, M. A. (1999) *Contemporary Curriculum Discourses* (Pinar, W F., Ed.). New York: Peter Lang Publishing.

Rorty, R. (1979). *Philosophy and the Mirror of Nature.* Princeton, New Jersey: Princeton University Press.

Schubert, W. (1986). *Curriculum: Perspective, Paradigm, and Possibility.* New York: Macmillan.

Schwab, J.J. (1969a, November). The Practical: A Language for Curriculum. *School Review, 78,* 1-23.

Schwab, J.J. (1969b). *College Curriculum and Student Protest.* Chicago: University of Chicago Press.

Schwab, J J. (1971). The Practical: Arts of the Eclectic. *School Review, 79,* 493-542.

Schwab, J.J. (1973, August). The Practical 3: Translation into Curriculum. *School Review, 81,* 501-522.

Schwab, J.J. (1977). Translating Scholarship into Curriculum. In S. Fox & G. Rosenfield (Eds.), *From the Scholar to the Classroom: Translating Jewish Tradition into Curriculum.* New York: Melton Center for Jewish Education.

Schwab, J.J. (1978). Testing and the Curriculum. In I. Westbury & N. J. Wilkof (Eds.), *Science, Curriculum, and Liberal Education.* Chicago: University of Chicago Press.

Schwab, J.J. (1983). The Practical 4: Something for Curriculum Professors to Do. *Curriculum Inquiry, 13*(3), 239-265.

Simon, R. (1999). Election, Ambivalence, and the Pedagogy of Jewish Particularity. In H. S. Shaprio (Ed.), *Strangers in the Land: Pedagogy, Modernity, and Jewish Identity.* New York: Peter Lang Publishing.

Smith, F. (1990). *To Think.* New York: Teachers College Press.

Steinsaltz, A.. (1976). *The Essential Talmud.* Chaya, G, (Trans.). New York: Basic Books.

Steinsaltz, A.. (1990). *The Talmud: The Steinsaltz Edition, Bava Metzia.* New York: Random House.

Steinsaltz, A.. (1995). *The Talmud: The Steinsaltz Edition,* Ta'anit. New York: Random House.

Stone, I. (1998). *Reading Levinas/Reading Talmud: An Introduction.* Philadelphia: Jewish Publication Society."

Tennyson, Alfred. (1952) "The Lotus-Eaters." In *The Victorian Age.* (Bowyer, John Wilson & Brooks, John Lee, eds.). New York: Appleton-Century-Crofts.

Thoreau, H. D. (1970). *Walden; or Life in the Woods.* (Van Doren Stern, P. ed.). New York: Barnes and Noble Books.

Tyler R. (1949/1971). *Basic Principles of Curriculum and Instruction.* Chicago: University of Chicago Press.

Tyler, R. (1977). The Curricular Deliberation. In S. Fox & G. Rosenfield (Eds.), *From the Scholar to the Classroom: Translating Jewish Tradition into Curriculum.* New York: Melton Research Center for Jewish Education.

Tyler, R. (1984). Personal Reflections on The Practical 4. *Curriculum Inquiry, 14*(1), 97-102.

Walter, M. (1996). Curriculum Topics through Problem Posing. In R. Corwin (Ed.), *Talking Mathematics: Supporting Children's Voices.* Portsmouth, NH: Heinemann.

Wankowski, J., & Reid, W. (1982, Summer). The Psychology of Curriculum Theorizing. *Journal of Curriculum Theorizing,* 4(2), 112-131.

Wells H.G. (1992). *The Time Machine.* New York: Tor Publication.

Westbury, I., & Wilkof, N. (Eds.). (1978). *Science Curriculum, and Liberal Education: Selected Essays.* Chicago: University of Chicago Press.

Willis, G., Schubert, W.H., et al. (Eds.). (1993). *The American Curriculum: A Documentary History.* Westport, CT: Praeger.

COMPLICATED CONVERSATION

A BOOK SERIES OF CURRICULUM STUDIES

This series employs research completed in various disciplines to construct textbooks that will enable public school teachers to reoccupy a vacated public domain—not simply as "consumers" of knowledge, but as active participants in a "complicated conversation" that they themselves will lead. In drawing promiscuously but critically from various academic disciplines and from popular culture, this series will attempt to create a conceptual montage for the teacher who understands that positionality as aspiring to reconstruct a "public" space. *Complicated Conversation* works to resuscitate the progressive project—an educational project in which self-realization and democratization are inevitably intertwined; its task as the new century begins is nothing less than the intellectual formation of a public sphere in education.

The series editor is:

Dr. William F. Pinar
Department of Curriculum and Instruction
223 Peabody Hall
Louisiana State University
Baton Rouge, LA 70803-4728